Organic Methods for Vegetable Gardening in Florida

UNIVERSITY PRESS OF FLORIDA

Florida A&M University, Tallahassee
Florida Atlantic University, Boca Raton
Florida Gulf Coast University, Ft. Myers
Florida International University, Miami
Florida State University, Tallahassee
New College of Florida, Sarasota
University of Central Florida, Orlando
University of Florida, Gainesville
University of North Florida, Jacksonville
University of South Florida, Tampa
University of West Florida, Pensacola

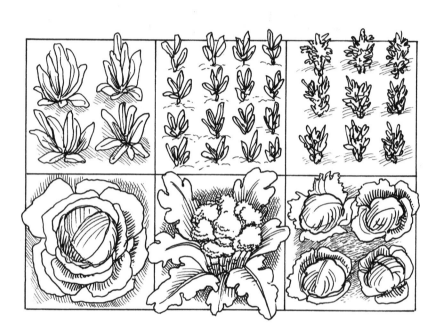

Organic Methods for Vegetable Gardening in Florida

GINNY STIBOLT AND MELISSA CONTRERAS

With illustrations by Marjorie Shropshire

University Press of Florida

Gainesville · Tallahassee · Tampa · Boca Raton

Pensacola · Orlando · Miami · Jacksonville · Ft. Myers · Sarasota

VIVA FLORIDA 500
1513–2013

A Florida Quincentennial Book

Library of Congress Cataloging-in-Publication Data
Stibolt, Ginny.
Organic methods for vegetable gardening in Florida / Ginny Stibolt and Melissa
Contreras ; With illustrations by Marjorie Shropshire.
p. cm.
Includes index.
ISBN 978-0-8130-4401-9 (alk. paper)
    1. Organic gardening—Florida. 2. Vegetable gardening—Florida. I. Contreras,
Melissa. II. Shropshire, Marjorie. III. Title.
SB453.5.S85 2013
635.9'8709759—dc23   2012039456

University Press of Florida
15 Northwest 15th Street
Gainesville, FL 32611-2079
http://www.upf.com

This book is dedicated to Florida's organic farmers and all growers who use organic methods in their gardens. We all benefit from their efforts.

Contents

Foreword

Gardening today can be one of the most relaxing and enriching endeavors in which an individual can get involved. And *organic* gardening is enriching not just for the individual but also for the community. You see, organic gardening inspires questions: How do we grow this wonderful food without synthetic chemicals? What is compost? How does it work? What's the natural predator of this problematic insect? Where does our watershed begin? And where does it end? And once one person begins to ask questions, inevitably more folks will chime in, too.

Indeed, the power of organic agriculture lies there—with the inquisitive nature of innovative ideas. When people ask questions, they begin to think. And even if it's only a few people asking questions in the beginning, like the handful of folks who revived organic agriculture in this country in the '60s and '70s, it has the potential to inspire more people to question the status quo and for something positive to grow.

I was lucky enough to be on the scene back then and was among some of the early organic farmers in Florida in this latest flush of organic farming and gardening. I've participated in and tried to help nurture the growth of the organic community and industry locally, regionally, and internationally. But it all started for me in my uncle Henry's garden. We connected, walking through the garden looking at it, talking about it, appreciating it. We were active, we got dirty, and I got hooked. We picked various things and brought them into the family home to smiles and gratitude in the waiting kitchen. I convinced my parents to let me grow watermelons (my Dad would let me grow only one thing) in our backyard in Texas. A decade later in 1973, I became a Florida organic gardener and then a watermelon farmer!

And that's really what it's all about—providing opportunities for people to get outside, maybe get a little dirty, to feel the soil in their hands and the sun on their skin. It creates a place and a space for relationships to be formed, both with nature and with each other. The joy and learning that happens when children have the chance to grow food is remarkable. The lifelong skills and knowledge they develop by understanding how food is grown, how food should taste, and how to cook healthfully and simply can benefit our whole society and the planet.

Our Florida non-profit organization has been trying to help open minds, hearts, and hands to the potential of organic gardening and farming for over twenty years. Now the seeds have germinated and the interest continues to sprout nationwide—from the White House Garden to the USDA People's Garden on the National Mall, to homes, schools, community locations and farms. Gardens can take many shapes. We have a GIFT Garden program to install raised bed organic gardens in low-income people's homes so they can have better access to fresh organic food for their family. A true hand up, not a hand out, as the garden can help supply fresh organic food for many years. We hope to see the program expand to new areas. A couple members in a neighborhood can be the force that helps create a community garden to improve the landscape, the feel, and the food for many. There are several examples of facilities, institutions, and schools using community gardens to achieve multiple benefits.

No doubt, when families grow food for themselves, they contribute to our communities' resilience and capacity for self-sufficient survival. For Florida's food security in particular, this should be a crucial component of life skills development and natural disaster readiness as we prepare for potential changes in our climate and potential emergencies in interstate trade and food distribution at a time of increasing energy prices. As a peninsula, we are in greater need to be aware of our vulnerability to unforeseen disruptions. Growing food for our own families and communities is certainly one of the best ways we can stay healthy now and on down the road.

Through the decades I heard over and over how organic farming and gardening just isn't possible in Florida, there are just too many challenges. The soil is too poor, it's too wet, too dry, too hot, too hard. While the "experts and authorities" kept saying it couldn't be done, there was an ever-growing number of farmers and gardeners who just kept doing it. Their proof is in the delicious tasting produce that continued to come out of organic farms and gardens. Don't forget, organic gardening and farming isn't really the new way, it is the way that has over *10,000 years* of real testing and practice. Even though some Western folks get a lot of credit, they learned from ancient culture's practices that have been refined over the years—good crop rotation, embracing biodiversity, conserving and building top soil, seed saving, companion planting, recycling of nutrient resources, intercropping, practices that just make sense in living biological systems. These topics are explained by Melissa and Ginny in the book in easy to digest language.

In truth, we have an even greater opportunity in Florida than in many states because our climate allows us to grow food nearly year-round. All through fall, winter, and spring there is an opportunity to have a bounty to be shared. Even in summer, with a little bit of learning, we can manage the heat and use that time for appropriate crops or to help rebuild our soils with cover crops or appreciate the resting of fallow earth. Florida gardeners have needed an organic vegetable gardening book like this. Melissa and Ginny have included many Florida crops not normally covered, such as chayote, corn salad, Malabar spinach, and sugar cane, and they have arranged the crops by family so crop rotation will be easier for you to accomplish. Folks have told us they need information, and this book provides a great, comprehensive resource to manage some of our uniquely tropical and sub-tropical challenges—all organically.

In fact, that might be the best part: we don't have to use poison or toxic chemicals to grow food. You don't need patented seeds tied to using a seed company's chemicals. You just need to be resourceful and innovative, and with a little guidance, and maybe a few friends, you'll be on your way to a bounty out your back door.

Picking fresh organic peas, tomatoes, beans, fruit, or veggies at their peak of ripeness and enjoying them makes one think about true food security, food safety, and sustainability, about how we treat our earth and resources and how well they treat us back. Freezing or preserving part of the harvest and enjoying a treat later brings a smile to our faces and an excitement toward "next year."

So, after you read a little, get up off the couch, look to see where you may have some space at home or in your community available to do a little gardening, think what you might like to grow and eat, and make it happen. May you get rain when you need it, have sunshine when you don't, feel only minimal frustration and abundant joy as you come to know, have, and appreciate your relationship with your garden.

Marty Mesh
Executive Director, Florida Certified Organic Growers and Consumers, Inc.
www.foginfo.org

Preface

We are excited about this project and believe that vegetable gardeners have needed a book like this for a long time. Many books on vegetable gardening have quickly dismissed organic methods in just a paragraph or two, but now the tide is turning. Gardeners want to know more about how to grow beautiful vegetables without using synthetic fertilizers or poisons. Although we started this project as active vegetable gardeners, researching and writing this book has been an educational adventure for both of us.

We first met in the fall of 2009 when Ginny was on a book tour to support *Sustainable Gardening for Florida*. Melissa invited Ginny to speak at The Edible Garden Festival, at Fairchild Tropical Botanic Garden.

Later, when approached by the University Press of Florida to write an organic gardening book for Florida, Ginny thought immediately of Melissa. Melissa is a Master Gardener located in south Florida who has taken her passion public through her work at Fairchild and as the creator of the Urban Oasis Project. Having one of us in north Florida and the other in south Florida is important because growing edibles varies significantly from one end of the state to the other. We met in person a few times during the writing process, but most of our collaboration took place via Google Docs, e-mail, and telephone.

A major advantage of working with the University Press of Florida is the feedback we received from the expert readers who rigorously reviewed our manuscript. We'd like to thank Mickie Swisher and Steve

xiv · Preface

Christman for their thorough reviews. We also enlisted the help of several informal readers. Thanks go to Rose Broome, Victoria Freeman, Frank Macaluso, Helen Marshall, Marty Mesh, and Kevin Songer. We'd also like to thank the professors of the Organic Agriculture Institute, including Glenn Hall, Oscar Liburd, Robert McSorely, Amy Simonne, Mickie Swisher, Danielle Treadwell, and Xin Zhao, who made themselves and their work available to us. In addition, we would like to thank Joyce DiBenedetto-Colton, Gabriele Marewski, Andres Mejides, Margie Pikarsky, Tim Rowan, Chris and Eva Worden, Art Friedrich, Florida Organic Growers, and Miami Dade County Extension. Thanks also go to the numerous other growers who along the way have shaped our knowledge and this book. Nevertheless, any remaining errors or miscalculations are our own.

While most of the photographs are ours, we'd like to thank Nathan Ballentine, Emilia and Cesar V. Contreras, Sarva Deslauriers, Nell Foster, Antonio Guadamuz, Robert Rozell, Ann Schmidt, and Kevin Songer for allowing us to use their photos in order to tell a more complete story. And thanks go to Marjorie Shropshire for her beautiful illustrations—they add clarity to the text.

We would like to thank our families and spouses, Dean Avery and Cesar A. Contreras, for their support and encouragement.

Lastly, our thanks go to you, our readers. We've been thinking of you throughout this process, and we hope our book will be helpful to you in your vegetable gardening endeavors.

To learn more about updates, events, speaking engagements, and reviews related to this book, check out our website: http://www.FloridaVegetableGardening.com.

Happy Gardening,
Ginny Stibolt and Melissa Contreras

Organic Methods for Vegetable Gardening in Florida

The Movement toward Gardening Organically in Florida

Growing your own food is gaining in popularity, and organic produce is the fastest growing segment of the food industry. Indeed, it seems there is a perfect storm of conditions that appeal to people who grow food in a down economy, who are concerned about food safety, and who support locally grown food.

The interest in local food is multifaceted and ranges from reducing one's carbon footprint to supporting local economies and propagating and conserving heirloom and regional crop species. And what is more local than produce grown a few steps from your front or back door?

Vegetable, Fruit, Herb, or Spice—What's Covered in This Book?

Technically, a vegetable is any edible part of a plant that is not the fruit. A vegetable can take the form of leaves, stems, tubers, flowers, or roots. While we think of tomatoes, squash, corn, beans, and peas as vegetables, they are technically fruit crops because we consume the part that contains or surrounds the seeds. Politically, there's no predicting what will qualify as a fruit or a vegetable. In 1893 the U.S. Supreme Court declared that for the purposes of for taxing and tariff laws, tomatoes were vegetables; in 1979 the European Union's Jam Directive, which sets the standards for the amount of fruit in jams, declared that carrots are fruits.

The strong odors herbs produce are probably intended to ward off bugs and slugs that might eat them, but those scented chemicals make them oh so attractive to cooks. Usually, the aromatic parts of plants that are not associated with the fruit are called herbs and those that are part of the fruit are called spices. Some crop plants can be both an herb and a spice. Dill is a good example: when we consume the feathery leaves in salads, spreads, or stews, it's an herb, but when we collect the pungent-smelling seeds to use in pickling or flavoring, then it's a spice. Many herbs are herbaceous, meaning they lack woody stems and generally die back each year. But some herbs, like rosemary, are woody.

The vegetables and herbs covered in this book are those defined in the broad, culinary sense and include the traditional crops that grow well in Florida. Edible flowers such as nasturtiums and marigolds plus edible native plants such as meadow garlic and spotted horsemint are also included.

Growing trees or shrubs that bear fruit or nuts—such as blueberries, grapes, citrus, pecans, dates, coconuts, bananas, and many others—is a wonderful idea when you have the room and the right environment. Fruits and nuts certainly add more variety to your harvest, and growing them is an important part of sustainable, ecosystem-wide gardening. Because the growing methods involved are vastly different from that of the classic crop vegetables, this book does not cover Florida's woody crops.

Gardening Organically

There are many reasons why organic gardening methods work well, even for small, family gardens. The main reason is that you work *with* Mother Nature, not against her, by building fertile soil naturally, by inviting beneficial bugs and other organisms to your garden, by recycling plant materials, and by providing the ideal conditions for your crops. Many people think that organically grown foods are not only safer but also tastier and more nutritious. But because you're looking at this book, you're probably aware of the benefits of organic produce and are looking for a straightforward and scientifically accurate treatment of the topic. So let's get started!

Defining Organic

The chemical definition of an organic compound is one that includes carbon and hydrogen, along with other naturally occurring elements. Anything that is or once was alive is made of organic materials because the vast majority of life on our planet depends in some way on carbon-based sugars formed by green plants during the magical process of photosynthesis. For example, when advised to add organic material to your soil, you could reach for compost, dead leaves, wood chips, manure from herbivores, or worm castings. Materials that have been predigested (i.e., compost, manures, and worm castings) provide nutrients in a more readily available form to the plants in your garden than do more recognizable materials such as dead leaves or wood chips, but they're all organic.

Pure sand, on the other hand, is inorganic because it's composed of various rocks and minerals that have never been alive. Fertilizers that have been manufactured with chemicals not derived from organic sources are also not organic. Some people label them "chemical fertilizers," but everything consists of chemicals—either alone as elements or combined as compounds. More accurate terms are artificial or synthetic fertilizers.

J. I. Rodale coined another use of the word "organic" in the 1940s when he started *Organic Gardening* magazine and wrote about the practice of farming without artificial chemicals. In 1990 Congress passed the Organic Food Production Act, authorizing the U.S. Department of Agriculture (USDA) to establish a nationwide definition for organic food and standards for organic certification.

In 1995, the National Organic Standards Board defined organic agriculture as "an ecological production management system that promotes and enhances biodiversity, biological cycles, and soil biological activity. It is based on minimal use of off-farm inputs and on management practices that restore, maintain, and enhance ecological harmony."

Becoming a certified organic grower is a rigorous process. For instance, if an organic farmer uses hay as mulch, that hay must be free of any artificial chemical residues and all the seeds to grow it must have come from organic gardens. If the local government sends a mosquito insecticide truck to spray an area near the garden, the pesticide-free environment will have been compromised unless the truck is using an organic insecticide that is approved for certified growers such as Bt (*Bacillus thuringensis*).

This book is not a guide to certification, but there are many ways any gardener can incorporate organic methods for growing safe and nutritious produce in Florida or anywhere.

Organic Products

Just because a product carries an organic label does not necessarily mean that it won't damage the environment; it means only that it's derived from animals or plants. Poisons, organic or not, kill both beneficial and pesky bugs, and their use should be minimized or eliminated as you work on integrated pest management (IPM), as discussed in chapter 9. The main problem with organic poisons is that people either overuse them or do not carefully follow the instructions for use, assuming that because the products are organic, they must be safe at any level of usage.

The USDA maintains a list of pesticides that organic farmers are allowed to use. Some of these are substances that are toxic only to a targeted group of pests, while others provide physical barriers to pests, such as sticky papers or diatomaceous earth whose sharp edges slice the undersides of caterpillars, worms, and slugs. Some last only a short time before degrading into harmless byproducts.

Record Keeping

Even if you're not planning to become a certified organic grower, record keeping is an important practice of a successful gardener. A journal can be a simple hand-written notebook or a fancy computer spreadsheet or document. At a minimum, record these items each season:

- A chart or map of your growing areas marked with the crops that were planted
- The source of your seed or seedling, its cultivar (or variety) name, and its stated resistance to diseases
- The date of planting (if it's a seedling you raised, record when it was started as well)
- Whether bugs or disease attacked your crop and what action you took
- When you began to harvest and the date of your final harvest (with your judgment on its success)
- The following crop or cover crop

Organic Crop Quality

Some people equate organic vegetables with ugly, worm-eaten, or substandard produce. They think or have been convinced that farmers and gardeners must apply pesticides and use artificial fertilizers to have perfect-looking fruits and vegetables. They are surprised when they learn that most organic growers produce beautiful and bountiful harvests. The best way to accomplish this is by providing the ideal growing conditions for your crops so they'll grow as quickly as possible. This goal of a beautiful and bountiful harvest is revisited throughout this book. If a crop shows signs of distress, act promptly to help it or call it a loss, yank it out, and start with the next rotation. Gardening (organic or not) is always subject to Mother Nature's whims. A crop may be fantastically successful one year, and less so the next for no apparent reason—from your perspective, you applied the same gardening techniques.

When First Lady Michelle Obama and the White House chef Sam Kass organized the installation of a 1,100-square-foot organic vegetable garden on the White House property in 2009, many people, especially those in the business of chemically supported agriculture, were quick to criticize, saying that the produce would be ugly and the harvest small. The criticism quickly died down when the harvests were beautiful and bountiful. The White House garden has also been used for educational purposes—not only to spread the word about growing your own vegetables but also about eating a healthier diet. In addition, the garden has changed the way the White House chefs plan the menus. This garden has been an inspiration to many.

Permaculture

Permaculture, a term coined in the 1970s by Australian ecologist Bill Mollison and his student David Holmgren, is often followed by the description "sustainable living." Organic gardening methods and consideration of the whole ecosystem when designing gardens are important pieces of permaculture. Planting perennial or woody crops in the garden and making the best use of available resources are also included. But the permaculture movement extends beyond gardening and agriculture to political topics, such as urban planning, sociology, ethics, overpopulation, and reducing people's reliance upon industrial systems.

Dealing with Florida's Climate

Floridians can drive 833.2 miles, from Pensacola to Key West, and never leave the state. Few other states can boast this distance! Our state's seven distinct USDA plant hardiness zones make covering gardening in all of Florida a special challenge. Most vegetable gardening books (organic or not) are of little use in Florida because "the rules are different here," and furthermore, the rules in Pensacola are different from those in Miami.

To make these differences more manageable, this book divides the state into three regions—north, central, and south—and provides recommended planting times for the three regions as part of the discussion of each vegetable. This information is also available in the regional month-by-month gardener's calendars presented in appendix 1. Suggested planting times are approximations and your actual climate may differ depending upon your proximity to large bodies of water and prevailing winds. This is why it's important to keep a journal, so you can learn from actual experience what works best for your location and with the most recent temperatures. It's also a good idea to check in with neighbors, garden clubs, Master Gardeners, and extension agents in your area for advice on what to grow when.

In Florida, it's not only the cold temperatures that limit our growing seasons but also the sustained warm periods. For instance, in more temperate climates, tomatoes do great in the middle of summer, but here, when the nighttime temperatures are consistently above 70°F, the fruit won't set. While there are some tomatoes that have been bred for heat, mid-summer is simply not tomato time in Florida—rather, we must plant our seedlings as soon as possible in the spring and again at the end of summer for a fall crop. Many stores sell tomato plants

Map showing north, central and south Florida. Courtesy of USDA.

(organic and not) throughout the summer even though they will not be successful. Educated gardeners will not buy them. So pay attention to the suggested planting times for your section of the state and time your crop plantings for the greatest success.

You may be able to extend your growing season further into the warm periods by creating some shade. This can be accomplished with portable shade houses or tents, or under the shade of trees in containers or raised beds so that your vegetables are not competing with tree roots for water. Plan for afternoon shade by siting the beds on the east side of a building, pergola, or tall climbing crop. Shade won't help set fruit on your tomatoes or reduce the summertime boom in bug populations, but you may be able to extend the season for leafy greens and other cool weather vegetables.

Florida's gardeners can grow cool-weather crops right through the winter months. But when planting in zone 8A in Florida's Panhandle and maybe in zone 8B during cold winters, row covers, blankets, or hoop houses might be called for during the coldest periods.

Growing crops during the shortest days of the year limits the choices for some vegetables. If you grow onions, you'll need to choose a short-day variety to be successful. Winter growing may also limit your sun exposure, if there are trees or buildings near the garden. Winter shadows may engulf an area that has good sun in the summer.

Rainfall: Too Much or Too Little

While Florida normally has its fair share of precipitation, with an average annual rainfall ranging from thirty-nine to sixty-four inches, its seven-month dry season (from November through June) also coincides with the best temperatures for growing cool-weather crops

Table 1. Monthly Rainfall in Inches						
	Pensacola	Apalachicola	Jacksonville	Tampa	Miami	Key West	Average per Month
Jan.	5.34	4.87	3.69	2.27	1.88	2.22	3.378
Feb.	4.68	3.76	3.15	2.67	2.07	1.51	2.973
Mar.	6.40	4.95	3.93	2.84	2.56	1.86	3.757
Apr.	3.89	3.00	3.14	1.80	3.36	2.06	2.875
May	4.40	2.62	3.48	2.85	5.52	3.48	3.725
June	6.39	4.30	5.37	5.50	8.54	4.57	5.778
July	8.02	7.31	5.97	6.49	5.79	3.27	6.142
Aug.	6.85	7.29	6.87	7.60	8.63	5.40	7.107
Sept.	5.75	7.10	7.90	6.54	8.38	5.45	6.853
Oct.	4.13	4.18	3.86	2.29	6.19	4.34	4.165
Nov.	4.46	3.62	2.34	1.62	3.43	2.64	3.018
Dec.	3.97	3.51	2.64	2.30	2.18	2.14	2.790
Total	64.28	56.51	52.34	44.77	58.53	38.94	52.562

Source: http://www.noaa.gov.
Notes: The table shows the thirty-year average for rainfall in Florida. June–October are considered the wet season (5 mos.), and rainfall averages 6.01 inches per month. Rainfall during the dry season (7 mos.) averages 3.22 inches per month.

and with the beginning of the warm-weather crop season. On average, the dry season months have only half the monthly rainfall as the five months of the wet season. This presents a significant challenge to Florida's gardeners because most crops require regular and deep irrigation. For all crops there are critical times when irrigation is a must—for instance, when seedlings have recently germinated or have been transplanted.

During the wet season, storms can dump several inches of rain in a day or two. This can cause several problems in your vegetable gardens:

- Saturated soil creates sustained puddling in low areas, causing crop failure due to lack of oxygen in the soil, root rot, and fungal attacks; most crop plants have poor tolerance for wetness.
- Garden beds erode and smaller plants are uprooted as large volumes of water rush through.
- Nutrients in the soil can be washed away.
- Tropical storms can carry salt spray a mile or more inland; most crops are not salt tolerant.

Most of these problems can be mitigated by using contained raised beds or container gardens, which provide better drainage, are protected from erosion, and can easily be refreshed with new soil amendments to replace lost nutrients. They also make it easier to flush away salts that have accumulated.

Humidity

While there is often a break in Florida's high humidity during the winter months, gardeners need to be aware that constant moisture in the air produces conditions that favor fungal attacks. Fungi can cause problems such as the damping off of newly sprouted seedlings, and various wilts, molds, and rusts. Preventive or defensive gardening practices include choosing fungus-resistant varieties, irrigating carefully so leaves don't get wet, sprouting seeds in a more sterile environment, and removing infected plants from the garden quickly and disposing of them properly.

Gardening and Florida's Myriad Soil Types

Growing vegetables in Florida's soil—from the red Georgia clay substrate in the Panhandle to the limestone rock in the Keys and the acidic sandy soil between—can present a significant challenge. While there is a lot of agriculture throughout Florida and large growers have obviously figured out how to grow successful crops, the small farmer may be better off avoiding the soil problem entirely by building raised beds.

Florida soils vary greatly from region to region, county to county, and within even smaller areas. Muck, marl, sand, clay, and rock—we have it all. The invention of the rock plow in the 1950s allowed farmers in south Florida to grow crops directly on the solid limestone substrate. The soil in Miami–Dade County is very alkaline—with a pH between 7.5 and 8.5—because of that limestone.

Raised beds and lots of compost solve these problems for the home gardener. Small organic farmers bring in lots of organic matter and use cover crops to build more soil.

Gardening in Florida Offers More Opportunities than Obstacles

Of all the advantages of Florida gardening, year-round harvests are probably the favorite of most gardeners. Being prepared for the obstacles that could negatively affect your crops is the best way to maximize your yields. The mission of this book is to help you have fun eating from your landscape.

Resources

For the USDA website on organic gardening, see http://www.ams. usda.gov/AMSv1.0/nop.

For the Florida Organic Growers Association, see http://www. foginfo.org.

Check the University of Florida's Institute of Food and Agricultural Sciences (IFAS) resource pages for organic production: http://edis. ifas.ufl.edu/topic_organic_gardening; http://edis.ifas.ufl.edu/topic_ organic_production and http://smallfarms.ifas.ufl.edu/organic_ production/organic_vegetables.html.

The National Sustainable Agriculture Information Service (AT TRA) provides a range of documents and publications pertaining to organic agriculture: http://attra.ncat.org.

The Florida Automated Weather Network provides information on rain and evaporation rates that can be useful for growers: http://fawn. ifas.ufl.edu/.

2

Siting and Arranging the Edible Garden

When many people think of growing vegetables, they picture a large rectangular plot in the backyard or a field filled with crops growing in long, widely spaced rows that must be plowed every year. You could do all that extra work to create such a plot, but now there are smarter ways to grow edibles. And you can grow plenty of fresh produce, even if your space is limited. Three of the most important ways to garden smarter is to rethink the backyard-only location, the widely spaced rows, and the annual plowing. Some of the problems with the traditional vegetable garden setup and regimen include the following:

Annual plowing—Besides being a lot of work, it disturbs the soil structure, making it more prone to drought and erosion, kills beneficial worms and other soil inhabitants, and unearths lots of weed seeds.

Widely spaced rows—While they may be a reasonable setup for large farming operations that use machinery (motorized or animal drawn), for the small grower the spaces between the rows can amount to three to four times more area to weed and water. Also, walking between the rows compacts the soil; once the soil has been compacted, it may not drain well and will need to be plowed before planting.

Native soil—In some regions of Florida, the soil is not suitable for growing edibles. The limestone, clay, sand, or salty soils make it difficult to grow a successful in-the-ground edible garden without a lot of extra effort.

The backyard—While it may offer a suitable, sunny location for some, many people are growing wonderful edibles in the front yard, patio, balcony, or porch. Some of these edibles are planted in cottage gardens where herbs, vegetables, and ornamental plants all grow together, while others are planted in containers or raised beds.

Growing Requirements

Plants will flourish if they are grown in their optimum environment, and gardeners will reap the benefit with a bountiful and wonderfully tasty crop. When plants are stressed by unfavorable conditions, their growth slows. When this happens, the plants are more susceptible to damage by bugs, fungi, or disease. Edible root crops may become bitter, small, or misshapen. Likewise, leafy crops may become bitter and bolt early as suffering plants attempt to complete their life cycles quickly to produce some seed before dying.

Mother Nature produces some less-than-ideal conditions, with unseasonably hot or cold spells and droughts or torrential tropical storms, but most of the growing requirements can be met when the gardener pays attention to the details. Siting the edible garden is an important and controllable detail.

Exposure

Most vegetables—particularly the fruiting crops like tomatoes, cucumbers, beans, and melons—do best when they receive six to eight hours of full sun. Leafy vegetables such as lettuces and chard or root crops like carrots and beets might grow well enough with less than six hours of direct sun, and may do better with some late afternoon shade for relief from Florida's hot sun, especially in south Florida.

So when you are looking for places to plant your edibles, time the sun exposure in both the summer and the winter. You'll be surprised by the long shadows cast by trees or buildings in the winter when neither had much effect in the summer. Enterprising winter gardeners can extend the season by planting their crops in garden wagons and moving the plants to the sunniest locations during the day or rolling them into the garage or some other shelter for the really cold nights.

In coastal Florida—which comprises 1,350 miles of coastline and an additional 2,276 miles of tidal shoreline—there are two more exposures to consider: salty spray from persistent sea breezes and saline groundwater. With very few exceptions, crop plants should be shielded from both. Locate your edible garden on the leeward side of buildings, solid fences, or tall, dense evergreen hedgerows to reduce damage from wind and salt spray. Wind speed can increase in the narrow spaces between buildings, solid walls, or other impenetrable objects in the landscape, so be aware of this effect and, if possible, locate your garden away these corridors or block the wind with thick hedges or fences. Sometimes the groundwater in locations close to waterways tends to be saline. If your garden is in such an area, you'll need to build raised beds or use container gardens.

Roots

When deciding where to site your edible garden, consider the nearby trees and shrubs, not only because of their shade but also their roots. A tree's roots can extend another 30 percent or more beyond its drip line. Some trees, such as maples and sweet gums, have root systems that are particularly shallow and wide spreading. The majority of the water that the roots soak up is pumped straight through the tree, and evaporates through the pores on its leaves—this process is called transpiration. A full-sized oak tree can transpire more than 400 gallons of water in a single summer day.

Essentially, you don't want your vegetables competing with these larger plants for water and nutrients—the trees will always win, even if you install raised beds. For your winter garden, consider whether nearby trees are deciduous; when deciduous trees become dormant in the winter and lose their leaves, their roots do not soak up nearly as much water or nutrients and their shade is much less of a problem. As soon as their leaves pop out in the spring, though, the water-pumping machine starts again.

Trees are valuable assets in ecosystem gardening, so consider their health, too. Excess walking, cutting roots, and piling soil within a tree's drip line are likely to harm the tree over time.

Drainage

Most vegetable crops hate wet feet! No matter how you arrange your plantings, you must plan for drainage. Anywhere in Florida can receive several inches of rain in a day, so think about where all of that water will go. Standing water means the soil has become saturated and its air pockets have been eliminated; under these conditions, the roots can't function properly and the plants may die. Anaerobic microbes will replace the normal aerobic ones in the soil, causing the soil to smell sour and inviting fungal infestation. There's a reason all those acres of swampland were drained before big agriculture could start planting crops in the Everglades region.

When siting your edible garden, avoid areas with persistent or seasonal wetness; that said, if that low spot in your yard is also the sunniest, then you will need to find ways to deal with the extra water. You could build a nearby pond or rain garden to collect the water in a concentrated area, leaving a drier space for your vegetables. Even then, you would be wise to install extra-tall raised beds to ensure that your crops stay relatively dry. One advantage of building a pond large enough to have a reliable water level is that you may be able to use that water for irrigation. The pond will also invite beneficial insects, frogs, and birds to the area, all of which are important parts of ecosystem gardening. Nevertheless, be sure to have the water tested before you use it.

If you are planning in-the-ground garden beds, locate them on a slight slope so the water can drain away. If your garden site has no slope, dig a series of trenches around the beds with catch basins to stop

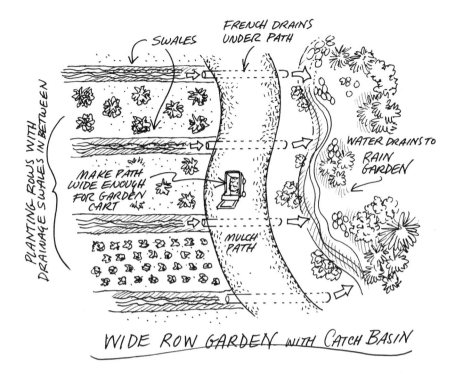

FRENCH DRAINS UNDER PATH

SWALES

WATER DRAINS TO RAIN GARDEN

PLANTING ROWS WITH DRAINAGE SWALES IN BETWEEN

MAKE PATH WIDE ENOUGH FOR GARDEN CART

MULCH PATH

WIDE ROW GARDEN with CATCH BASIN

the water and allow the sediment to settle. At the change in seasons, you can dig out the captured soil and layer it back into the garden or add it to your compost pile. This way, you don't lose your precious soil and you reduce the amount of sediment and pollution coming from your property.

You can place raised beds on hard surfaces such as patios, driveways, hard limestone, or rock-hard clay. Be sure to test the drainage before you plant to avoid giving your plants wet feet. When working on a hard surface, build your raised beds at least eight inches deep—deeper beds can accommodate a wider variety of crops.

Irrigation

For the purposes of locating your garden, you need to consider how you will provide water to your crops. (For a detailed description of irrigation options, see chapter 8.) Your edibles will need extra irrigation during Florida's seven-month dry season, which lasts from November through June and corresponds to our most productive seasons—winter and spring.

Self-irrigating containers have a water reservoir in the bottom and keep the soil damp through wicking action. You will still need to make sure that the water doesn't run out, but using this type of container does mean that you will have to worry about watering less often. For the weekend gardener, this may be the perfect setup.

If your garden proves too difficult to water, your enthusiasm for gardening may wane and your crops will suffer. So whether you're growing vegetables on your own property or in a community garden, be sure to plan for irrigation.

Landscape Usage

While you can grow edibles in many places in the landscape, how you and your family use the area will affect the success of your garden. If the sunniest spot lies along the driveway, you will need to build sturdy, raised beds that drivers can easily see and that can withstand a nudge from a tire if a driver overshoots the turning radius.

If you have small children or are designing a school garden, you can encourage the kids to participate in the edible garden by planting easy- and fast-growing vegetables. Design the beds so that kids can reach into the growing area to weed and harvest without walking on the soil where the crops grow. If you place the edibles next to a play area for kids or dogs, use sturdy (but removable) fencing so that errant balls, Frisbees, or other toys don't damage the crops. (Don't allow cats and dogs into the growing or composting areas. The nice loose soil you've worked hard to build provides an irresistible sandbox for cats and a lovely digging spot for dogs. Fence them out—for your health and safety.)

Many cooks love to locate the herb garden just outside the kitchen door so they can easily collect just the right herb for their savory recipes. Most herbs are tolerant of hot and somewhat drier conditions, so if you have a hot microclimate next to a southwest-facing wall, consider using it for an herb garden.

If you intend to grow tall or rangy edibles, plant them in the back corners on the north side of the beds or in other out-of-the-way locations so that they don't crowd or shade the other crops or look too sloppy. For instance, pumpkins or gourds are likely to spread thirty feet or more in a long season; plant them next to a meadow or along an edge where they can scramble through the tall grasses or up a nearby tree. If you are planting perennial crops such as Jerusalem artichoke or sugarcane, plan for their needs away from the hustle and bustle of the short-term crops and their continual rotations. Tall perennials like these could also form an effective barrier at the periphery of your garden.

Many home gardeners are more successful when they grow their vegetables close to their houses. Living close to your garden makes you more likely to spot a problem, pull a few weeds, or quickly irrigate wilted seedlings. Gardeners who locate their gardens some distance from their living areas might visit less often, and less frequent tending increases the chances of something going wrong.

Growing among Ornamentals

Many crops are every bit as attractive as plants grown as ornamentals, and whole books have been written about integrating edibles into your landscape at large. Whether your yard is formal or informal, edibles are appropriate additions to your plantings. Many gardeners are rethinking the old idea of separating the "pretty" part of the yard from the practical, productive parts.

For example, you might plant attractive, formal herb gardens inside a border of trimmed rosemary hedges. Less formal cottage-style gardens provide a riot of color and texture when planted with edibles including those with edible flowers such as roses and nasturtiums. Why not plant a border of garlic chives instead of liriope? In a sunny front yard in south Florida, you can integrate a stand of edible pineapple plants into your bromeliad collection. Pineapples are low-maintenance and attractive plantings year-round, but they get even better, for both the eyes and the taste buds, when they bear fruit.

A ruffle of leaf lettuces of various colors creates a beautiful border for any garden, whether it's in the ground or in a decorative container. Colorful and cold-weather loving, cabbages are bold replacements for your warm-weather flowers. Once you start integrating edibles into your landscape, you'll wonder why you hadn't started sooner—it's addictive to have your garden and eat it too.

Intensive Gardening Methods

As discussed at the beginning of this chapter, widely spaced rows are not the ideal setup for smaller growing operations, primarily because it means maintaining large areas of unplanted soil.

The other design flaw in long-row gardening for smaller operations is that your crop will mature at the same time and probably yield more produce than you can use. It's unlikely that a single family will be able to consume forty or more cabbages all at once. You will create "just-in-time" vegetable harvests if your planting schedule includes only what you can comfortably consume. If you plant only a few cabbages at the beginning of the cool season, and then three or four weeks later plant a few more, you might have three or four rounds of cabbage before the hot weather arrives. This way, you'll be able to consume the cabbages more comfortably. Even if you are growing extra crops to donate to needy families or soup kitchens, the receiving parties will appreciate a good variety of crops.

Many old-timers planted all the seeds from a package in a row and then stabbed the packet with a stick and stuck it the soil as a marker. This method makes it easy to remember what we planted where, but (and this is a big *but*) this method of sowing seeds usually results in way too many seeds being planted at one time. Upon sprouting, the densely planted seedlings must be drastically thinned in order to provide enough room for the remaining plants to grow. If the thinning isn't accomplished soon enough, or not at all, the whole crop will suffer from the crowded conditions. What a waste of time, money, and garden space!

Most small growers favor a more intensive and logical planting arrangement to grow crops more efficiently. Plant fewer seeds in properly prepared soil at just the right distance from each other to reduce the amount of weeding and thinning. Seed tapes ensure proper spacing and have the added advantage of allowing you to see where you've planted seeds so you don't overseed an already-planted area. Smaller gardens also require less water for irrigation than large ones. Plant small areas with a single crop adjacent to other small plantings of crops from different families. The exception would be a crop like corn, which requires a large number of plants in close proximity to one another for pollination to occur.

Intensive gardening requires some extra planning, but the results are well worth the effort and offer many key benefits:

- Decreased weeding, soil building, and water use because the wide spaces between rows are eliminated;
- Increased plant growth because the soil is not compressed;
- Decreased labor because the seeds are properly spaced so little or no thinning is required;
- Fewer chances of gardenwide infestation of bugs or disease because crops belonging to the same families are separated and rotated to different areas in the following seasons;
- Less waste because we have planned ahead for reasonably sized harvests.

Vertical Gardening

Vertical gardening is a technique well suited to small garden spaces. One type of vertical gardening involves incorporating trellises, nets, strings, cages, or poles for supporting vining and sprawling plants in your in-ground or raised beds. This will maximize your yield per square foot. Cucumbers, tomatoes, melons, and pole beans are good candidates for this treatment. Some plants entwine themselves onto the support, while others may need to be tied. Heavy fruits such as melons and pumpkins require slings for extra support, but elevating them above the ground makes them less likely to rot or to be eaten by slugs or insect larvae. Another type of trellis arrangement that works well for heavy fruit is an A-frame constructed with small ladders tied together at the top. Insert shelves on the rungs at various levels, and as a fruit is formed just place it on a shelf—no sling necessary.

Remember that a vertical planting will cast a shadow, so position it on the north side of the bed to avoid shading sun-loving crops. You can take advantage of the shade it does provide by planting shade-tolerant crops near the trellis. Because plants growing vertically are more exposed to the elements than nonstaked plants, they dry out more quickly and may need more frequent irrigation. On the other hand, being fast-drying and above the soil are advantages for plants that are susceptible to fungal diseases.

Green Wall Gardening

A green wall garden, which is a garden composed of various containers that are filled with soil and strapped to or hung by a support system, is another type of vertical gardening. The wall could be a stand-alone structure built specifically to support a garden or a part of an existing structure like a pergola on the south- or west-facing side of a building or shed. Before you start planning your garden, evaluate your wall, noting in particular its support capability and its vulnerability to the damp conditions that frequently occur near plants.

There are various ways to provide pockets of soil on your wall large enough to grow small crops such as lettuces and other small greens, radishes, strawberries, green onions, thyme, chives, or other small herbs. Given the limited amount of soil, you will need to provide ample space for each plant; after you have harvested the crop, dump all the old soil into your working compost pile, and start your next crop in new soil.

Gutters—Mount an array of plastic gutters on a vertical structure, having drilled holes in the bottoms for drainage. Then, add end pieces, and fill with soil.

Shoe organizers—Various closet-organizing systems use hanging shoe-holding bags made of cloth or plastic. Shoe organizers provide an easy way to set up a wall garden. Hang the shoe holder on a strong support and fill each pocket with soil. If you use the plastic shoe bags, be sure to poke at least one small hole in the bottom of each compartment for drainage.

Fabric tubes—Tubes made of landscape fabric can be filled with soil and strapped to a strong vertical structure. Plant your seedlings in cuts made near the top of the tube. You can make your own or purchase commercially made systems.

Hanging pots—A green wall could also be outfitted with a series of hanging pots of various sizes, with alternating hanger lengths providing the best coverage. You may also hang the pots from each other by hooking lower pots to the rim of the higher pots. Before you hang too many pots test the strength of the support system.

Window boxes—A series of window boxes made of coconut fiber supported in a metal frame or in a solid product made of wood, fake wood, or plastic can be hung on a wall or railing. These boxes offer enough soil and space to grow a greater variety of crops.

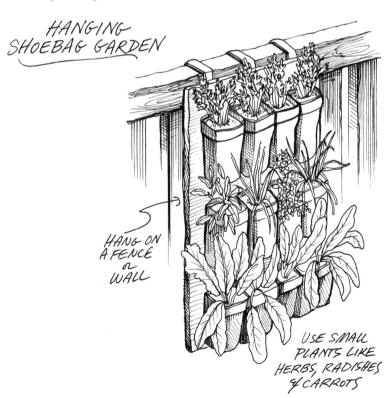

HANGING
SHOEBAG GARDEN

HANG ON
A FENCE
or
WALL

USE SMALL
PLANTS LIKE
HERBS, RADISHES
& CARROTS

However you arrange your green wall, ensure that there is plenty of sun, good airflow, adequate irrigation, and good drainage. Green walls are the ultimate in space-saving edible gardens.

Green Roof Gardening

An increasing number of buildings are being constructed across the country with energy-saving green roof systems. Here in Florida, the systems that work best are those that collect rainwater in cisterns and reuse it for irrigation or that irrigate using the condensate from air conditioner compressors. Green roofs are braced to withstand the weight of the soil and fare much better than "normal" roofs in hurricane-force winds. There are two types of green roofs:

(1) Intensive green roofs are designed to accommodate frequent human access and a variety of planters and plants, including shrubs and small trees.

(2) Extensive green roofs, which are often built at fairly steep angles, do not accommodate frequent human traffic and are usually planted with a solid field of low-care, drought-tolerant, low-growing perennials.

Only intensive green roofs are suitable for edible gardens. Building a green roof system is a major expense, but if you have access to an intensive green roof, you can plant a fantastic edible garden. The sun exposure a roof offers is hard to beat, but keep in mind that the wind will be stronger and the heat greater. You will probably need to supplement the automated irrigation system with a manual system to keep your plants from wilting in the rooftop heat and drying winds. Also, be sure to make the vertical parts of your garden strong enough to withstand the winds, especially when covered with your vining crops.

Square-Foot Gardening

In 1976, Mel Bartholomew, an efficiency specialist, came up with the concept of square-foot gardening, and in 1981 he published his best-selling book. Now he has updated his system in a new book, *All New*

Square Foot Gardening (2005), which offers many more logical ideas for efficient gardening. His enthusiasm is contagious.

The main idea is to create a grid in your planting area marked with string, slats from old Venetian blinds, or inexpensive one-inch-wide wood lath. The grid should be no wider than four feet, and because you should never walk in your garden, you will need to position the grid so you can tend each of the square-foot sections.

Within each square you sow seeds such that the plants will be properly spaced according to their needs. For instance, one square could accommodate four leafy lettuce plants, so you would space the seeds or seedlings so the center of each quarter square foot contains one lettuce plant. If you are sowing seeds directly into the soil, plant two or three seeds in each of the four shallow holes. After they sprout, choose the best of the seedlings and cut the others away with a small pair of scissors. For radishes or carrots, plant sixteen seeds per square foot; for cabbages or peppers, just one. This precalculated number of plants

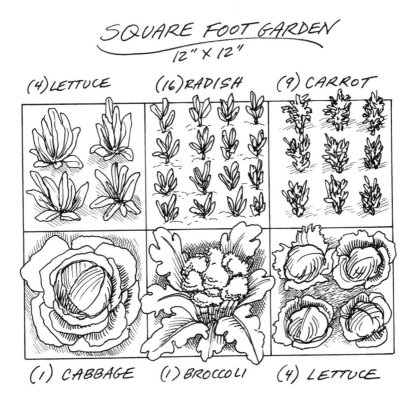

SQUARE FOOT GARDEN
12" X 12"

(4) LETTUCE   (16) RADISH   (9) CARROT

(1) CABBAGE   (1) BROCCOLI   (4) LETTUCE

makes it easier to consider just how many carrots (and other crops) you'll want at one time. The other advantage to this pattern of seed sowing is the knowledge that anything that sprouts outside of the grid pattern is probably a weed.

Wide-Row Planting

Instead of planting a single row of plants in your garden, planting in a wide row squeezes more crop plants into a small area without sacrificing the proper spacing between plants. Wide rows are typically six- to twenty-inches wide with four to eight inches of well-mulched space between rows. For easy maintenance, build the rows no more than four feet across. You can think of this arrangement as a variation on the square-foot garden, where seedlings are planted or seeds sown so that there is the proper spacing between the plants.

In the wide-row planting method, the space between the rows is relatively narrow and is not for walking, although it does provide more space between crops than a square-foot garden where the only intervening space is that one-inch-wide lath. This extra space also serves as a trench for easy runoff in the event of a heavy rainstorm—an important feature in Florida. The trench should be heavily mulched to keep the weeds out and the moisture in. The heavy mulch also prevents erosion. Also, your garden toads will love that mulch for keeping cool on a hot day.

You can also use the space between the rows for trench composting, but only before you plant or before your plants are mature enough to have an extensive root system. (For more on composting—trench and otherwise—see chapter 3.)

You can accomplish wide-row gardening using raised beds or in-ground gardens, and this may be the most flexible arrangement for small growers who farm without the aid of tractors.

Keyhole Gardens

U-shaped keyhole gardens provide the highest ratio of gardening space to walking space. They are usually raised beds about three feet wide with a narrow path cut into the top of the U. The end of the access path at the bottom of the U can be enlarged to provide more room for the gardener to turn in all directions. The name keyhole comes from the shape of the access path. Once in the center, the gardener can reach the whole bed.

Several keyhole gardens can be set up together in a row—each with its own access path. If you have the room, you could set up another set of keyhole beds oriented in the opposite direction so that the tops of

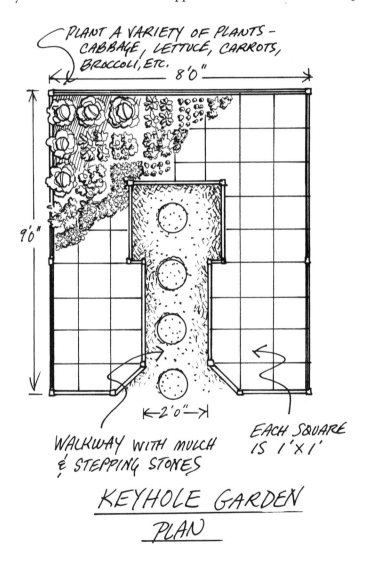

PLANT A VARIETY OF PLANTS —
CABBAGE, LETTUCE, CARROTS,
BROCCOLI, ETC.

8'0"

9'6"

2'0"

WALKWAY WITH MULCH
& STEPPING STONES

EACH SQUARE
IS 1'×1'

KEYHOLE GARDEN
PLAN

the U's face each other, with a path between the two sets wide enough to accommodate a garden cart.

Within the U-shaped beds, you could arrange your plantings based on a modified square-foot pattern or a radiating wide-row pattern. Many permaculture proponents recommend this arrangement for its efficient use of space.

Mounds

Whether you are using square-foot gardens, wide rows, or keyhole gardens, there are some unruly crops like squash, cucumbers, or melons that just won't conform to our artificial boundaries. For these outsized crops, mounds are a good solution.

A typical mound is two feet in diameter and piled a foot high above the soil level. If the mound is in a sandy area with good drainage, you should probably start with a thick layer of dead leaves or other dense organic material that will help hold moisture in the mound. For crops with high nutrient demands, add a shovel full of composted manure under the center of the mound. Build the rest of the mound with compost and soil.

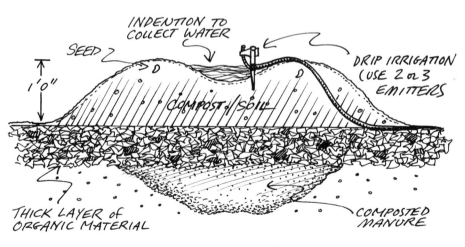

CROSS SECTION of a SQUASH MOUND

Make a good-sized indentation in the center of the mound to collect water so that it's available to your crop. According to the size of the crop, plant between two and four seeds at regular intervals around the rim of the mound. Some people say that mounds are not necessary in Florida, but the erratic rainfall means that during dry spells these crops, especially melons, will require lots of additional irrigation. The indentation in the mound will ensure that the water doesn't roll away. Arrange your drip system so that two or three emitters fill this indentation. Plant fewer vines per mound if you'll be hand watering, or if the amount of water is limited.

Intercropping

There are several methods of intercropping, all of which combine crops to take advantage of the temporal, spatial, or physical characteristics that allow them to grow well together. Here are some examples:

- Sow the seeds of a fast-growing crop with those of a slow-growing crop, so the fast grower is harvested before the slow-growing crop matures. For example, plant forty-day radishes around your newly planted bell pepper seedlings—you'll harvest the radishes and recompost and remulch the area long before the heat of summer when the peppers start to produce.
- Plant a cool-weather crop on the north side of a summer crop a few weeks before harvest time. Until it's harvested, the summer crop will shade the cool weather crop, giving it a good start. Be careful not to damage your new fall crop when cleaning up the summer crop. You may, for example, wish to snip off the plants you are removing at, or just below, the soil level to avoid disrupting the roots of your new crop. The old roots will then become part of the organic material in the soil.
- Use the physical characteristics of one plant to complement those of another. When you plant corn, pole beans, and squash together on the same hill, the beans crawl up the corn stalk and the large squash leaves shade the ground, discouraging weeds. Native Americans called this arrangement the Three

Sisters because it represented a complete vegetable diet. To grow your own Three Sisters, create a hill that is two to three feet in diameter and work in a large amount of compost and composted manure to supply nutrients for all three crops and plant the corn first.

Companion Planting

Much has been written about which plants work well together, and often the various human emotions, such as love and hate, accompany these descriptions. At the end of the day, extension agents, university professors, and other professionals have been unable to verify most of the anecdotal benefits of companion planting.

There are some properties to watch out for, like the allelopathic chemicals exuded by crop plants such as broccoli and sunflowers, or trees such as the walnut, Australian pine, eucalyptus, and others. You may have noticed this phenomenon under your bird feeder, where the hulls of sunflower seeds inhibit the germination of many other types of seeds. Armed with this knowledge, use spent sunflower parts as mulch in areas such as paths where you want to suppress weeds, but don't use them to mulch desirable plants. Feel free to put them in your compost pile, where they'll be mixed with lots of other plant material and the decomposers will digest the chemicals. If you plant broccoli in your vegetable garden, don't plant another cabbage crop in the same spot for two seasons.

It's also beneficial to plant flowers among your fruiting crops as they will attract pollinators. So go ahead and plant marigolds next to your tomatoes; you'll get a tough, good-looking border to attract pollinators, but don't count on the marigolds to prevent nematodes from attacking the tomato roots. While it is true that marigolds repel nematodes from their own roots, this repellence does not transfer to nearby crops. You could plant marigolds as a cover crop and then turn them into the soil to reduce the nematode population. Better yet, choose tomato cultivars that have been bred to resist nematodes, and be sure to plant those tomatoes in a different section of the garden the following year.

Legume crops such as beans or peas can provide their own fertilizer via symbiotic nitrogen-fixing bacteria in their root nodules, but this process does little for the fertility in the surrounding soil until the end of the season. Legumes are an excellent choice for a green manure because as you turn them under, that newly fixed nitrogen is added to the available nutrients in the soil. It is also good to keep track of legumes in your crop sequencing; because you won't have added composted manure to their space in the garden, be sure to add some for the next nonlegume crop in the rotation.

So take the advice on companion planting with a grain of salt, and keep notes about your crops in your garden log.

Raised Beds

The first rule about raised beds is that they must be set up and sized such that you can access all areas without stepping into the bed. The working areas between the beds should be wide enough to accommodate wheelbarrows or garden carts. If you build your raised beds on top of lawn areas, it's a good idea to get rid of the grass between the beds, too. It will be too hard to mow and trim, plus it probably won't grow well with all the trampling the area will receive. Strip off the sod and place it upside down in the lowest layer in your raised beds, unless it contains deep-rooted perennial weeds such as dollar weed, Florida betony, or torpedo grass. After you have removed the grass, line the paths with a thick layer of wood chips or other mulch. You could also use stepping-stones or pavers for a more solid footing, especially if the people tending the garden will be in wheelchairs.

The height of the raised beds above the surrounding land could range from a mere six inches to two feet or more. If the bed is only six to eight inches high, you may need to work the soil as described for a regular, in-the-ground garden plot, especially if deep-rooted or persistent weeds grow in that area. Another option is to bar the persistent weeds with a solid sheet of weed barrier cloth attached to the bottom of the raised bed framing. Keep in mind that in using weed barrier cloth, you are also limiting yourself to crops with shallow root systems, as roots will not readily grow beyond the weed barrier.

The ideal height of the bed and the depth of the workable soil will depend upon such factors as the underlying surface, whether you'll need easy accessibility, and the crops you will be planting. Leaf lettuce, radishes, and many herbs require soil depths of only six inches, but larger or perennial crops do best in deeper soil. Potatoes and other root crops may need eighteen to twenty-four or more inches of soil. Choose crops that have the best chance of succeeding in your beds. Don't scrimp on root space.

Keep in mind that the higher you make the walls, the more soil or other materials you will need for fill and the more pressure there will be on the walls. Beds with higher walls require sturdier construction and more drainage holes along the bottom of the sides than shallower beds do. On the other hand, a greater mass of soil does a better job of holding moisture and maintaining more even temperatures.

Material and Design Choices for Raised Beds

The sides of most raised beds are made of wood; it is readily available, comes in a variety of sizes, is easy to work with, and looks good in the landscape. Don't use pressure-treated lumber or creosoted railroad ties where you grow your edibles as the treated wood releases chemicals into the soil. Plan on replacing the lumber after several years if you use standard pine. A more durable wood such as red cedar will last longer.

Fake wood lumber, made from recycled plastic products or a combination of recycled plastic and sawdust, may cost a little more initially, but it is probably the most sustainable choice. It has (mostly) the look of wood, comes in the same sizes and shapes; and because it's made from recycled materials, it won't warp, and it will last for many years.

You could also use cement blocks or bricks to construct your raised beds. For low-walled beds, the bricks could be stacked loosely, but you may find that you'll need metal or wooden stakes to hold them in place once you start working in the beds. This arrangement offers good flexibility, because you can reconfigure your bed's size and shape as your needs change. If, on the other hand, you are designing a higher-walled bed, you may need to mortar the blocks in place. Keep in mind that if you use cement and mortar the soil near the walls will be more al-kaline. It is best, in this case, to plant your acid-craving crops such as tomatoes away from the walls. If you use mortared or more permanent walls, plan for your irrigation and drainage before you start installing the walls.

You can purchase complete a raised-bed system or kit, with pre-cut lumber, made out of either wood or fake wood, that snaps together to form containers for your beds of various sizes and shapes. Using a kit will certainly make the job of creating the raised beds easier, but it may also limit you to certain sizes or shapes.

Straw-Bale Gardens

You can also create a raised bed garden by planting directly in one or more bales of hay or straw. This arrangement can be a good idea for crops that have had problems with soil-borne pests such as root-knot nematodes or for areas with lousy soil.

To begin, add some compost or composted manure to the center of the bale, where you will plant your crop. If you plan to use just one bale, lay it flat, use a garden fork to dig out a hole in the middle of the

STRAW BALE GARDEN

SWEET POTATO VINES GROWING IN STRAW BALES

bale that's about one half the surface, and then fill the hole with your compost and soil mixture. How deep you dig your hole will depend upon what you are planting—five or six inches for lettuce; eight to ten inches for carrots or larger crops like tomatoes, potatoes, or squash. For a larger straw-bale garden, tie several bales together with twine.

Before planting your bale gardens, let them sit for several days, and water them thoroughly each day. After planting keep a close eye on the soil moisture—you may find that these gardens require more frequent irrigation. At the end of the growing season, add the straw and soil mix to your compost pile or use for mulch.

Tray Beds

Tray gardens are relatively lightweight and are built to be portable. Construct the sides with 1 × 6, 2 × 6, or 2 × 8 lumber (wood or fake wood) with good corner bracing. If you plan to carry the garden by hand on a regular basis, three feet by three feet is probably the maximum size. You can also size your tray to fit on top of a support such as a table or cart. To reduce the weight of the tray, fashion the bottom out of half-inch gauge galvanized hardware cloth and secure it to the inside of the sides with heavy staples or nails. Run two or three 2 × 4s parallel to one another across the bottom and screw them into the sides. Space the bottom boards such that they fit onto your cart, saw horses, or other support structure. Line the bottom and sides with heavy-duty weed barrier cloth to contain the soil and to allow for drainage. If you enjoy repurposing and recycling, old drawers make good tray gardens, as long as they have adequate drainage.

Tray gardens require a lighter and more absorbent soil mixture than other gardens do. A good mix is two parts compost, one part vermiculite, and one part coconut coir. Wet the soil mixture before you place it in the tray to ensure that the moisture is evenly distributed—both vermiculite and coconut coir are highly absorbent and take in a surprising amount of water.

Container Gardens

If you have only a balcony or patio to grow your edibles on, then hanging or freestanding containers are your only option. Container gardens can also complement more traditional edible gardens. For instance, you may wish to contain mint and other aggressive spreaders in pots, which can be artfully arranged in or around your in-ground herb garden. Then again, you could plant your whole herb garden in an array of containers.

Container Types and Materials

Standard flowerpots and planters with built-in drainage come in a variety of types, sizes, and shapes. Here are some pros and cons to consider when deciding which containers to use:

Clay/terra cotta—This is the standard pot material, and some people think that all the others are pale imitations. Clay is heavy, offering good stability for tall plantings, but it's also harder to move when full of soil, and it's breakable. Clay is porous, retains heat, and will require more irrigation. It comes in many styles and sizes, ages well, and in most parts of Florida, the weather is not cold enough to crack it.

Cast concrete—While it is less breakable than clay, it may sweeten the soil, making it a poor choice for acid-loving plants. Otherwise, it has many of the same advantages and disadvantages as clay.

Glazed clay or ceramic—While it offers the heft of clay or cement, it is not as porous, and it is heavy and breakable. It comes in many beautiful colors and patterns.

Resin, fiberglass, or plastic—Pots made from these materials are impervious, inexpensive, and lightweight and come in many of the same sizes and shapes as clay. They do not retain heat or lose water like clay does. These pots will last a long time, but may crack or split, and the colors may fade in the sun.

Lumber (wood or fake wood)—Lumber provides good insulation and blends in with a natural landscape. It is used most often for window boxes and patio planters. Untreated wood will rot over several years and will last much longer if you use liner pots to keep the wood from directly contacting the soil. Don't use treated wood for edible plants. Fake wood is more durable.

Metal—Metals conducts heat, exposing roots to rapid temperature fluctuations. Some metals rust quickly when in contact with soil. Use a liner pot for the best results, especially if the container will be exposed to full sun. If you are planting edibles, make sure that the soil doesn't contact the metal—some metals are poisonous and can leach into damp soil.

Hanging or mounted planters—These containers can be fashioned from wire baskets lined with sphagnum moss or coconut fiber mats or be made of a solid material like plastic or wood. Some folks really like the special upside-down hanging pots for growing tomatoes, and they are a good option if you have a sturdy and sunny place to hang them.

Woven or nonwoven fabric—Use these as a stand-alone container or as a liner pot placed inside a heavy decorative container. Growing in cloth ensures that the plants won't become root bound and the soil is aerated. When roots reach the side of the pot, they sense the air and stop growing in that direction in a process called air pruning. If you use this type of container as a liner in a nondraining pot, set it on an inexpensive plastic catch tray with drainage holes and set that tray on some stones in the bottom of the container. You can purchase ready-made cloth pots, sew your own using high-end weed barrier cloth, or use inexpensive, reusable cloth shopping bags. The shopping bags won't last as long, but they'll last a couple of years and are readily available. Some folks use the bags for shopping until the handles give way and then use them for planting.

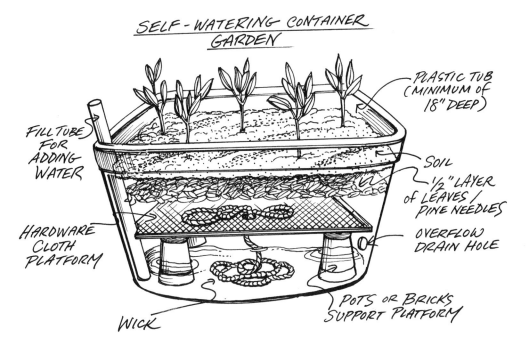

SELF-WATERING CONTAINER GARDEN

PLASTIC TUB (MINIMUM OF 18" DEEP)

FILL TUBE FOR ADDING WATER

SOIL

½" LAYER of LEAVES / PINE NEEDLES

HARDWARE CLOTH PLATFORM

OVERFLOW DRAIN HOLE

WICK

POTS OR BRICKS SUPPORT PLATFORM

Self-Watering Containers

Self-watering containers include a reservoir for holding water, which is drawn up and into the soil through wicks. The key to a self-watering system is the wick, which ensures that the soil does not become totally saturated. These containers work well if you can't water often enough. You can purchase manufactured self-watering containers or build your own.

Planting and Caring for Container Gardens

Before you start planting, whether you are using a new pot or reusing an old one, it is a good practice to rinse or scrub out the pot to remove salts, disease-carrying organisms, or chemicals used in manufacturing. If it is a porous pot, such as clay, cement, or wood, thoroughly wet down the interior of the container. If it is a fabric pot, soak it in a bucket of rain barrel water.

Despite the conventional wisdom, covering the bottom of a container with three or more inches of gravel is not recommended. The layer of gravel or potshards actually impedes drainage. Because water tends to hang together, it does not travel from the fine substrate of the soil to the coarse gravel mixture until the soil is saturated. Plus, plants are under enough stress in containers; don't add to their stress by reducing the depth of the soil in the pot with that layer of gravel. Prevent soil from washing out of the drainage holes by placing a piece of screen or nonwoven weed barrier cloth, or even a few dried leaves or pine needles over the holes before adding the soil. For the best drainage, use a tall pot.

You can plant the container with a single crop or an attractive combination of two or three. When combining different types of plants in a container, do your homework to find out whether they are compatible. They should, for example, require the same soil type and irrigation level. If possible, choose plants whose roots will occupy different depths of the pot. For instance, you could arrange a ring of parsley around the perimeter for a good border and then plant a few lettuce plants in the center. The lettuce has fibrous roots while the parsley's taproots will draw moisture from deeper in the soil. The lettuce will probably be harvested before the parsley, and you could then replant the center with another crop. If a plant is an aggressive spreader, a container may be the best place to grow it, preferably on its own—it would crowd out other species in no time. It may be easiest to use multiple pots, each with a monoculture; this way, they can be arranged in a pleasing manner, and you won't have to worry about compatibility.

To create a garden in a hanging wire basket with a coconut fiber mat or sphagnum moss liner, it's best to plant well-developed seedlings in a fairly heavy soil mixture—the aeration in this case is so extreme that your plants will appreciate the extra moisture retention. You can plant several plants across the top of the soil, and add more plants to the sides. To plant the sides of your container, place just a little soil in the bottom, and cut slits in the coconut mat or sphagnum liner in three to five places. Slip the plants, roots first, into those slits. Fill in the rest of the soil up to the bottom of the root balls of your top plants and then position the top plants so their root balls alternate with the side plants' roots to reduce competition. Have fun arranging your edibles—with some planning, they can look every bit as delicious as an entirely ornamental planter.

Strawberry pots, with their pocket-like openings around the sides, enable you to grow several different plants in one container. Insert the root mass of each plant into an opening from the outside of the pot. One problem with this container is that water doesn't always reach the plants in the lowest openings. Before you fill the pot with your soil mixture, insert a piece of bamboo or PVC pipe with holes drilled into it every few inches and its bottom end sealed so that the top sits just above the soil surface. Attach some screen over the top hole. When you water the container, pour water through the screen so the water fills the tube and seeps into the bottom of the pot.

Location, Location, Location

Of all the variables to consider when planning your edible garden, location and arrangement are the two that will make the difference between a successful crop and a mediocre one. Fortunately, growers have the most control over siting their edible gardens.

Resources

Mel Bartholomew, *All New Square Foot Gardening* (Brentwood, Tennessee: Cool Springs Press, 2005).

For information and supplies for setting up your own square-foot garden, check out the associated website www.squarefootgardening.com.

Rosalind Creasy, *Edible Landscaping* (San Francisco: Sierra Club Books, 2010).

For more about planting tubes, go to http://www.tubeplanters.com.

For information about green roof systems, go to http://edis.ifas.ufl.edu/ep240.

3

Soil Building

In organic gardening, it all starts with the soil. Before we can grow anything successfully, we must first have soil that is rich in organic matter; is filled with microbes, worms, bugs, and other critters; and has good tilth. A soil with good tilth has both good porosity and good water retention.

Soil Basics

In a natural environment, plants and animals litter the soil with their waste as they live and die. As a result, soil found in native habitats is a complex ecosystem of bacteria, fungi, nematodes, earthworms, ants, salamanders, toads, insects and their larvae, voles, and more, all living in a substrate of minerals and humus. In woodlands, that wonderful, earthy smell of good soil that all gardeners love is caused by actinomycetes, a type of soil bacteria. The minerals are some mixture of rocks, sand, silt, and clay. The humus or organic matter consists of fully or partially digested plant and animal parts. As humus breaks down into simple compounds, it provides a living for the decomposers, and eventually yields nutrients for plants. Just think what a mess we would have if we did not have those soil inhabitants to clean up all that dead stuff.

In undisturbed landscapes, the soil is layered in a pattern called the soil horizon. The top layer or duff consists of organic litter, such as dead leaves and twigs, which serve as Mother Nature's mulch. Topsoil, the next layer, contains a lot of humus (digested organic materials) and may itself consist of several more layers. Under the topsoil lies the subsoil, which contains very little organic material, and then comes the bedrock layer. The soil's inhabitants are found mainly in the top two layers of the horizon.

One gram of soil (about one-fifth of a teaspoon) could contain as many as one hundred million bacteria, one million actinomycetes, and one hundred thousand fungi—if strung together, their filaments or hyphae would measure about sixteen feet in length. This same gram of soil could also contain hundreds of nematodes living on the damp surfaces of the soil particles and maybe a few insect eggs or larvae and some earthworm cocoons. The exact proportions of each of these organisms will depend on soil conditions, such as moisture, aeration, amount of humus, and what's been growing in the soil. Chemical conditions such as acidity will change the balance of organism populations. Fungi are more plentiful in acidic soils, while actinomycetes and other bacteria prefer more alkaline conditions.

Beneficial Soil Inhabitants

Here are some of the more obvious soil inhabitants that are important in your soil's ecosystem and beneficial to your plants.

Earthworms

Earthworms keep the soil aerated and digest organic materials in the soil so nutrients are more available to plants. In most of Florida, a pile of wet, dead leaves or a compost pile on the ground will attract earthworms in just a few days.

Mycorrhizae

This type of fungus often forms a symbiotic relationship with plant roots. Some of these fungi invade the root tissues, while others simply live among the roots. The root tissues exude sugars or starches that the fungi ingest, while the fungi's thin hyphae work to extract nutrients and greater amounts of water from the surrounding soil. Plants growing with the aid of mycorrhizae do much better than plants in sterile soils. Some companies sell mycorrhizae spores for inoculating sterile soils, but if you are using good compost to enrich your soil, you will not need them. Furthermore, those alien spores may harm the indigenous fungi.

Nematodes

These microscopic worms live in the soil. While we hear about the destructive ones, such as root-knot nematodes, most are benign or beneficial and play important roles in soil ecosystems. Some prey on the destructive nematodes and others consume harmful fungi.

Rhizobia

These include several types of soil bacteria that form symbiotic relationships with plants in the bean family (i.e., the legumes), such as clover, peas, and beans. These bacteria invade the legume roots and form root nodules. The bacteria absorb nitrogen from the air in the soil and create ammonia (NH_3), which is advantageous to the plant. In turn, the bacteria receive sugars from the plant. While air is 78 percent nitrogen, plants cannot use it in its gaseous state. Many legumes can grow vigorously where other plants fail, which is one reason gardeners use legumes as cover crops.

Soil Nutrients

The minerals and the humus determine the acidity of the soil. From Miami southward, the minerals consist mostly of limestone, so the soil (what there is of it) is quite alkaline. In much of peninsular Florida, the soil is mostly acidic and sandy. In parts of the Panhandle, the red Georgia clay predominates. You should test your soil before you begin any big project. As your extension agent would say, "Don't guess; do the test." A complete soil test will assess the acidity, or pH, of your soil, plus its major nutrients. You can also test for heavy metals, and for *E. coli*, Salmonella, or other pathogens if your garden's location and history indicate that there might be a problem. Again, your extension agent can help you to determine whether this type of testing is necessary.

Three of the sixteen elements necessary for plant growth come from the air and water—these are hydrogen (H), oxygen (O), and carbon (C). The remaining thirteen nutrients must come from the soil and are absorbed through a plant's roots.

Soil nutrients are not all needed in equal quantities—there are macronutrients and micronutrients. The three primary macronutrients are nitrogen (N), phosphorus (P), and potassium (K). The secondary macronutrients are calcium (Ca), magnesium (Mg), and sulfur (S). Micronutrients, while essential for plant growth, are required only in tiny quantities. The micronutrients are boron (B), copper (Cu), iron (Fe), chloride (Cl), manganese (Mn), molybdenum (Mo), and zinc (Zn).

Native soil might not provide enough nutrients to support the vigorous growth required for the best crop production. Successful vegetable growers amend the soil with several organic substances to provide a variety of nutrients including the micronutrients. Some organics are labeled with exact nutrient quantities, while others come only with estimates. Follow the guidelines on your product so that you don't overload your soil with too much of one substance.

Amending your soil with various nonorganic conditioners, such as lime, will alter its chemistry temporarily, but the best way to change the nature of your soil for the long run is to add enough organic materials year after year to neutralize imbalances. Raised beds and containers provide a much faster way to control the soil chemistry.

Enriching the Soil

Soil texture is a function of the relative proportions of sand, silt, and clay particles. These proportions are not readily changed, and, in fact, if you add sand to clayey soil, you could end up with a hard cement-like concoction. The key to improving the structure of your soil, be it sandy or clayey, is more organic matter. Soil structure derives from the manner in which soil particles are assembled as aggregates. Your aim is to achieve a loose, crumbly, or granular aggregation of particles. A handful of moist soil should have different sized, mostly rounded particles with enough body to hold together under gentle pressure. As icky as it may sound, the glue holding your soil together is made of the leftovers (poop, slime, and body parts) from its inhabitants.

When preparing your vegetable garden, you'll want to use the richest soil mixture you can find, except where you plan to plant your legume crops and some herbs, which appreciate a leaner mixture. The best time to work on your soil is before you start planting. If you're preparing a bed for a perennial crop, you won't have good access to the soil in the root zone again until you dig it up to divide it; plan on enriching the soil for your annual crops between each rotation.

Florida's warm climate raises the metabolism of its soil organisms, and they don't take a holiday in the winter. Because our soil's microbes are always working, they require more organic material for energy. Fortunately, compost production in Florida is also greater than elsewhere in the country because our long growing seasons produce more material to compost, and compost piles or bins are more efficient. A highly managed compost system in Florida could turn out finished compost in two or three months; compare that to the six months to two years it takes in places with cold winters. Sustainable landscape management will produce enough compost to keep the soil enriched. It's a balance. (For more details on composting, see the "Composting" section, beginning on page 54)

Organic Soil and Amendments

Not all of these amendments may be allowed in certified organic operations. Approved materials will have "OMRI-listed" label on the package. Don't add concentrated minerals such as phosphorus or phosphate unless a soil test indicates a low level of phosphorus—much of the soil in Florida contains an abundance of phosphorous.

Alfalfa Meal

This amendment is rich in minerals and nitrogen. Add it to compost or directly to the soil. You can also make an emulsion and apply it as a liquid fertilizer.

Bentonite Clay

Its high affinity for water makes bentonite clay a useful addition to sandy soils. It occurs in nature in two main types—a sodium type and a calcium type. The sodium type has a much higher rate of water retention, up to five times its own weight.

Bentonite clay layered several inches thick can form a seal that prevents water from penetrating the soil. This characteristic may be useful for gardeners who wish to create ponds with high water retention or to seal the garden layer from contaminated soils below. In the latter case, bring in the experts before you start growing edibles.

Blood Meal

This amendment is rich in organic nitrogen. Use it in your compost or apply it directly to the soil prior to planting a heavy-feeding crop. Some vegan operations may object to this animal product.

Coconut Coir

Made from coconut shells, coconut coir (pronounced core) provides a nonacidic substitute for peat moss when a sterile, fine medium is required, such as when you are starting seeds. Coir pots are also available for starting seeds that don't like to be transplanted—just tear out the bottom when placing in the soil and the rest will decompose.

Coffee Grounds

While some gardeners use them only in their compost, you can also add coffee grounds directly to the soil, either as a topdressing or by digging them in. Too much coffee will shed water, so use the grounds in moderation.

Compost

Most organic gardeners strive to make enough of their own compost. But you can also purchase bagged organic compost, which is made from a variety of substances. If the compost is labeled "organic," it should be free of artificial chemicals. The original substances may not be listed on the bag, but you may be able to contact the producer to find out what they were. You need to know whether it's mostly composted manure, as you risk creating a soil mixture too rich in nitrogen. Also, make sure the compost is "finished"; in other words, it should not resemble its original ingredients. *Warning*: The compost and mulch that is often available at Florida landfills consists mostly of shredded yard trash. This compost could contain herbicides, pesticides, other artificial chemicals, and even pieces of plastic bags.

Fish Emulsion

This product comes in several different forms: dry powder, concentrated liquid, or combined with an organic liquid fertilizer and seaweed. Fish emulsion is rich in many nutrients, particularly calcium. The extracts are useful for feeding new seedlings and for giving heavy feeders a mid-season boost. Most fish emulsions are made with scrap fish from the oceans and are considered to be an organic amendment, but emulsions from fish farms may not be.

Greensand or Glauconite

This amendment is a greenish layer found in sedimentary limestone that contains marine potash, silica, iron oxide, magnesium, lime, phosphoric acid, and other trace minerals. It's particularly useful for tomato plants because it supplies the calcium necessary for preventing blossom end-rot. Some say that it improves the flavor of tomatoes, too.

Manures

Composted herbivore or fowl manures provide a renewable resource for nitrogen-rich soil amendments. Use thoroughly composted or pelleted manures, and mix them with compost to avoid burning your plants with too much nitrogen. Manures that you add to soil where you're growing edibles that don't touch the ground, like tomatoes, should be composted for at least ninety days before being applied; increase this time to one hundred twenty days for edibles that do come into contact with the soil, like carrots. Horse manure mixed with straw bedding shoveled from stalls also contains urine, which provides even more nitrogen.

Handle raw or partially composted manures with special gloves and boots designated for this activity, and don't wear them in the planting areas. Also thoroughly clean any tools you use to work the manure and then wipe them down with alcohol.

Do not use the manure of carnivores such dogs or cats because they could harbor *E. coli* and other disease-causing organisms. Also, keep the cats out of the garden with a good fence—you don't want your lovely soil to be their sandbox.

Organic Soil

Unfortunately, there is no standard in place for what can be sold as "soil." Organic soil (packaged or bagged) will contain no artificial chemicals, but some brands may include a lot of sticks, wood chips, or hard, dry lumps of soil. These brands could work okay in the bottom of the bed or container, but they would not be suitable for starting seeds or for the top layer of your soil, where you'll be planting seeds or seedlings. So buy one bag and open it up to see what it looks like before you purchase a large quantity.

Peat Moss

This is a traditional humus-rich garden product, but it takes centuries to form in sphagnum moss bogs and is therefore not sustainable. Also, it's highly acidic and has very few available nutrients.

Seaweed or Kelp

Seaweed products come in several different forms: dry powder, concentrated liquid, or in combination with an organic liquid fertilizer such as fish emulsion. Seaweed is rich in nutrients and provides soil with a good general enrichment. The extracts are generally mixed with water and are useful for feeding new seedlings and for giving heavy feeders a mid-season boost.

Spent Mushroom Soil

Mushroom farms create wonderful enriched soils in which to raise their fungal crops, only to throw it away after one season so that stray spores do not contaminate the next crop. You can use it in your edible beds without fear of too many mushrooms, because your sunny conditions are not conducive to mushroom growth.

Wood Ash

Wood ashes are alkaline and contain potassium, some phosphorus and magnesium, and some trace elements, but no nitrogen. Their nutritional value varies with the species of wood. It's probably best to incorporate ashes into your compost pile. You may also add them directly to the soil, but not where you plant potatoes or other acid-loving crops.

Wood Chips

Often available for free from arborists, the chips will eventually decompose into a rich soil. It is best used as mulch for walking areas between beds, but a thick layer of wood chips could also be used to smother weeds as a no-till alternative for preparing a garden bed. The problem with adding wood chips directly to the soil is that while they are decomposing, the microbes working on them will create a nitrogen deficit in the surrounding soil.

Worm Castings

Another type of manure is available from vermiculture operations—either your own or from large worm farms. Of course, you'll want to work to attract earthworms to your garden so you'll have an unending supply. See appendix 2 for more information on animal manures.

Preparing the Soil for Vegetables

If you plan to garden where there is little or no soil or where the soil is not suitable for growing vegetables, use raised beds or containers with imported soil. In areas where the soil can be rehabilitated, in-the-ground beds offer gardeners the most flexibility in terms of size and opportunity for expansion in the future. Lucky for us, the soil in much of Florida is sandy. This soil type is the easiest to remedy because it is easy to dig and drainage is never a problem. Clayey soil is hard to dig and good drainage may be harder to achieve. On the other hand, clayey soil may contain more of the needed trace elements, has better water retention, and will require less irrigation. For either type of soil, the steps to make it work well for an edible garden are approximately the same: add organic material. Lots of it.

There are many methods for preparing soil for planting. There is no one magic way to accomplish this for every situation, and each method has its advantages and disadvantages.

Roto-Till or Plow the Whole Field

The traditional approach to farming calls for plowing the whole field. If your gardening area is large or if you have hard, clayey soil, you could use this technique to get started. First, wait until the soil is relatively dry. Before or after you plow, add a six-inch-thick layer of compost, composted manure, earthworm castings, or spent mushroom soil to the planting areas. Then let the plowed, enriched soil sit for a few days before you plant.

Advantages: uproots existing weeds; reduces growers' manual labor through the use of machinery.

Disadvantages: stirs up new weed seeds; disturbs the existing soil horizon and ecosystem; prepares soil where nothing will be planted; loose soil is more apt to erode, becoming a source of pollution in nearby waterways; requires the use of machinery that is expensive to rent or own.

Roto-Till or Plow Wide Rows

More efficient than plowing the whole field would be to plow only those areas you intend to plant. You could, for example, plow wide rows measuring up to four feet across and leave the walking area between the rows unplowed. This approach leaves you with a raised-bed-like arrangement, with the plants optimally spaced within the wide row. You will need to do something to kill or suppress the weeds in the unplanted areas—some growers use black plastic sheets as mulch, while others use a cover crop or a thick layer of wood chips.

Advantages: uproots weeds in the planting areas; reduces growers' manual labor through the use of machinery; requires soil amendments to be added only where needed.

Disadvantages: see those listed under plowing the whole field.

In-Ground Composting or Double Digging

If your beds are relatively small and the soil is poor, in-ground composting is an effective method for enriching the soil. At least six weeks before planting time, complete the following steps. First, remove all the weeds or grass. Next, remove the soil to a depth of one shovel, loosen the soil in the bottom of the hole with a garden fork, and then add alternating three-inch layers of composted horse or cow manure, dried leaves or other "brown" materials, freshly pulled weeds, grass clippings, or other "green" materials, and the original soil. Repeat these layers at least three times and mulch the top with a thick layer of easily removed mulch such as leaves, pine needles, or straw to keep it moist and to prevent weeds from growing. The new soil level will be eight to ten inches higher than the original soil level. Keep the soil moist, but not wet, while you wait the six to eight weeks for the composting to complete. The soil level will sink during this time as the decomposers work, but it should remain higher than the original soil; this difference in height will help you to identify the amended areas. When you are ready to plant, rake away the top mulch, smooth out the soil, and arrange your plot in wide rows or squares for planting.

This in-ground composting, sometimes called double digging, is a one-time treatment. To keep the soil rich after this treatment, add new compost, earthworm castings, or composted manure between crops.

Advantages: requires only a one-time treatment; uproots weeds; creates rich soil relatively quickly.

Disadvantages: requires too much labor for clayey soil or large gardens; requires a waiting period of six to eight weeks while the composting takes place; disturbs the soil horizon and ecosystem (but since it's a one-time treatment, the soil recovers quickly); makes the plot somewhat susceptible to erosion until the soil settles down.

No-Till Farming

No-till farming is often praised for its preservation of the soil horizon, but often the large-scale growers that use this method also use an herbicide to kill all the weeds first—not an approved organic farming practice. Some organic gardeners use a propane flaming system to scorch the top few inches of soil or soil solarization. These methods kill the weed seeds and any other organisms living in that top layer of soil.

The weed treatment is usually followed by an application of compost to enrich the soil. The microbes in the compost will eventually work the newly applied compost into the soil.

Advantages: is less labor-intensive, especially for large operations; results in less erosion of the original soil; leaves soil ecosystems undisturbed, providing better support for plants' root systems.

Disadvantages: makes planting seeds or seedlings more difficult because the soil is not loosened; requires the use of specialized equipment; makes amending the soil more difficult, and those amendments that lie on top of the soil erode quickly.

Layered Gardening #1

This no-till method is suitable for smaller operations. First, remove woody plants and deep-rooted or persistent weeds such as dollar weed, torpedo grass, Florida betony, or catbrier. Next, place a layer of paper (four or five sheets of newspaper or one layer of corrugated cardboard will do) on the soil, wet it down, and cover it with six to eight inches of compost or other organic soil. Let it sit for a few days before you plant your crops. Mulch well around the edges so that the soil doesn't erode away in the first heavy downpour.

You may also create your own compost on top of the paper in place of the finished compost or soil. Lay down alternating three-inch-thick layers of green and brown materials until you achieve a total height of eight to ten inches, and then cover these layers with an easily removed mulch such as hay or pine needles. Water the area well and keep it moist, but not soaking wet, for at least six weeks before you plant it.

Advantages: requires less labor because there's no digging; results in less erosion of the original soil; leaves soil ecosystems undisturbed, providing better support for plants' root systems.

Disadvantages: removing large quantities of deep-rooted weeds from an area is a lot of work and it destroys the soil horizon; a heavy rainstorm could wash away your raised and exposed layer of soil, unless you build sides around it.

Layered Gardening #2

This is yet another no-till method. First, remove woody plants and deep-rooted or persistent weeds such as dollar weed, torpedo grass, Florida betony, or catbrier. Next, place an eight-to-twelve-inch layer of arborists' wood chips on the planting areas and the surrounding walking areas. Let it sit for at least six weeks to kill the surface plants and to allow the process of composting to begin. The chips will settle during this time, and the soil underneath will suffer a nitrogen deficit while the composting decomposers are working on the chips. When it's almost time to plant, rake away the chips, and add a three-inch layer of compost or organic soil. Let this layer settle for a few days before planting your seeds or seedlings.

This is a one-time procedure; in future seasons, just add more compost to the planting areas.

Advantages: requires less labor because there's no digging; results in less erosion of the original soil; leaves soil ecosystems undisturbed, providing better support for plants' root systems.

Disadvantages: in an area with too many deep-rooted problems, risks ruining the soil horizon by the time you have removed them all; delays planting; requires a good source for the wood chips.

Soil Solarization

In the summer, cover your soil with clear plastic for at least six weeks. Anchor down the plastic with soil on all sides to retain the heat and keep it from blowing away. This procedure will produce enough heat to kill weed seeds, nematodes, and other soil inhabitants to a depth of three to four inches. You could use this method in conjunction with no-till farming or on previously tilled beds.

Advantages: provides an effective, nonchemical method of reducing problems with weeds and nematodes.

Disadvantages: takes a fair amount of expense and labor to install; removes that bed from your planting rotation for at least six weeks; also kills the beneficial microbes, so it may take a while before your soil becomes a working ecosystem.

Mulching

Organic mulches, such as wood chips, sawdust, pine needles, straw, or bark nuggets, will suppress weeds, help the soil hold in moisture, prevent the soil surface from crusting, and help prevent erosion on level grades or gentle slopes. Because they are organic, these mulches will eventually add compost to the soil. Mulching with organic materials in a garden area is called sheet composting; mulch is slow to decompose because it does not have enough mass to raise the temperature of the soil.

The best organic mulches for the planting areas in your edible gardens are those that can easily be raked away after a harvest, such as straw or pine needles. Removing the mulch between plantings is important; doing so allows you to clear out that area of the garden, work in more compost or other amendments, prepare the soil for the next crop, and then plant. The chunkier mulches such as wood chips and bark nuggets or the fine mulches such as sawdust tend to stick in or combine with the soil and are not easily removed with a leaf rake. Also, the fine or chunky mulches will reduce the amount of nitrogen in the soil as they are decomposing, so don't use them for your planting areas. They are great options for mulching the walkways around your beds and are good additions to your compost.

If you are using a short wide-row method of arranging your beds, with four- to ten-inch-wide trenches between the rows, you'll want the mulch layer between the rows to be six or more inches deep so the mulched trench is nearly level with the planting area. The best mulches for the trenches are those that are easiest to arrange in the trench, and again straw or pine needles are the best candidates. You can also accomplish trench composting between the rows by digging the trench to at least ten inches, layering the trench with seven inches of kitchen scraps, including calcium-rich eggshells, and filling in the last three inches with a layer of soil topped with straw or pine needles.

Many professional growers use plastic sheeting as mulch between widely separated rows to absolutely stop weeds. Because the plastic is impervious to water, these growers use drip irrigation to deliver water to the crops. This method of weed suppression takes a fair amount of effort and money to install. Also, plastic does nothing to build up the soil, and some gardeners find it incompatible with their organic plan.

Composting

Composting is a form of recycling. Instead of throwing away kitchen scraps or stuffing the dead leaves and other yard trimmings into unsustainable plastic bags and leaving them for pickup, gardeners can deposit Mother Nature's offerings in a compost pile. A couple of months later, dark, nutrient-rich compost will be ready for you to use as a soil amendment.

You may wish to consider sizing your edibles garden according to your volume of compost. That means that you have enough compost to generously enrich the beds before planting your next set of crops. The larger your compost operation, the more crops you can support.

While there are many methods of setting up a compost system, here are some general composting guidelines.

- When constructing a new pile, use equal amounts of green and brown materials in alternating layers: *brown materials* are mostly dry and are high in carbon (examples include dead leaves, wood chips, pine needles, straw, dryer lint, and shredded paper); *green materials* are softer, moister, and higher in nitrogen (examples include freshly pulled weeds, grass clippings, coffee grounds, kitchen scraps, manure, and invasive waterweeds like hydrilla and water hyacinths).
- To produce the richest compost with all the micronutrients

necessary for plant growth, compost many types of materials. For instance, eggshells provide a good supply of calcium in the soil and will decrease the occurrence of blossom end-rot in your tomatoes.

- Do add gardening waste, but not diseased plants or noxious weeds with aggressive roots or tubers. Regular weeds and sod are fine, though. If weeds sprout from the pile, pull them out and put them on top of the pile to dry.

- Don't use materials that have been treated with poisons. It doesn't matter whether these pesticides are made from organic or artificial materials; they'll still damage the decomposers in the compost and to the plants you grow in it later, and it may affect your organic status. The heat in an active compost pile will break down some of the poisons, but it's hard to predict to what extent.

- You may add manure from horses, cows, rabbits, and other herbivores or manures from chickens and turkeys that are omnivores, but don't use pet or human feces. They could introduce harmful bacteria into the soil.

- Do add kitchen scraps, but not meat, oils, or dairy products. Following this practice keeps the odors down and discourages raccoons, possums, crows, or other scavengers from raiding your pile.

- Don't add twigs larger in diameter than your finger unless you run them through a chipper. In general, the more finely chopped the initial materials are, the faster they'll decompose.

- The more often you turn the pile, the faster it will become fully composted. "Turning" refers to rearranging the pile so that the materials on the top end up on the bottom and those on the outside end up on the inside. Turning also discourages weeds and tree roots from invading your pile.

- Keep your compost moist but not wet. In drier periods, create an indentation on the top of the pile so water is more easily absorbed, and add a bucket of water each week. In the wet seasons, create a peak on the top of the pile, and cover it with pine needles, straw, or some other material that will shed the water—you may even use a tarp during really wet periods. Cover the whole pile with a layer of pine needles, straw, or other persistent mulch to keep the weeds at bay.

- If your compost smells like ammonia, then it is too wet or contains too much green material. If the compost smells sour or more like rotten eggs, then it likely contains anaerobic decomposers. To solve either of these odor problems, turn the pile to introduce air, add some dry brown material, and leave the pile uncovered until it becomes just moist to the touch. A good compost pile should not stink.

- Compost piles need to have enough mass for the microbes' activity to raise their temperature. The rule of thumb is that the sides of an open pile each need to be at least three feet long, but the pile should be no greater than five feet in any one direction in order to allow air to penetrate it. In the initial stages of composting, the temperature of the pile will rise to 140°F or more.

- Do not purchase worms for your compost unless it is entirely contained and the worms have no way of escaping into your soil. Use only earthworms that you find in your landscape for the compost pile, and then not until it cools down a bit.

- Enclosing your compost in a bin is optional. A closed bin will be neater and easier to turn, but it will limit the volume of compost you can make at one time. It's not a good idea to construct bins with pressure-treated wood or railroad ties because their poisons can leach into the compost. Compost piles constructed directly on the ground will attract earthworms and other beneficial soil inhabitants.

- Make sure to construct your open compost pile at least two feet from any building and 300 feet from any waterway. Direct all runoff from the compost to a heavily vegetated swale, hedgerow, or wooded area—especially if you use manures.

- Don't add lime to your compost pile, even if your original materials are acidic. The decomposers will neutralize most of the acidity and lime could kill many of them.

- Use caution when composting poison ivy, poisonwood, or

Brazilian pepper. Urushiol, the oily toxin that causes a rash in many people, survives for a year or more after the plant is killed. If you decide to compost these poisonous-to-touch plants, protect yourself with long sleeves and gloves when handling the compost.

- If you use compost before it is ready, its decomposers will absorb the nitrogen from the surrounding soil as they work, causing your plants to suffer from a shortage of nitrogen. The timing of your projects may require that you do this. If so, add an extra nitrogen source such as composted manure to your soil to supply the need. If you're using compost as a mulch, unfinished compost can offer some weed control.

Locating Compost Piles

Open compost piles can look messy. Here are a few strategies for disguising or hiding your composting areas.

- You could create a spot hidden from view with cinder blocks dry-stacked into two or three U-shapes. Lay the blocks so that their hollow spaces are horizontal to let air into the piles. A space like this can also be used to store containers and other gardening items that don't need to be covered. While partial shade works well for compost in Florida's heat, remember these areas may have high foot traffic, so plan to keep the working area ten or more feet from the base of trees.
- If you don't have a good shady spot, create almost instant shade with vines. Construct a cylinder with chicken wire or other fencing that is at least three feet tall and three feet in diameter. Dump three or four shovels-full of manure (composted or bagged) on the bottom. Fill the cage with composting material, making sure to alternate green, brown, and thin, soil layers until the mound rises above the top of the cage, like an ice-cream cone with an indentation on top. Then plant three or more fast growing vines next to the bottom of the cage. Plant vegetables such as indeterminate tomatoes, cucumbers,

squash, or pole beans. The compost inside the cage will create a lovely environment for these plants' vigorous growth. At the end of the season, after you have harvested your vegetables, cut down the vines, and harvest your compost. The material will shrink significantly during the season.

- Recycle used, wooden shipping pallets to build the sides, and maybe the bottom, of your compost bin. You can wire, tie, or nail them together to create three-sided bins. You may find that two vertical posts set into the ground at the back corner of the bin will stabilize the structure. These bins allow for good aeration, and you make use of materials that might otherwise have been discarded. The untreated wood will last for a few years before it rots and becomes part of the compost.

- Another option is trench composting. Dig a narrow trench at the edge of a garden bed or between planting areas. The trench should be deep enough to allow you to cover the newly added kitchen scraps with an inch or two of soil and then four to six inches of straw or pine needles to make the top of the trench even with the planting area.

- Use a sixty-gallon plastic garbage can. Drill several half-inch holes in the bottom and several more on each side of the bottom fifth of the can. Also drill several holes in the lid. Dig a hole in the ground deep enough for the holes on the side of the can to sit below the soil surface, then fill in soil around the can. Add composting material and keep the can covered with the lid.

Composting Management Styles

You can control how soon your compost will be finished or ready to use in your garden areas by adjusting your level of management. The less work you put in, the longer it will take.

Passive Composting

Maintaining a passive compost pile requires the least amount of work, but it also takes the longest to produce good compost. As you gather clippings, weeds, or other appropriate organic materials, toss them on the top of the pile until it gets either too big for its spot or taller than five feet, and then start a new pile. When you think about it, throw an earthworm or two on top of the pile.

In four or five months or when it starts to shrink, check the middle of the first pile. If you can still see distinct shapes of the original matter, it's not done yet; if, on the other hand, the materials have become dark brown and crumbly, the compost is finished. To harvest the compost, disassemble the pile and shovel the finished compost into a container for use in your garden. Then place the newer undecomposed materials from the top and sides of the old pile on a new pile, and start again.

It's probably not a good idea to add kitchen scraps to a totally passive pile because the process is so slow that the kitchen waste may start to smell. In a case like this, you could maintain a passive pile for your yard waste and use a different method, such as trench composting, for your kitchen waste.

Moderately Managed Compost

With this method, you build an entire pile in just a few days and don't add newer materials to it while it's ripening. Instead, you accumulate your new materials in a new passive pile that you can use in the next managed pile.

Here is one method of constructing a moderately managed pile: For either a freestanding pile or one maintained in an open bin, arrange your materials by category—green or brown. Often the best tool for composting work is a pitchfork or garden fork, although a shovel will be more suitable for wood chips, soil, and the like. Create a four-inch-thick layer of brown materials followed by an equally thick green layer, and then spread a shovel-full of garden soil or finished compost evenly over the pile. The soil introduces microbes at different levels, so the pile will start to "work" sooner. Poke numerous holes through the top of the soil layer with your garden fork. This works to settle the pile as you build it, and creates passageways between the layers. Moisten the soil layer with a gallon of water—nonchlorinated, if possible. Water from a rain barrel is perfect. Skip the water if your green materials are wet, such as fresh water hyacinths, hydrilla, or rinsed seaweed.

Repeat these layers until the pile is three to five feet tall. Create an indentation on the top of the pile and pour a gallon or two of water into it. If you stop the construction halfway through the process, end with a thicker brown layer to hold in the moisture. When you continue, scrape away a little of that top layer before adding the next green layer. When you finish, cover the pile with a layer of persistent mulching material such as a mixture of pine needles and dead leaves or straw to keep the pile moist and to retard weed growth on the outside.

If you kept your ratio of green to brown materials and there is enough moisture, the pile should heat up after one day. After a week or two, turn the pile to aerate it and keep the heat up. You'll obliterate the layers when you turn it, but that's okay—the layers are mostly for creating the proper ratio of green to brown materials. This is when you'll be happy to have a location for a second pile; it's much easier to fork the pile into the empty bin or space, ensuring that the top ends up on the bottom, than to mix a pile up in place. If the weather is dry, water your pile every week or so. If it's very rainy, you may need to cover it with a tarp for a while. The pile should be damp, but not wet, or it will start to smell. After that first turning, turn the pile when you get to it. The more frequently you turn it, the faster it will ripen.

Highly Managed Compost

For an open pile, start it as you would a moderately managed pile, but use a chipper to chop your materials to a finer texture. You'll need a compost thermometer. You want to keep the temperature of the pile between 110°F and 150°F. After each turning, the temperature will rise at first, and then decline after a few days—when it does, turn it again. This keeps the microbial activity at the highest rate. After a month or so, when the temperature no longer increases after a turning, add some worms from the garden. There will probably be some worms in your pile already, but adding more at this stage will hasten the process. When the pile cools down, turn it every week or two to keep it mixed and aerated.

Highly managed open piles are a lot of work, but if you are composting manures or need the compost for a project, these procedures do speed up the process. Using a closed compost system in a barrel that turns on its axis makes the job of turning very easy. After you add your materials, turn the compost by rotating the bin. The frequent rotation ensures that the compost is well aerated, which allows the microbes to work full time. The compost in a closed system could be ready in as little as a month or two, but watch out for too much moisture. An enclosed system is usually smaller, but because the composting rate is so much higher and the labor involved so much less, it may be worth it in the long run. And for small lots or for courtyard and balcony gardening, a closed bin may be the only reasonable option.

Vermiculture, or composting with special composting worms, is a highly managed system because you can't starve your worms or let them dry out. Some folks use this method for composting their kitchen scraps. Use shredded and dampened black-ink-only newspaper as your brown material and the kitchen scraps as your green material. To harvest the compost, lure the worms to new food, then clean up their leavings. It is important that no worms from these systems be allowed to escape (or you may cause a worm population explosion to the detriment of natural ecosystems), so place your finished compost in an airtight container for a week or two and search it for leftover or newly hatched worms before you introduce it to outdoor soils.

Using Compost in the Garden

At the end of the composting process, your compost should be dark brown and crumbly and should not resemble its original ingredients. Some people recommend sifting the compost through a hardware cloth screen with half-inch or one-inch mesh; this extra step does have the added benefit of separating out the materials that have not completely decayed. Screening your compost will give it a more uniform appearance and will make it more useful for starting seeds, but beyond this its value will not significantly increase.

The nutrients your compost contains depend upon the starting materials and the decomposers. If you've used nutrient-rich materials such as manure or waterweeds, your compost may contain relatively high amounts of usable nitrogen (N), phosphorus (P), potassium (K), in addition to secondary and trace elements. If your starting materials were lean in nutrients, such as shredded paper, dryer lint, and grass clippings, your compost might look rich but you may need to use more of it to get enough microbes working. Nevertheless, it will be an important additive to your soil. It's probably a good idea to send your compost in for a complete soil test every so often so that you know what you're working with.

Keep in mind that compost is not used in the same way as an artificial fertilizer; it's applied more generously and becomes part of the soil. After you apply compost as a top dressing next to your crops, it won't take long for it to disappear. This doesn't mean that it's stopped working; it indicates that the compost microbes have worked their way into the soil and the organic materials in the compost have provided food for the soil's ecosystem.

As the microbes live and die, they break down the animal and plant parts in your soil and release the nutrients in a form that's useful for plants. When fungi dominate the soil, as is the case in most wooded areas, nitrogen will be released as ammonium (NH_4). When bacteria dominate the soil, most of the nitrogen is released as a nitrate (NO_3), which is the form that vegetables and other herbaceous plants prefer. You can alter your compost in favor of bacteria by adding more green materials to it. Compost with a higher proportion of brown, carbon-rich materials will contain more fungal decomposers. In the end, though, this mostly doesn't matter because the compost will adjust to the environment in which it's placed. After repeated applications of compost over several seasons, your soil will be in much better shape. It will start to resemble compost.

At the beginning of each season, work compost into your vegetable beds. After the initial clearing of weeds or plowing under of the green manure such as clover, apply three inches of compost in the planting areas and work it into soil. You could also mix it with composted animal manure to boost the nutrients it offers to heavy feeders such as tomatoes or squash.

During the growing season, add more compost to your beds in and around the vegetables. This will keep the weeds down and introduce new microbes into the soil.

Compost Tea and Compost Extract

Three liquids can be produced from your compost pile. Of the three, compost extract is the most beneficial for your garden.

Compost Leachate

Compost leachate is the liquid that seeps out of the bottom of the compost pile. While rich in soluble nutrients, the leachate in the early stage of composting may also contain pathogens. Reduce the amount of leachate produced by using less water and adding more brown material to your pile. Make sure this liquid has a safe place to drain into—a dry well, a rain garden, a thick hedgerow, or a densely wooded area.

Compost Extract

Compost extract (or unaerated compost tea) is made from completed or finished compost suspended in a cloth bag in a barrel of water for a day or so. Don't soak it too long, or anaerobic microbes will replace the aerobic ones, causing the pile to stink. This compost tea can be used as a liquid fertilizer to enhance soil microbes, and it's an important boost for growing seedlings that have one or two real leaves. Note that if you're using city water, you'll need to let the water sit for a day or more until the chlorine dissipates before using it. Also, never use water from a system with a water softener; the water contains too many salts.

Your compost extract should be an almost black or dark brown liquid that smells sweet or earthy—dilute it so that it looks more like tea before you use it. If it smells sour, don't use it on your plants. Just throw it onto your working compost pile and start over. Once it has a good smell, use your extract liberally in your garden.

Compost extract has many uses, but it is most beneficial as a liquid fertilizer for your seedlings and container gardens. Applying compost in liquid form will enhance its nutrient delivery and provide the soil with good microbes. Compost extract makes your compost more versatile and go further.

Enhanced Compost Tea

Enhanced compost tea is made from compost extract that has been fermented or brewed with added sugars to culture the microbes. To produce large populations of microorganisms, this process requires active aeration using a bubbler. Enhanced compost tea has been widely touted as a foliar spray for reducing pathogens, but university and scientific studies have not verified its efficacy in disease control. It is not registered as a pesticide and cannot legally be recommended or applied as one. Compost tea creates an artificially high culture of compost microbes. You don't know what microbes are in your compost; you could be growing *E. coli* or other pathogens in this highly enriched environment. Use the extract with the "normal" levels of microbes.

Healthy Soil Is the Key to Organic Gardening

The time and energy you invest in enriching the soil for your edible gardens will pay you back with larger yields of better quality edibles. Soil enrichment is a good investment.

Resources

The U.S. Department of Agriculture provides a detailed report on the soil for every county in Florida; see http://soils.usda.gov/survey/online_surveys/florida/.

For articles on compost tea and more, go to the website of the Washington State extension agent Dr. Linda Chalker-Scott at http://www.informedgardener.com.

For details on soil additives, see the University of Florida's IFAS document "Introduction to Organic Crop Production," http://edis.ifas.ufl.edu/cvl18.

The Minnesota Institute for Sustainable Agriculture provides a booklet on dealing with contamination in urban soils: http://misadocuments.info/Urban_Soil_Contaminants.pdf.

For the extension article "Organic Soil Fertility," go to http://www.extension.org/pages/18565/organic-soil-fertility

See also Jeff Lowenfels and Wayne Lewis, *Teaming with Microbes* (Portland, Ore.: Timber Press, 2006).

4

Seed-Sowing, Propagation, and Planting Techniques

Planting seeds and watching them sprout and grow into robust plants is one of gardening's great pleasures. Starting plants from organically grown seed stock is probably the best way to guarantee that your seedlings have not been exposed to pesticides, synthetic fertilizer applications, and genetic modification. Planting your own seeds gives you the peace of mind of controlling their environment, from seed to table. It's disappointing when seeds don't sprout or when your seedlings are chopped off by a cutworm, crowded out by a jungle of Florida's weeds, or attacked by a damping-off fungus. Growing plants from seed may be Mother Nature's miracle, but there are ways to increase your odds of success.

Seeds are not the only way to propagate plants. Many crops naturally use asexual or seedless methods of plant propagation. Some examples of seedless propagation are the formation of bulblets on wild garlic or walking onions, the layering of a rosemary bush or a tomato vine, or the spreading rhizomes of a mint plant. Growers can also induce asexual reproduction taking cuttings and making divisions. See "Seedless, or Asexual Crop Propagation" beginning on page 77 for ideas on asexual propagation.

Seeds and Seedlings

The Seed

Seeds are the products of the sexual reproduction of plants. Some plants have both male and female parts in the same flower, making self-pollination possible, while other plants require pollination from a different flower. Plants employ various methods to enforce the cross-pollination that provides greater vigor and variability. These variations are key to helping the overall plant populations adjust to a new area or to changing conditions in their original environment. When you harvest the seeds from your best-performing crops, you are more likely to end up with a strain of plants that has adapted to your particular environment. This holds true only for open-pollinated plants because the seedlings produced from cultivars or hybrid plants may vary significantly from the parent plants.

Fertile seeds contain a plant embryo, and under the proper conditions, each seed will germinate to produce a healthy young plant known as a "seedling." The seed contains several parts: the seed coat; one or two preformed seed leaves called cotyledons; the radicle, which grows downward to form the root; the epicotyl, which grows upward to form the shoot above the cotyledon leaves; and usually enough stored food to supply the seed with the energy to germinate and get to the point where it can start the process of photosynthesis. Once the seedling starts photosynthesizing, the new plant can produce its own energy for living.

The cache of food in the seed is a combination of sugar, starch, protein, and oil. In fact, these high levels of nutrients have made seed crops a staple in the human diet for thousands of years. In corn, for example, the stored food is called endosperm and takes up the majority of the seed volume, with a small embryo located off to the side. Once an ear of corn has been picked, the endosperm begins to change from sweet to starchy; this is why fresh-picked corn is noticeably sweeter and why farmers work so hard to get corn to the consumer as quickly as possible. Some plants, such as beans, store the food within the fat cotyledons or seed leaves, so there is little or no endosperm. Depending

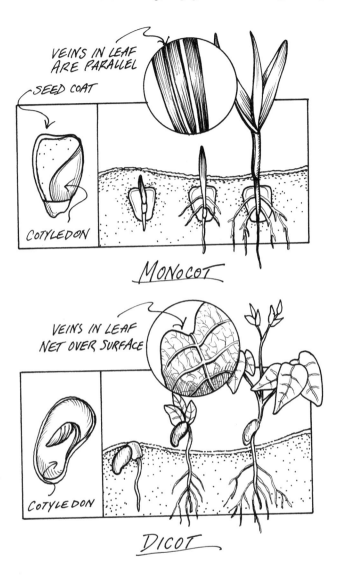

upon how it's formed, the stored food may have up to three sets of genes (triploid); some humans have trouble completely digesting this type of food and may produce gas (methane) as it passes through their digestive systems.

A plant with one cotyledon is called a monocot. In our vegetable gardens, the monocot crops include corn or any of the other grasses, pineapples, and the onion family. The leaves of monocots have parallel veins and monocot flower parts, such as petals and sepals, that cluster in threes or multiples of three. Plants that have two cotyledons are called dicots, and these include the vast majority of plants in our vegetable gardens. The veins in the leaves of dicots form a net throughout the leaf surface. Dicot flower parts are usually arranged in multiples of four or five.

When a seed sprouts, the radicle grows first to anchor the seed and absorb water and nutrients. Next, the cotyledon leaves emerge and turn green, after which the true leaves are produced. The size and shape of the cotyledon leaves provide a recognizable clue to the identity of some plants. Other plants have less distinct cotyledon leaves and the plant may not be easily identifiable until the first true leaves are formed. Growers who have taken care to plant their seeds in an orderly fashion have a better chance of telling desirable plants from weeds; the seedlings growing in their grid-like pattern are more likely to be the crop plants, while those growing outside of the pattern are more likely to be weeds.

When you plant seeds directly in the garden, Florida's weeds will also invite themselves into your nicely prepared soil. It's a good idea to prepare an area in the garden as you would were you planting seeds, and then to leave it unplanted. This is your test area for noting which weeds or volunteers are likely to sprout in your real garden beds. This way, you'll be able to distinguish them from the sprouts of the seeds you planted.

Some gardening experts advise against planting seeds when it's hot and humid to avoid fungi. Unfortunately, if we followed this advice in Florida, we'd never get our seeds in the ground! If you can manage it, choose fungus-resistant varieties and irrigate your garden early in the morning to allow the leaves of the seedlings to dry before nightfall, thereby reducing the probability of a fungal attack.

Obtaining Seeds

Most small or casual vegetable growers buy their seeds from seed companies, and these days you can usually find organically produced seeds. You may also purchase some of your seeds from local garden clubs or Master Gardeners or at more formal seed-exchange organizations. Some of these seeds will be great, but quality and germination rates do vary. If possible, purchase seed that is recommended for Florida.

If you're just beginning your edible gardening adventures, commercial seed sources may work best because seed companies have the resources to produce seeds with resistance to diseases and pests. On tomato-seed packs, look for "V," "F," and "N" after the varietal name, which indicate that it is resistant to Verticilium wilt, Fusarium wilt, and nematode damage, respectively. In Florida, it's also best to look for varieties that are heat resistant.

Once you gain some experience, you can start saving your own seed. If you have a surplus, maybe you could participate in a seed-exchange program.

Planting Seeds in the Garden

To increase the germination rate of your seeds, avoid problems with fungal infections, and suppress the weed seeds, use a sterile top dressing of treated soil, vermiculite, or unfertilized potting mix. Compost that has gone through a hot phase also works well. The native soil (without amendments) may carry diseases or may form a crust that could impede seedling growth.

Follow the directions on the seed packet for pretreating the seeds for sprouting. For instance, parsley takes fourteen to twenty-one days to germinate, but soaking the seeds in water overnight will significantly decrease the time between sowing and germination—this is called seed priming. Pretreatment often produces a more uniform germination rate. The earlier you know that there is a germination problem, the quicker you can sow additional seeds to grow enough to fulfill your harvest plan.

On planting day, thoroughly moisten the soil so that it's damp to a depth of at least two inches, and layer your sterile top dressing an inch thick on the planting area. Then plant only one to three seeds in each hole according to the size and the suggested spacing; for tiny seeds, you could mix the seed with sand and broadcast the mixture thinly on your planting surface. Be sure to label your rows or areas so that you know what you have planted in each. Thoroughly moisten the top dressing with a fine spray of water.

Don't plant too many seeds; instead, plan for "just-in-time" crops. To do this, first estimate how large a harvest you could use, whether it's for just you and your family or for others. Then plant just slightly more than the amount you estimated. Although nothing is certain in gardening, prudently planning the size of your harvest ensures that you won't end up with way too much of a good thing.

Just-in-Time Crops

The most successful harvests are those that provide you and your family with plenty of what will be consumed, but not so much that food goes to waste. The planned quantity could leave enough for any canning, drying, or freezing you intend to do. Planting extra in order to share the surplus with a soup kitchen, needy families, or other charitable causes is certainly a noble enterprise, but you should determine what their needs are before you start planting. Your needs will be much greater if you're planting for a farmers market or CSA clients, but having a plan will keep your harvests in balance, no matter their size.

If you are a family gardener, plant crops that your family will want to eat, especially when you are just starting your edible endeavors. Add a few new crops each season to expand your horizons and find new vegetables to enjoy. It's disheartening to spend weeks tending a crop only to find out that everyone hates eating it, so go slow on the new stuff.

Once you decide on what to plant, plant only enough to provide a reasonable quantity for your stated needs. You can achieve this by planting only two to three seeds in each planting hole or by broadcasting your tiny seeds thinly. When the seeds sprout, wait until one or two sets of true leaves emerge, then chose the best-looking seedlings and snip away the extra ones. If appropriate, lay in a layer of mulch between the seedlings to keep the soil moist and to retard the weeds. This will ensure that each plant has enough room to grow well. It also saves you time because you won't have to thin the seedlings or deal with as many weeds. Your goal as a grower is to provide the ideal conditions for your crops so that they can grow quickly and can produce the best harvest possible.

Plant the next round of seeds so as your first set of crops has run its course, the next round is ready to harvest. For example, if you are planting forty-day radishes (the number of days to harvest is usually listed on the seed package), plant the first crop as soon as cool weather sets in. Then, two or three weeks later, plant the next crop. At forty days, you'll start pulling up the first radishes and continue harvesting for the next week or two. By the time you've finished harvesting the first set, the next round of radishes will be nearly ready. Continue planting new seeds every three weeks or so until it's time to plant your tomatoes and peppers. The last round of radishes can be planted around these warm weather crops while they're small. You will have harvested the radishes by the time the tomatoes and peppers really start growing. At that point, add some extra compost or composted manure, topped with mulch, around the tomato or pepper plants where the radishes were growing.

Planting Seeds in a Controlled Environment

While some large-seeded plants like beans, sunflowers, squashes, or root crops like carrots and beets do best when planted directly in the garden, others are more successful when given a head start away from the insects and snails for a few weeks and then transplanted into your beds. If you're working on a sustainable multicropped vegetable plot, starting seeds elsewhere gives the current crop six to eight more weeks in the soil. Also, older seedlings started in pots are more likely to survive than tiny sprouts sown directly into the wilds of your garden. Planting viable seedlings makes it easier to get just the right spacing because the uncertainty of germination and initial seedling development is no longer a factor.

There are several strategies for starting seeds in pots or flats, but whichever method you choose, keep the seedlings close at hand so you can see when they begin to wilt or need other attention. Follow the directions listed on the seed packet for planting depth and whether to presoak the seeds. Poke holes in the soil for each seed, or scatter the smaller seeds on top of the soil and cover them with a sterile medium such as vermiculite or powdered coir. To ensure that the seeds come into good contact with the soil, gently pat or tamp the soil once the seeds are sown.

There are a number of different ways to start seeds, but these two methods will get you started:

1. Plant several seeds in each little pot. When they sprout, save only the two or three best seedlings, and cut off the rest at the soil line. Continue to grow the remaining seedlings in the pots until they are ready to set out in the garden. Or, re-pot them, as they grow, into larger pots—this process is called "potting up."

2. Sow the seeds into a flat where they will sprout quite thickly. After one or two of their first real leaves appear, transplant the seedlings into the starter pots, where they'll have more room to grow. Depending upon how big they are and how well they take to transplanting, you could plant them singly or in groups of two or three to a pot. This is a delicate transplant because the seedlings are so small. Handle each one as little as possible and don't squeeze the stem; instead, use the tough cotyledon (seed leaves) or root mass as a handle, or, if they are too small to pick up with your fingers, handle them with an old kitchen fork or tweezers. Even though this method adds an extra step, it has the advantage of eliminating the germination issue because you're dealing only with seeds that have sprouted and are growing well. This is probably the best way to handle seeds that you've stored for three years or longer.

For seedling pots, you could use four-inch plastic pots, recycled yogurt tubs, or other hard-sided containers. Be sure to wash them well and poke some holes in the bottoms for drainage. You could also use egg cartons or other fiber containers. Some folks make planting cups by folding several layers of newspaper (black and white pages only) and holding them together with a paperclip. When you're ready to plant, remove the paperclip and sink the newspaper cup directly into the soil. You could also tie a bunch of toilet paper tubes together so they stand upright, stuff the bottom of each tube with a wad of newspaper so soil doesn't run out, fill each tube with your starter mix, and then plant a couple of seeds in each. As with the newspaper cup, you can sink this tube right into your garden. Tear open the bottom of the tube to encourage good root growth, but leave the top in place as a built-in collar to protect the seedling against cutworms.

Fill your containers with a thoroughly moistened, seed-starter soil mix; a good bet is a combination of vermiculite, compost, and coconut coir in approximately equal amounts. You could also purchase an organic seed-starter medium. It's best not to use peat moss; it's acidic, has no nutrients, and it may actually dry out your seedlings. Gardeners have used garden soil to start seedlings for thousands upon thousands of years, but it may harbor injurious organisms and weed seeds, so keep a close watch if you decide to go this route.

The general rule of thumb is to provide your seedlings with gentle bottom heat in order to promote good germination, especially for tomatoes and peppers, but this step may not be necessary in the warmer sections of Florida. With the exception of midwinter months in northern Florida, we can set our seeds outside in the middle of the day during cooler weather. Morning is probably the best time to set out your seedlings during the hotter months, but if you can, move them into the shade for the afternoon so they don't dry out as quickly. Natural light is best for good growth. If you're working inside, set them under and close to white florescent bulbs, and leave the lights on for twelve to sixteen hours a day. If the seedlings become spindly, they need more light.

You can irrigate your seedlings by placing your containers in a pan of water for twenty minutes each day; don't let your seeds sit in water all day. You could also use a soft mist to water them from the top. Be sure to test your irrigation to be sure that the water is soaking into the soil. You want to train the roots to grow down, not to come up to the surface in search of water.

Good air circulation helps prevent fungal problems. If you're growing your seedlings indoors, set up a small fan to blow air across your seedlings for an hour or two each day. This airflow will also help them to build strong stems.

One or two weeks after your seedlings sprout, begin to fertilize them weekly with diluted compost extract or a gentle organic fertilizer such as highly diluted fish or seaweed emulsion. Once they have one or two sets of true leaves, start hardening them off by setting them outside in the vicinity of where they will be planted. This is also the time to taper off their extra irrigation. This way their stems will build up strength to endure the breezes and their leaves will become accustomed to the sun exposure. Be sure to bring them in on cold nights.

Storing Unused Seeds

Because you'll be planting only the seeds you'll need for your just-in-time harvest, you'll probably have some seeds left over. If you treat them right, you can use them for the next few years.

Seeds are living organisms in a semidormant state, and while some seeds may survive for years, others are more fragile. To maintain their dormancy, store your seeds in a cool, dark location with low humidity—an opaque container in the refrigerator works well.

Invest in small, resealable plastic bags with a white area that can be labeled with an indelible marker. Record the seed name, along with the cultivar, source, and year, directly on the bag. If you have a lot of seed to store, remove the seeds from their original envelope and pour them into the bag to save space and to prevent spillage from opened envelopes. Store the seed bags in a larger opaque container. If you have more than one container for your seeds, divide the seeds alphabetically and label your larger containers. This way, you'll know where to start looking for your seeds. Yes, this organization takes time, but, like keeping a detailed garden journal, it will save you time in the long run and help you to take good care of your seed investment.

Once you are ready to sow the seeds you have saved, test their viability by soaking them in water for a few hours. The ones that are still alive will usually sink to the bottom, while the dead ones will float on the surface. Some people carry the germination test one step further by actually germinating a batch of test seeds in moistened paper towels. This way you'll know how densely to plant the seeds. If you have a sixty-percent germination rate, you'll need to plant at least two seeds in every planting hole.

Choosing Seedlings from a Nursery

You could let someone else do the work of nurturing seedlings and purchase them when they are ready to plant. Buying seedlings certainly saves on labor, but, in addition to the extra cost, there are some disadvantages. The selection of cultivars will be severely limited to only the most popular ones, and even if they are sold in Florida, they may not be suitable for your climate. You won't know how the plants have been treated—obviously, they've survived if they are on the shelf, but they may have been overfertilized or overwatered. Those that are labeled organic should have been treated well by the grower, but who knows how they've been treated at the store?

Look for plants with thick top growth and good green color; existing blooms or fruits are not usually an advantage but rather mean that they've been forced. A more telling way to judge the seedlings health and potential is by examining their roots. Slip a plant or two out of its pot to see what's happening below the soil. If the roots are white and just beginning to fill out the bottom of the pot, then the seedling is ready to plant. If the roots have formed a solid mass inside the pot, then the plant has been in the pot for too long. If the roots are still white, go ahead and purchase it, but rinse away the soil and spread the roots out upon planting. If they are tan or mushy, don't buy the plant.

Purchasing seedlings does give you a head start. So if your harvest plans change or your own seedlings bite the dust, then go ahead and buy someone else's seedlings.

Planting Seedlings

It's best to prepare the garden beds where you'll plant your seedlings a week or two ahead of time. Remove the weeds, especially the deep-rooted ones. Work in your compost and other organic matter, and cover the area with an easily removed mulch such as pine needles or straw.

The day before transplanting your seedlings (either your own or ones you've purchased), soak the plants in their pots. Create your planting areas, be they wide rows or square feet, and then measure out the positions for each plant. Soak the beds until they are moist to a depth of two to three inches. Have some mulch on hand to place on the bed in order to moderate the temperature and the moisture level. If possible, choose a cloudy day to plant, provide some temporary shade, or plant early in the evening so that the seedlings won't be baked in Florida's hot sun right away.

Turn the pots upside down or sideways, depending upon the plant size, and urge the root ball out by squeezing the pot, poking your finger into a drainage hole, or by slicing around the inside of the pot with an old table knife. Put two fingers across the top of the pot with the plant stem between them then tip the pot up so that the plant falls into your hand. Handle the plant by the root ball. It's important not to pull the plants out by their stems because you could damage the cell walls, preventing the ready flow of water up through the plant. Removing the plant from its container will be unnecessary, if you've used containers made from newspaper or cardboard rolls because you can just sink the whole container into the soil.

If there are two or three plants in the pot, carefully separate them. Your seedlings should each have a large mass of roots. Dig a hole in your garden that's deep enough for the roots to extend downward. Fill in the hole with soil or compost, and provide support for the stems. Unlike trees and shrubs, seedlings can tolerate having soil packed up higher around their stems. In the case of tomatoes and a few other crops, adventitious roots will sprout from the buried stem to significantly increase the total root mass. (But keep grafted tomato seedlings at the original soil level to ensure that the graft remains above the ground.) Water the seedlings thoroughly to eliminate large air pockets around their roots. Prop up the plants again so that they are upright and not stuck in the mud. Finally, mulch around (but not touching) the seedlings.

If you have had problems with cutworms, place a collar made of paper or foil around each plant; with any luck, your seedlings will be too large and tough for cutworms by the time they are planted.

For the next week or two, check your seedlings every day and water them as needed to prevent them from drying out. They are vulnerable at this stage because their roots have been compromised. If they wilt, you have only a short window of opportunity to revive them. If you do not rehydrate your seedlings quickly, they will die. Once they adjust and really start growing, you won't need to be quite so vigilant.

Seedless, or Asexual, Crop Propagation

This is the point at which we perform the mathematical oxymoron—multiply by dividing. Asexual, or vegetative, propagation means that each new plant is a clone of the parent plant—there is no genetic variability. There are several methods for achieving seedless propagation—some occur naturally, while others are forced by the grower.

Underground Crop Terms

A true bulb is a plant embryo encased in fleshy modified leaves that contain food reserves for the plant. The roots of the bulb emerge from a basal plate on the bottom, while the embryonic plant and layers of fat leaves emerge from the top. Onions and their relatives are the only crops that form true bulbs.

Corms are modified stems that look like bulbs, but they don't have basal plates nor the layers of modified leaves.

Rhizomes, sometimes called rootstocks, are thickened stems that grow horizontally. Ginger produces edible rhizomes.

Taproot vegetables include radishes, carrots, turnips, and beets. The swollen root is harvested whole and is not normally used in propagation.

Tubers, or underground stems that store food, have knobby or lumpy surfaces with growth buds (eyes) from which the shoots of

continued

continued

the new plant emerge. Irish potatoes are the best-known example, and Jerusalem artichokes, true yams, and daylilies also produce tubers.

Tuberous roots look similar to tubers but are actually swollen roots, not modified stems. They don't sprout from eyes, but from one end (called the "crown"), and they grow in clumps. The sweet potato is a good example of a tuberous root.

Bulbs

Members of the onion family (Alliaceae) produce a true bulb. Some onions, including walking onions and meadow garlic, also produce a scape, a stem bearing a group of small bulblets and sometimes flowers. An initial leaf often sprouts from the bulblets, which allows the little bulbs to start growing while attached to the mother plant. You can harvest the bulblets for replanting or for consuming, but if you leave them on the stem, they will eventually become too heavy, causing the stem to fall over and allowing the onion to "walk," albeit slowly and randomly, across the garden.

Compound bulbs such as garlic divide themselves into cloves separated by papery skins. If you save several entire bulbs of garlic over the summer, each one could produce eight to twenty new plants the next season. Buying whole bulbs is the most common way to purchase garlic for growing; seeds are not usually available.

When you plant new bulbs or bulblets, give them additional irrigation. After that, too much irrigation could cause the bulbs to rot.

Cuttings

If you've ever snipped off a sprig of basil or other member of the mint family (Lamiaceae) and placed it in water, you've probably noticed how quickly and easily it develops roots. Cuttings, such as the ones you can buy in a store's organic produce department or at a farmers market, provide the grower with additional sources of crop plants. In addition, you can make cuttings from your own the garden to increase your number of plants such as sweet potatoes, strawberries, tomatoes, or any member of the mint family.

Growers may take cuttings to avoid hazardous periods in the garden. For instance, the grower could harvest a portion of the basil before mid-summer when fungal attacks are likely, root the cuttings in water or sand away from the garden, and then replant the cuttings in a container or different section of the garden toward the end of summer to produce a second (or third) good harvest after the summer doldrums. The same strategy works for tomatoes, which often begin to fail once the nighttime temperatures remain above 70°F. You can root cuttings from tomatoes in damp sand in a cool place away from the garden, and then set the new plants back out in the soil when the nighttime temperatures begin to fall.

When making cuttings, it's best to choose stems with good terminal growth buds. Cut a section long enough for you to remove the leaves from the lower three to five inches of the stem and sink this part of the stem into water or sand with at least three additional inches above the water or soil line. Some plants root easily, while others may need to be dipped in rooting hormone in order to stimulate adventitious root formation from stem tissue.

While successful cuttings normally have lots of roots, those formed in water will differ in structure from those formed in the soil because cuttings absorb oxygen differently when their roots are submerged. Once planted in the garden, supply these cuttings with additional irrigation for a week or two until the plants put on some new growth or until they stop wilting in the middle of the day.

Cuttings should be taken only from healthy plants, but even then a cutting may harbor diseases such as a fungal wilt, so keep that in mind. It may be more prudent to plant new seeds or to purchase new slips of crops that are not susceptible to various diseases.

Divisions

Gardeners can divide perennials that spread via rhizomes or by bunching when they are dormant or at harvest time when the whole plant including its roots or bulbs is dug up. For many plants, being divided periodically increases their vigor. Plus, the grower is able to expand his or her crop.

Treat these newly planted starts as you would any other transplant. If it's a bulb, water it once, at the time of planting. For other plants, supply them with additional irrigation until they recover.

Layering

Layering, a variation on cutting, occurs when a stem comes in contact with the soil and puts out roots. This may happen naturally in the garden, but growers can force this adventitious rooting by weighting down a stem with a rock or a handful of soil. Once new roots have formed, cut the layered stem away from the mother plant, dig up the rooted portion, and then replant it in a temporary pot or elsewhere in the garden.

Rosemary is a commonly layered crop: as the shrub expands, stems lay on the ground and root. Being a member of the mint family, rosemary is also a good candidate for cuttings.

Some growers like to bury the stems of their squash plants in order to encourage the formation of new roots farther up on the stems. Doing so may offset any damage from stem borers. Sweet potato vines can also be layered to start new plants.

Tubers

Tubers are modified stems that develop in a seemingly random pattern several buds or eyes from which shoots can sprout. The typical method of propagating tubers is to cut the tuber into pieces that each contain two or three eyes (growth buds), and plant the pieces at the proper spacing to allow for good growth. It's best to use certified seed potatoes for your crops because they won't have been treated with sprout-inhibiting chemicals. Of course, while they are called "seed potatoes," they are really not seeds at all.

Plant Propagation

If you want to use organic growing methods in your edible gardens, propagating your own plants is one way to make sure that the seedlings, roots, tubers, and cuttings have been handled without pesticides. Giving your crops a great start will make it easier for them to produce a bountiful harvest.

Resources

For more on seed production and sources of organic vegetable seeds, go to http://edis.ifas.ufl.edu/hs227.

The Organic Materials Review Institute (OMRI) provides information on organic growing, including sources of organic seeds, at http://www.omri.org/seeds.

5

Florida's Vegetables

The crops, including the culinary herbs and native edible plants (but not including fruiting trees and shrubs), are organized by family, and within their family alphabetically by their official names. The authorities on family names and Latin binomials are the Atlas of Florida Vascular Plants and, secondarily, the U.S. Department of Agriculture. There are several reasons for choosing this arrangement, but probably the most important is to provide you with an easy reference to consult when planning your crop rotation—essentially, crops in the same family rotate together.

Unless otherwise mentioned, you can assume that the crop requires moderately rich, well-drained soil and as much sun as possible. Also check out appendix 1 for month-by-month guides for each of the three regions—north, central, and south Florida.

Specific cultivars or varieties of crops are not listed here because there are too many and new ones are being developed each year. Rather, general categories, such as short-day onions or soft-necked garlic, are provided to start you off on the right track. Your extension agent will have data sheets and online information for specific mainstream crops. You can also find many online publications on the Electronic Data Information Service (EDIS) website: http://edis.ifas.ufl.edu. Because the extension service can provide only general guidelines, it's important for you to keep track of which crops work best for your situation in your garden log.

Each crop is classified as EASY, MODERATE, DIFFICULT, or NOT RECOMMENDED, depending on the region. For instance, pineapple is ranked EASY in south Florida, but MODERATE in central and north Florida because it requires protection from cold weather and would need to be moved inside for a portion of the season. These ratings are subjective, and your experience could be different.

For the recommended spacing between plants, refer to the instructions on your seed packets. Different varieties and cultivars may require different spacing—some sunflowers are two feet tall, while others grow to twelve feet or more. The goal is to allow enough space for your crop plants, while leaving very little soil exposed for the weeds. Feel free to modify the density of your plantings to suit your situation and growing style.

Recipe Gardens

When selecting the plants to grow in your garden, the best advice is to grow what you and your family are likely to consume. You might further narrow the field by selecting the vegetables you need for your favorite recipes. Time your plantings so that you can harvest all the ingredients at the same time. Here are a few recipes whose ingredients you can pull straight from the garden:

Cabbage Soup—This soup is a delicious combination of cool-weather vegetables and perennial herbs. Plant cabbage, broccoli leaves, purple and red carrots, kale, chard, sweet onions, bunching onions, white radishes, garlic, rosemary, and sage. If you alter the ratio of carrots to greens, you could end up with carrot soup instead.

Salsa or Pizza—Plant garlic, onions, cilantro, parsley, oregano, basil, tomatoes, tomatillos, green bell peppers, and jalapeno peppers. If you're lucky, you'll also have a lemon or lime tree for supplying juice for the salsa.

continued

continued

Stir Fry—For best results, choose vegetables that are relatively firm so that they don't fall apart during cooking. Plant some cool-weather crops such as onions, carrots, radishes, broccoli, bok choy, fennel, kale, sugar-snap peas, and meadow garlic. Also, plant some warm-weather crops such as bunching onions, sweet or hot peppers, various types of squash, eggplant, sweet potato, Jerusalem artichoke, beans, rosemary, and garlic, which is actually a cool-weather crop that's harvested in early summer.

Tempura—Plant squash, for both its blossoms and its fruits; daylilies, for both its roots and its flower buds; various onions; green peppers; sugar-snap peas; and sweet potatoes. Slice dense vegetables thinly so that they cook quickly.

Veggie Chips—Kale and other veggies make delicious, crispy chips that are an addictive alternative to commercial potato chips. Plant kale, collards, Swiss chard, or other greens—be creative! Thinly sliced root vegetables work, too. Even potatoes!

To make your own veggie chips, mix olive oil with sea salt, black pepper, or other of your favorite spices. Coat the leaves (washed and thoroughly dried; whole or cut) or root-crop slices with the oil mixture. Spread the mixture in a single layer on cookie sheets and bake them at 400°F for about five minutes on each side—longer for root crops. Be careful not to burn them!

Aizoaceae

The ice plant family (Aizoaceae) contains a number of ornamentals, but New Zealand spinach is its only commercial crop.

NEW ZEALAND SPINACH (*Tetragonia tetragonoides*) is a vining or sprawling annual or short-lived perennial in frost-free areas. The dark green leaves look, taste, and cook somewhat like spinach. It is tolerant of heat, salt, and drought.
Regions: EASY, in N, C, S.

Planting: Soak the seeds overnight and plant them after the last frost. The "seeds" are actually little capsules that each contain three or four true seeds, so after germination, choose the strongest seedling and chop off the others.

Growing: Full sun or slight shade; more shade in south Florida.

Maintaining: While the plants can survive droughty conditions, they taste better if given consistent moisture. Cut back the plants two or three times during the season to keep them bushy.

Harvesting: Cut leaves as needed to use at any time after the vines become established.

Using: Use the leaves as you would spinach. Like spinach, this plant contains oxalic acid, so cook it or serve it raw with vinegar to dissolve the oxalate crystals.

Alliaceae

The onion family (Alliaceae) has, in the past, been included in the lily (Liliaceae) and the Amaryllis (Amarylliaceae) families. Members of the *Allium* genus form bulbs or bulb-like stem enlargements; onions that form only stem enlargements, and not bulbs, are called bunching onions and often multiply if left in place. If allowed to flower, these plants form a specialized stem called a scape that could bear all the flowers in a spherical flower head, as is the case with chives, all bulblets, as with garlic, or a combination of flowers and bulblets, as with meadow garlic.

Members of this family may be harvested and eaten at any point during their life cycles. In our gardens, most onions and garlics are treated as long-season annuals, but there are some important perennials in this family, including chives, garlic chives, scallions, meadow garlic, and walking onions. Because many onions are cool-weather crops, plant short-day or day-neutral onions in Florida—never long-day onions. Generally, the onions and garlics are drought tolerant, but if you want larger bulbs and lusher greens, irrigate them regularly through dry periods and add extra compost when planting. Keep these plants well weeded because most members of the onion family have shallow roots and don't compete well with aggressive weeds.

When you cut into an onion or one of its relatives, chemicals inside the plant cells that are ordinarily kept separate mix with each other and with the air to form a volatile sulfur compound that makes your eyes water. Some onion varieties are milder, but the same compounds that draw tears also ward off insects that might feed on the onions. In fact, onion or garlic slurry makes an effective bug repellent that can be used in organic gardens.

The seeds of plants in the onion family are tiny and germinate slowly and somewhat erratically. Many gardeners germinate onion seeds in flats and transplant seedlings into the garden in early fall. Others grow the seeds until little bulbs form, and then remove them from the soil and let them dry out. The small bulbs are called sets and can be stored until the next season. Growing plants from sets or seedlings makes it easy to plant the onions at the perfect spacing.

CHIVES (*Allium schoenoprasum*) is a perennial in northern and central Florida, but it's grown as an annual in south Florida.
Regions: EASY, in N, C; MODERATE, in S.
Planting: Plant bulbs at any time during the year. Plant the seeds directly in the garden in fall or spring.
Growing: Full sun or slight shade; more shade in south Florida.
Maintaining: Provide moderate moisture and keep them well weeded. After two or three years, when the leaves become smaller due to overcrowding, dig out all the bulbs, separate them, and replant. After they bloom, the scape will die back. At this point, you may either pull out the dead stems or cut them off to keep the area tidy.
Harvesting: Cut leaves as needed. While many cooks use only the leaves, you can also dig out the bulbs to use at any time of the year. Save enough bulbs to plant for next year's crop.
Using: Use the leaves in salads and stir-fries; since they are hollow, add them only at the very last minute when frying or cooking. Finely chopped chives are often used as a topping for baked potatoes and creamed soups. The lavender flowers are edible as well, and you can use them in salads or as a colorful garnish. The edible bulbs are best cooked in stir-fries or soups.

GARLIC (*Allium sativum*) is a long-season annual; use only the soft-neck varieties in Florida. Garlic produces no seeds, so only the bulbs are sold. Each compound bulb consists of a dozen or more cloves separated by layers of thin, papery skin. If you grow enough garlic, the vampires will leave you alone.

Regions: EASY, in N; MODERATE, in C, S.

Planting: In north Florida, plant the cloves two inches deep and three inches apart in the fall. In central and south Florida, place the bulbs in the refrigerator in an opaque container for a month or longer before planting, and get them into the ground just before the cool winter weather sets in for your area. After planting, cover the bulbs with a two-inch layer of straw or pine-needle mulch to minimize temperature fluctuations in the soil.

Growing: Full sun or slight shade; no standing water or soggy soil.

Maintaining: Keep them weeded and let the soil dry out completely between waterings. When the leaves begin to yellow, stop watering.

Harvesting: While you could pull the bulbs at any time, this is one member of the onion family that improves with age. Immature bulbs don't have the size or flavor that you want from garlic. Harvest them when the soil is completely dry. The traditional method of drying the bulbs is to braid the leaves together and hang them in a dry shed or garage. Save some bulbs to plant for next year's crop; you'll get ten to twenty plants from each bulb.

Using: Use garlic to flavor soups and sauces. Freshly harvested "green" garlic tends to be milder and softer than garlic that has been dried. Some people choose a few bulbs in the garden to sacrifice for their leaves, which can be cut finely and used for soups or sautéing. When you use the leaves for cooking, the bulbs usually won't grow as large. If your harvest is large and unlikely to be used within a few months, you can make a garlic and olive oil pesto to freeze: peel the cloves and put them in the blender with enough olive oil to make a paste. The olive oil also keeps the mixture from freezing solid, making it easy to flake off a chunk as needed. A quick way to peel the cloves is to bust open the bulb with the heel of your hand, and then put all the cloves in a covered plastic container and shake it hard for twenty seconds. Voilá! All the cloves are peeled.

GARLIC CHIVES (*Allium tuberosum*) is a heat-tolerant perennial that is often used instead of chives in south Florida and even as a border in ornamental beds. The leaves are flat, not hollow and round like chives, and have a mild garlicky or oniony flavor. Garlic chives tolerate poor soil conditions and erratic irrigation. If you allow the flowers to go to seed, you may find it growing "everywhere" in your landscape. In addition, it spreads via its rhizomes to form new clumps.

Regions: EASY, in N, C, S.

Planting: Plant bulbs an inch deep, five inches apart. Plant the seeds directly in the garden or flat in the fall or spring.

Growing: Full sun or slight shade; more shade in south Florida. Some growers blanch the lower stems by mounding soil around them. The white leaves are said to be milder and are often used in Asian recipes.

Maintaining: Keep them weeded. After two or three years, when the leaves become smaller due to overcrowding, dig out the clumps of bulbs, separate them, and replant into freshly composted soil.

Harvesting: Cut leaves as needed, being sure to cut them all the way to the ground. They lose their flavor quickly, so use them right away and don't dry them. The flowers are also edible, and it's a good idea to pick the flowers to control the amount of reseeding in small garden areas.

Using: Use the leaves in salads and stir-fries, but add them late in the cooking process, as they lose flavor when heated. The leaves are an important ingredient in Asian cooking and are often paired with raw foods. The flowers can be used in salads or as a colorful garnish. Few people use the bulbs or rhizomes, but if you do, slice them thinly and cook them.

LEEKS (*Allium ampeloprasum*) were developed in Europe and their mild taste makes them a favorite for soups. They form a thick stem at the base that continues fairly high into the plant. The flat, solid leaves are folded and grow on opposite sides of the stem, but no true bulb is formed.

Regions: EASY, in N, C, S.

Planting: Plant the seeds early in the fall and transplant them as eight-to-ten-inch seedlings into a ten-inch-deep trench in winter or early spring. As the plants grow, carefully fill in the trench with soil to create a mound around each plant, taking care to avoid getting soil into the folds of the leaves. The resulting grit is nearly impossible to remove and may end up in your soup. Some growers wrap the stems with brown paper first. Whatever your method, covering the lower part of the plant keeps it white and sweet; it also encourages the stem to grow thicker.

Growing: Full sun in well-drained soil; does not tolerate standing water or persistent wetness.

Maintaining: Weeding is important, especially when you first plant the seedlings.

Harvesting: Harvest the plant at any time once the stem is one inch in diameter; most people wait until it's much larger. The leaves don't turn brown at the end of the growing season. Most farmers cut back the leaves at harvesting, to ten inches or so, but they could be left long and used as well.

Using: Cut through the stem and rinse out the grit. You can slice the stem thinly to use raw in salads, but most people either sauté the leeks or use them in soups and stews. Potato leek soup is a favorite.

MEADOW GARLIC (*Allium canadense*) is a perennial; grow it near your chives in the herb garden or next to the walking onions. It dies back during the summer months; keep track of where it is in your garden so that you don't over plant it with something else. In late fall it sends up new leaves, followed by a flowering stalk with a few white flowers and a bunch of bulblets, each with a single, curly leaf. A Florida native, it's not usually sold commercially, but once you find some, you won't need to purchase it again because it multiplies.

Regions: EASY, in N, C; NOT RECOMMENDED, in S.

Planting: Plant bulbs or bulblets from the flower heads an inch deep, two inches apart.

Growing: Full sun or slight shade.

Maintaining: Moderate moisture, but will tolerate wetter conditions. After the leaves die back for the summer, weed the area and apply an inch of compost topped by straw or pine needles. After a few years, when the leaves become smaller due to overcrowding, dig out all the bulbs, separate them, and replant.

Harvesting: Cut leaves as needed or harvest bulblets when available. The bulblets have a thin skin that you'll need to remove before using them. Or, dig out the bulbs to use at any time of the year.

Using: Use the leaves in salads and stir-fries—since they are solid, not hollow like chives, they hold their shape during frying. Use the bulbs or bulblets as you would any garlic; because they are mild, they can also be used raw in salads, preferably thinly sliced.

ONIONS (*Allium cepa*) are treated as a long-season annual in most places. In Florida, we plant onions in the fall and grow them through the winter months. Because of this, you want short-day or day-neutral onions. Onions have been under cultivation for thousands of years, and there are hundreds of varieties to choose from—sweet, strong, big, little, yellow, white, or purple. You can buy sets or seedlings for some popular varieties, but best way to obtain a variety is to purchase seeds. Because we Floridians don't live in the counties near Vidalia, Georgia, we can't call our sweet onions Vidalia onions. But our onions can be just as sweet, especially when eaten right out of the garden.

Regions: EASY, planting sets or seedlings in N, C, S; MODERATE, planting seeds in N, C, S.

Planting: Plant the seeds, seedlings, or sets directly in the garden, or start the seeds in a more controlled environment to produce your own seedlings or sets to plant later out in the garden. To produce a bulb crop, plant the seedlings or sets one inch deep and four inches apart. To produce onion greens, plant the sets two inches deep and only two inches apart.

Growing: Full sun in well-drained soil. Rich soil and consistent irrigation is important for good bulb development.

Maintaining: Weeding is necessary, especially as the seeds germinate or when you first plant the sets. The roots are shallow, so hand weeding is your only option. As the bulbs form, they emerge from the soil, exposing their top half—do not add more soil or compost around them at this time.

Harvesting: Cut leaves as needed if you're growing them for onion greens, but don't harvest the leaves if you're growing them for the bulb. You can harvest onions at any stage, but generally, when more than half of the leaves fall over, it's time to harvest. If you see a flower head forming, it's time to harvest that onion because the flower development will reduce the size of the bulb. Unless you'll be using the onions right away (within a week or two), wait until the soil is totally dry before harvesting the bulbs, and don't rinse them with water. You can cut the leaves off at the time of harvest or you can braid them together with other onions so that they can be hung in a dry space to prepare them for storage. If you do cut off the leaves, use them in cooking or toss them onto the compost pile.

Using: Use the young hollow leaves in salads, soups, and stir-fries for an extra-fresh onion flavor. Use the bulbs as you would any onion. Trim the brown from older leaves and chop them finely for frying or for tossing in a soup. Use the flowers in salads or cook them in stir-fries, soups, or tempura. The flower scape (stem) is tough and should be cooked.

The **SCALLION**, **WELSH ONION**, or **BUNCHING ONION** (*Allium fistulosum*) is a perennial bunching onion; grow it in an area where you do not plan to rotate the crops. It produces leaves throughout the year, but leaf production increases in the spring before the plant sends up a scape with its bunch of bulblets. It is sold commercially as seeds or seedlings. Once you find a variety that works well for you, with some good management, you won't need to purchase it again because it multiplies.

Regions: EASY, in N, C; MODERATE, in S.

Planting: Plant the seeds or seedlings directly in the garden in the fall to grow through the winter. Or plant the seeds in flats and move them to the garden as seedlings. To grow new greens or start your own population, use just the leaves of the scallions you purchased from the store or farmers market and plant the bottoms in your garden.

Growing: Full sun or slight shade. Some growers treat scallions like leeks and blanch the bottoms of the plants by mounding soil around the young plants as they grow.

Maintaining: Before the active growth period in the spring and again before the blooming period, weed the area and apply an inch of compost topped by straw or pine needles. When a large bunch has formed, dig them out, add some compost to the hole, replant one or two of the bulbs, and harvest the rest.

Harvesting: Cut leaves as needed or dig out the bulbs at any time of the year. Save enough bulbs to plant for next year's crop.

Using: Use the mild-tasting scallions raw or cooked.

WALKING ONION or **EGYPTIAN WALKING ONION** (*Allium* × *proliferum*) is a perennial bunching onion with no true bulb. It produces leaves throughout the year, but leaf production increases in the spring before the plant sends up a scape with its bunch of bulblets. The crop is believed to be a sterile hybrid of a standard onion (*A. cepa*) and a scallion (*A. fistulosum*). While it is sold commercially, you may have to look to specialty retailers to find it; once you find some, you won't need to purchase it again because it multiplies.

Regions: EASY, in N, C; MODERATE, in S.

Planting: Plant the sets, bulbs, or bulblets from the flower heads one inch deep, three inches apart any time during the year.

Growing: Full sun or slight shade.

Maintaining: Before the active growth period in the spring and again before the blooming period, weed the area and apply an inch of

---

Spring Onions versus Green Onions

Scallions, or bunching onions, are usually labeled green onions and are sold as a whole plant with a fat, but not bulbous, base. Spring onions, on the other hand, are young traditional onions that have been harvested early while their leaves are dark green. You can see the swelling of a small bulb at the bottom of the stem. Some of the green onions are walking onions.

Spring onions, green onions, and walking onions can be used interchangeably in cooking.

compost topped by straw or pine needles. When a large bunch has formed, dig them out, add some compost to the hole, replant one or two of the plants, and harvest the rest.

Harvesting: Cut leaves as needed or harvest the bulblets when available. Or dig out the whole plant to use at any time of the year. Save enough bulbs or bulblets to plan for next year's crop.

Using: Use the hollow leaves in salads, soups, and stir-fries. Use the whole plant as you would any onion, but since the base has a strong onion taste, most people think it's best cooked. The stalk of the scape is too tough to eat raw, but you can add it to soups, stir-fries, or a batch of mixed greens.

Amaranthaceae

The amaranth family (Amaranthaceae) includes crops grown for their leaves (spinach and swiss chard), their roots (beets), or their seeds (quinoa). Every part of the plants in this family contains oxalic acid, which can be an irritant for some people. Cooking these plants or dressing them with vinegar will effectively break down the acid and dissolve the oxalate crystals.

AMARANTH (*Amaranthus tricolor* or *A. cruentus*) is a heat-tolerant annual grown for its leaves, stems, and seeds. Growing these plants allows you to harvest salad greens through Florida's hot summer. The greens and stems are also suitable as cooked greens and as a substitute for spinach.

Regions: EASY, in N, C, S.

Planting: Plant the seeds directly in the garden when the soil temperature is above 70°F.

Growing: Full sun.

Maintaining: Irrigate after planting the seeds and for a week or two after they germinate; after that, only moderate irrigation is needed. Keep them cut back to promote new growth.

Harvesting: Harvest the leaves at any time after the plants are established.

Using: Use them raw or cooked as a spinach substitute.

BEETS (*Beta vulgaris* var. *crassa*) are a classic cool-weather, biennial, root crop and have been under cultivation for thousands of years. Commercially, sugar-beet crops now supply as much sugar as sugar cane. The tops are also edible (see swiss chard), but if you're growing the crop for the bulbous taproot, refrain from picking the leaves until harvest to allow for the best and quickest root formation. The leaves can still be used after you pull the plants out. Beets come in an array of colors, from dark maroon to yellow, white, or orange.

Regions: EASY, in N, C; MODERATE, in S. The northern part of the state will have a longer growing season. Caution: beets bolt easily in areas with longer days and warmer weather.

Planting: In the fall plant the seeds directly into deeply prepared garden soil with no rocks, sticks, or hard lumps. To grow large beets, go easy on the nitrogen-rich amendments—more nitrogen will produce a good leaf crop. Just barely cover the seeds with fine soil and water thoroughly several times a week. Three or four seeds may germinate from a single seed ball. Beets transplant better than carrots or other root crops do, so you may wish to plant them ahead of time and separate out the seedlings before planting them in the garden. Plant or thin the seedlings so that there is adequate room for root expansion, and keep in mind that a thinner taproot may grow another foot below the bulbous root that you harvest. Eat the thinnings as micro-greens.

Growing: Full sun or slight shade; more shade in south Florida. Beets appreciate an application of the micronutrients such as seaweed or fish emulsion during the growing season.

Maintaining: Consistent, deep irrigation will ensure that your plants develop good roots. Cut back on your irrigation two weeks before harvesting so that the roots don't crack.

Harvesting: Some growers pull up the largest beets first, leaving the small ones undisturbed so that they can develop further. Other growers harvest the whole crop at one time and use just the leaves from the plants with undeveloped bulbs. Beets are best if they are harvested when they are about two inches in diameter.

Using: While pickling beets and using them in soups are standard, try grating them into a salad or baking them to serve with butter as a warm vegetable on a cool night. The greens (chard) can be used raw or cooked as a spinach substitute.

CALLALOO or **JAMAICAN SPINACH** (*Amaranthus hybridus*) is easy to grow in the hot, humid summer months when other crops can't take the heat.

Regions: EASY, in N, C, S.

Planting: Plant the seeds directly in the garden when soil temperature reaches 70°F or more. Plant them in either of two ways: close and dense, if you intend to eat the thinned seedlings, or eight inches apart, for successive leaf harvests.

Growing: Full sun.

Maintaining: Irrigate after planting the seeds and for a week or two after they germinate; after that, irrigate only during extended droughts. Callaloo grows best in the hot, rainy season and is susceptible to spider mites if planted during the dry season.

Harvesting: Harvest the leaves, tender stems, and growing tips three to six weeks after planting. When the flower bud begins to form, cut it off at a foot or so below the tip of the plant, where the stem remains tender. The plant will regrow, forming several new side-growing tips. You can repeat this procedure until the plant becomes too woody to recut. Allow some heads to go to seed for replanting.

Using: Very tender, young plants may be eaten raw in salads. Like many greens, the boil-and-sauté method works very well. Do not overcook them, as the greens will soften too much and acquire a slimy texture. It is also very good added to soups and used in the place of spinach in your favorite spinach-pie recipe—be sure to add feta and Greek oregano to liven it up!

LAMB'S QUARTERS (*Chenopodium album*) is widely considered to be a weed. But you may find that this weed tastes better than many spinach varieties, and is much easier to grow. It's been collected in the wild throughout the state, so you may already have it growing in your yard. If not, you can purchase seeds from online suppliers (who, incidentally, are laughing all the way to the bank because you're buying weed seeds). Several species grow in Florida; *C. berlandieri* is a

Florida native, but it's the *album* species that you want. Once you've established it, you should have no trouble keeping a population going.
Regions: EASY, in N, C, S.
Planting: Plant the seeds directly in the garden in the fall. Plant more every few weeks, leaving enough space for growth. Some people grow them outside of the garden near the wildflowers they grow to attract pollinators—obviously they are not fussy.
Growing: Full sun or slight shade; more shade in south Florida.
Maintaining: Irrigate after planting the seeds and for a week or two after they germinate; after that, little additional irrigation is needed.
Harvesting: Harvest at any time. The stems on older plants are tough, so most people use only the leaves.
Using: Can be used raw or cooked as a spinach substitute.

ORACH (*Atriplex hortensis*) is a popular green in Europe that comes in many colors—most notably, red or purple. This fast-growing annual is tolerant of alkaline or salty soils and of some drought. These are valuable characteristics in Florida.
Regions: EASY, in N, C, S.
Planting: Plant the seeds directly in the garden every few weeks beginning in the fall.
Growing: Full sun or slight shade; more shade works well in south Florida.
Maintaining: Irrigate after planting the seeds and for a week or two after they germinate; after that, only moderate irrigation is needed. Keep them cut back to promote new growth.
Harvesting: Harvest the leaves at any time after the plant is established.
Using: Can be used raw or cooked as a spinach substitute. The red orachs don't lose their color when cooked and so provide interest when mixed with pasta or rice.

SPINACH (*Spinacea oleracea*) is a cool-weather annual that's a little temperamental in Florida. It requires rich soil, consistently cool temperatures, and moisture. There are many varieties and you may find one or two heat-tolerant varieties that work well for you; if not, try some of the spinach-substitute crops such as corn salad, lamb's quarter, Malabar spinach, or New Zealand spinach.

Regions: MODERATE, in N, C; DIFFICULT, in S.

Planting: Plant the seeds directly in the garden every two or three weeks beginning in the fall. You may want to plant them fairly thickly because they germinate erratically in warm soil, and with Florida's variable weather you never know when a warm day will come. You may have better luck with your earliest fall rotations if you start the seeds in a flat where can keep them cooler than they would be in the hot garden soil. After germination, thin the seedlings to their optimum spacing and then mulch them heavily to reduce their stress on warm days. Eat the thinnings as micro-greens.

Growing: Does best in richer-than-average soil. Full sun or slight shade; more shade in south Florida.

Maintaining: Irrigate after planting the seeds and consistently throughout their growing season. Once they dry out, they'll stop growing.

Harvesting: Harvest the leaves as needed or chop off the whole plant; if the conditions are right, chopped plants may regrow.

Using: Can be used raw or cooked; many people use a vinegar-based dressing when eating them raw. For cooked or steamed spinach, remove the leaves from the heat as soon as they wilt. Some people save the vitamin-rich cooking water to use in vegetable stocks.

SWISS CHARD or **CHARD** (*Beta vulgaris* var. *cicla*), a cool-weather biennial crop, is basically a beet that's been bred for the leaves. Some varieties are visually striking, with bright red or yellow stems; you should have no trouble integrating these plants into your flower gardens. The roots are also edible (see beets), but because you'll be harvesting its leaves, the taproot will be smaller. You can still eat the roots after you pull the plants out.

Regions: EASY, in N, C. MODERATE, in S. The northern part of the state will have a longer growing season.

Planting: Plant the seeds directly in the garden in the fall. Just barely cover the seeds with fine soil, and water them thoroughly several times a week. Three or four seeds may germinate from a single seed ball. You may wish to plant the seeds in trays and separate out the seedlings before planting them in the garden. Plant or thin the seedlings so that there is adequate room for root expansion. Eat the thinnings as micro-greens. Plant a second crop toward the end of winter—chard is somewhat heat tolerant and will continue producing leaves into the beginning of summer.

Growing: Full sun or slight shade; more shade late in the spring and in south Florida.

Maintaining: Consistent, moderate irrigation works best, but chard's large taproot makes it less sensitive than spinach to dry periods. Slugs and snails can be a problem, so keep a neat bed and be aggressive with your beer traps or diatomaceous earth to protect your crop.

Harvesting: Snip off the outer leaves as needed to maintain the growth of the inner stems and buds. Or, chop off all the leaves at once just above the soil line and wait for renewed growth.

Using: Chard can be used raw or cooked as a spinach substitute.

Apiaceae

The carrot family (Apiaceae) includes mostly biennials whose plants develop a thick taproot one year and flower the next; here in Florida, however, the majority will flower in the first year. The older name for this family, Umbelliferae, refers to the shape of the broad flower heads, which resemble umbrellas. Allow some of these crops to flower in order to attract the beneficial insects. Crops in this family include carrots, parsnips, parsley, and dill, any of which may attract the larvae of the black swallowtail butterfly. Some people transfer these distinctive banded caterpillars from their food crops to an extra bed of dill or parsley set aside for this purpose so that they can nurture the beautiful black swallowtail butterfly and eat their Apiaceae crops, too.

The carrot family also includes poison hemlock, a native of Europe, and spotted water hemlock (*Cicuta maculata*), which is found throughout Florida. These are some of the most poisonous plants in the country, so be careful if you're foraging for wild carrots.

CARROT (*Daucus carota*) is a biennial in colder regions, but in Florida, it can complete its life cycle in a single year if you leave it in the ground long enough. Carrot seeds were a requisite supply for many of the early colonists. The naturalized version of carrots, known as Queen Anne's lace, has become invasive in some parts of the country, but not in Florida. There are oodles of carrot cultivars, which take several forms and colors—try a few to find your favorites.

Regions: EASY, in N, C, S. The northern part of the state will have a longer growing season.

Planting: Begin planting this cool-weather crop in the fall and continue every third or fourth week through the winter. When sowing during the winter, wait for a warm spell so the soil is at least 50°F. Don't try to transplant the seedlings because disturbing the roots produces ugly carrots. Prepare the bed or wide row with deeply worked soil with no rocks, sticks, or hard lumps. When the carrot encounters a lump in its path, it will fork.

To plant the tiny seeds with enough space between them, mix the seed with sand, coffee grounds, or vermiculite and sow this mixture directly into a wide row. Just barely cover the seeds with fine soil or sand, and pat down the soil. Water them thoroughly several times a week. The seeds may take a week or two to germinate. Many gardeners recommend planting a few widely spaced radishes in with the carrots to mark the row. You'll harvest the radishes well before the carrots develop any significant growth. Thin the seedlings early so that there is adequate room for root expansion.

Growing: Full sun or slight shade; more shade in south Florida.

Maintaining: Irrigate moderately after the seedling stage. Cut back on your irrigation as the roots develop. Too much moisture at the end of the cycle could cause the roots to split or crack.

Harvesting: Pull up the largest carrots first and leave the small ones undisturbed so they can develop further. If the top of the root (the carrot) is exposed to the light, it may turn dark red. This will not affect the carrot's taste or edibility, but it may reduce its marketability.

Using: Rinse freshly pulled carrots with rain barrel water before bringing them inside to reduce the amount of mud you collect in your sink. Usually you just need to lightly scrub these carrots before using—peeling them is rarely needed.

Ugly Carrot Soup

Here's a hearty soup that is good served hot or cold and perfect for using up your ugly carrots (those that have split or forked) and other the end-of-the-season crops.

- ¼ cup of olive oil
- 1 or 2 medium chopped onions (with their greens)
- ⅔ cup chopped celery
- ¼ cup sunflower seeds (shelled)
- ¼ cup barley
- 1 tablespoon fresh rosemary
- 2 or 3 garlic cloves, chopped
- 8 to 12 fat carrots chopped or sliced thickly
- 6 to 8 cups of water
- spaghetti (an inch in diameter when held in a bunch) or 2 lasagna noodles, broken
- ½ to 1 cup of chopped greens (parsley, broccoli, or cabbage leaves, wild garlic leaves, or pretty much whatever needs harvesting)
- 1½ cups of nonfat plain yogurt
- ¼ cup grated Parmesan cheese
- finely chopped onion greens, chives, and fresh dill leaves for garnish

In a soup pot, heat the olive oil. Over a medium heat, brown the onions and their greens, celery, sunflower seeds, barley, rosemary, and garlic. Stir frequently. As the onions become translucent, add the carrots, stir for a few minutes, and then add the water. Bring the soup to a boil, and then simmer for about 25 minutes until the carrots become soft. Add the pasta and greens. Simmer for another 15 minutes until all the ingredients are soft. Remove from the heat, cool, and then run the soup through a blender or food processor until it is mostly smooth. Stir in the yogurt and Parmesan cheese. Garnish each bowl with a dollop of yogurt, onion greens, chives, dill, and freshly ground pepper to taste. If you add a lot of greens, the orange-yellow color will dull, but the soup will still taste carroty. Serves eight to ten.

CELERY (*Apium graveolens*) is a water-hungry, slow-growing annual. There are three types of celery: the standard celery you find in the grocery store, which is called Pascal; celeriac (*A. graveolens* var. *rapaceum*), which is grown for its bulbous roots; and cutting celery (*A. graveolens* var. *secalinum*). Celery is a cool-weather, but frost-sensitive, vegetable. In north Florida, celery is planted from January to March; in central Florida, from August to February; and in south Florida, from October to January. These planting times maximize its exposure to cool weather and minimize its exposure to heavy frosts after germination. To further complicate matters, too much cold weather during the early stage of growth may cause the plant to bolt.

Regions: Standard Pascal celery: DIFFICULT, in N, C, S. Cutting celery or celeriac: MODERATE, in N, C, S.

Planting: Plant the tiny seeds directly in the garden or in a flat to be transplanted into the garden as seedlings. After sowing, just barely cover the seeds with a finely sieved coir or compost. Water them with a fine spray so that you don't disturb them. Move the seedlings from the flat as soon as they each have three or four sets of true leaves.

Growing: Full sun or slight shade; many growers cover their celery crop with a thin fabric to provide shade in order to blanch the lower stems. The lighter green stems are said to be milder. Some of the newer varieties do not require shade.

Maintaining: Celery needs a lot of water and requires consistent and deep irrigation throughout its long season. If it's grown in a dry environment, it will be tough and stringy. This level of watering also attracts slugs and snails, so be prepared for them. The roots are dense, but shallow, so weed by hand.

Harvesting: With standard celery, cut the whole plant off below the base of the stalks. Stalks that are separated from the base tend to dry out quickly. For cutting celery, harvest the stalks as needed; the plants will regrow several times. Harvest celeriac when its root is the size of a softball. Chop all the side roots and stalks from the root, and either compost the tough stalks or use them in soups. The root will keep for several months in a cool, dry environment; once it starts to sprout, use it sooner rather than later.

Using: You'll enjoy the cutting celery—both the stalks and leaves—for its fresh, tangy taste in salads, stews, or wherever you would use celery. Celeriac root has much less starch than potatoes or turnips, but it can be used in similar ways—its fresh, crisp taste also complements salads.

CHERVIL (*Anthriscus cerefolium*) is a cool-weather annual grown for its aromatic, decorative leaves. It's used as a milder version of parsley, and like parsley it comes in both curly and flat-leaved varieties.
Regions: EASY, in N, C; MODERATE, in S.
Planting: Plant the tiny seeds directly in the garden in a moist, shady spot. Transplanting is not recommended because of the taproot.
Growing: Full shade to slight shade in a damp location.
Maintaining: Chervil will bolt at the slightest stress, so irrigate regularly.
Harvesting: Cut off the outer leaves as needed.
Using: Use the mild, aromatic leaves as garnish or in salads. It's also one of the traditional ingredients in herbes de Provence, a blend of dried herbs, but it loses much of its flavor when dried.

CILANTRO or **CORIANDER** (*Coriandrum sativum*) is a short-lived, fast-growing, cool-weather annual. Their tangy, citrusy flavor makes the leaves a popular addition to Mexican cooking, while the root is used in Thai cooking. The seeds are a spice called coriander.
Regions: EASY, in N, C, S. The northern part of the state will have a longer growing season.
Planting: Plant the seeds directly in the garden every few weeks starting in the fall. Like other members of this family, cilantro has a long taproot, so it doesn't transplant well unless it's young. Some cooks like to keep a series of pots of thickly planted cilantro available throughout the year. In the hot weather, keep your pot of cilantro out of the afternoon sun.
Growing: Full sun or slight shade; more shade in south Florida.
Maintaining: Provide moderate irrigation after the seedling stage. Cutting back the stems will postpone the flowering, but do allow some of the crop to flower, both to attract insects and to harvest some of the coriander.

Harvesting: Cut leaves as needed. They can be dried or frozen, but they are definitely best fresh.

Using: Use the leaves in salads, salsa, pesto, guacamole, and stir-fries, but add them late in the cooking process, as they lose flavor with heat. Use the seeds (coriander) in potato or pasta salads, sausages, marinades, or chutneys.

DILL (*Anethum graveolens*) is a short-lived, fast-growing, cool-weather annual. It provides both a classic herb and spice—the leaves are called dill weed, and used as a herb in salads or as a garnish while the seeds are used as a spice for pickling or in potato and pasta salads.

Regions: EASY, in N, C, S.

Planting: Plant the seeds directly in the garden every few weeks starting in the fall. Gardeners in colder areas in the northernmost part of the state may lose some of their dill to the cold, but dill will last through most Florida winters. Dill has a long taproot, so it doesn't transplant well after the seedling stage.

Growing: Full sun or slight shade; more shade in south Florida. Once the hot weather hits, dill bolts quickly. Some growers blanch the lower stems by mounding soil around them. The white stems are said to be milder, and are sometimes used in Asian cooking.

Maintaining: The long taproot makes dill somewhat drought tolerant after the seedling stage. Cutting back the stems will postpone the flowering, but do allow some to flower in order to attract the beneficial insects. Once you have allowed the dill to go to seed, it's likely to show up randomly in next year's garden.

Harvesting: Cut leaves as needed. They can be dried, but they are definitely better fresh. To harvest the seeds, wait until they turn brown, place the whole flower head in a bag, and then shake the seeds loose.

Using: Use the leaves uncooked as a garnish or in salads and dressings. If you cook dill, add it late in the cooking process, as it will lose flavor; it is good in soups and stir-fries. The seeds can be used not only in pickling, but also in potato or pasta salads. The stems can be sliced thinly and used in stir-fries or soups.

FENNEL (*Foeniculum vulgare*) includes two types: leaf fennel, which is a hardy perennial, and bulbing fennel, which is a more delicate annual. The bulbing type is called Florence fennel or finocchio (*F. vulgare* var. *azoricum*) and is the one commonly sold in supermarkets under the misnomer "anise." The fennel bulb is not really a bulb at all, but swollen stem at the base of the plant. Leaf fennel is rarely offered in grocery stores, but it is the source of the fennel seeds that are used as a spice or for medicinal purposes. The plant is available in bronze or green and is easy to grow as a perennial.

Regions: EASY, in N, C, S. The warmest parts of the state will yield year-round harvests of leaf fennel, while bulb fennel performs best in cooler temperatures; three months from seed to table.

Planting: Plant the seeds directly in the garden anytime after the last frost in north and central parts of state. In south Florida, plant it from October to January. Fennel may be allelopathic to some other garden plants like lettuce and radishes.

Growing: Full sun or partial shade. According to old gardeners' tales, fennel likes to grow alone. Try planting leaf fennel in the landscape, in mulched areas. It will reward you with lots of fern-like fronds in green or bronze. Wherever you plant it, plan for its height—some varieties can reach four or five feet.

Maintaining: Bulb fennel needs more water than the leaf varieties, which are quite drought tolerant.

Harvesting: Leaf type: cut stems from the side of the plant, oldest first; new stems will grow in their places. Bulb-type: when you are ready to use it, cut the bulb at its base, leaving the roots intact. It may resprout a bulb or two from the sides. Leaf fennel reseeds readily, while the bulb type may not.

Using: Bulb fennel is used for cooking, grilling, or in salads. Unfortunately, many people use the bulb and throw away the leaves, which can be used like leaf fennel. Leaf fennel is great in soups, fennel pesto, added to potato salad, or mixed into a green salad. Fennel and citrus were made for each other—try a fennel and citrus salad! Pet rabbits will love you forever if you give them a fennel stem in their daily salads!

PARSNIP (*Pastinaca sativa*) is a biennial that is similar to carrots, but with a paler root. This crop definitely needs at least one hard frost before it's harvested, so the farther north you are, the better your chances of success.

Regions: MODERATE, in N; NOT RECOMMENDED, for C, S.

Planting: Plant the seeds directly in the fall into deeply prepared garden soil with no rocks, sticks, or hard lumps. Just barely cover the seeds with fine soil and water them thoroughly several times a week. The seeds may take a week or two to germinate. Many gardeners recommend planting a few widely spaced radishes in with the parsnips to mark the row. You'll harvest the radishes well before the parsnips develop any significant growth. Don't try to transplant the seedlings because you'll disturb their roots and they may not recover. Thin the seedlings early so that there is adequate room for root expansion.

Growing: Full sun or slight shade.

Maintaining: Provide moderate moisture after the seedling stage. Cut back on your irrigation as the roots develop. Too much moisture at the end of the cycle could cause the roots to split or crack.

Harvesting: After at least one hard freeze, pull up the largest parsnips first and leave the small ones undisturbed to allow them to develop further.

Using: Rinse the freshly pulled parsnips with rain barrel water before bringing inside to reduce the amount of mud in your sink. Usually you just need to lightly scrub these roots before using them—peeling them is rarely necessary. You can eat them raw, but most people cook parsnips in soups or stews. Compost the leaves—do not eat them or give to your pets, as they are poisonous when ingested.

PARSLEY (*Petroselinum crispum*) is a biennial in colder regions, but in Florida, it usually completes its life cycle in a single year. When planted in the fall for a cool-weather start, parsley will grow well into the summer. Two major types: the curly leaf variety (*P. crispum* var. *crispum*) and the flat leaf or Italian variety (*P. crispum* var. *neapolitanum*). Some people think the flat-leafed varieties have a stronger flavor, while others cannot tell the difference—that ability is the result of a genetic difference in our taste genes.

Regions: EASY, in N, C, S. The northern part of the state will have a longer growing season. Parsley bolts as the hot, humid, Florida summer progresses.

Planting: Plant the seeds directly in the garden in the fall. Just barely cover the seeds with fine soil and water them thoroughly several times a week. The seeds may take four weeks or more to germinate. (The old gardeners' tale is that they go to hell and back before sprouting.) Soaking the seeds overnight before you plant them may decrease the germination time and produce a more uniform germination rate.

Growing: Full sun or slight shade; more shade in south Florida.

Maintaining: Provide moderate moisture after the seedling stage. Cutting back the flowering stems will postpone the flowering for a while, but do plan to keep some of the flowers to attract the beneficial insects. Once the plant flowers, it becomes somewhat bitter—again, those sensitive to the taste of the flat-leafed vs. curly parsleys will be more offended at this point.

Harvesting: Cut leaves as needed. They can be dried, but they are definitely better fresh.

Using: Use the leaves as a garnish and in salads, soups, and stir-fries. Parsley is a major ingredient in tabbouleh. You can make a parsley-based pesto to use during the cool months. Use your basil pesto recipe, but substitute the parsley for the basil—it's not the same, but you may like it just as much.

Asteraceae

The daisy family (Asteraceae) is huge and includes quite a few crops such as the many lettuces, stevia (a no-calorie sweetener), marigolds, and sunflowers. The sunflower produces the flower head typical of this family—the fertile central florets are arranged in a dizzying circular array, while the sterile ray florets look like petals. The flower heads of a lettuce look more like dandelions and have only fertile ray florets.

LETTUCES (*Lactuca sativa*) are beautiful and easy-to-grow cool-weather crops. In Florida, you can grow lettuce right through the winter. There are six main types of lettuce: head, butter head, leaf, Chinese, summer crisp, and romaine. Leaf lettuces and romaines are the easiest to grow and usually the most heat tolerant. You can purchase single varieties or assorted lettuce varieties—some mixtures, which include red, crinkled, and oak-leaf, make beautiful borders anywhere in your landscape. Mesclun is another beautiful mixture of lettuces and other leafy greens such as radicchio, arugula, swiss chard, and spinach.

Regions: EASY, in N, C, S. The northern part of the state will have a longer growing season.

Planting: Plant the seeds directly in the garden as soon as the weather starts to cool in the fall. Plant the seeds thinly and just barely cover them with fine soil because they need light to germinate. Water them thoroughly several times a week at the beginning of the growing cycle. The seeds should sprout in five to seven days. It's important to thin the seedlings so that they have adequate room to grow. Use the thinnings as micro-greens.

Growing: Full sun or slight shade; more shade may extend the season as warm weather starts, and afternoon shade is recommended for south Florida.

Maintaining: Provide moderate moisture after the seedling stage. Once the plant bolts, its leaves turn bitter.

Harvesting: For leaf or loose lettuces, cut leaves as needed from the outside working in or cut the whole plant at the base. If you leave the base in place, most lettuces will regrow, but harvest the regrowth leaves quickly because the plant will try to flower as soon as possible after the initial harvest. After the second or third harvest, pull the plants out and start a new crop.

Using: You know what to do with lettuce, but if you've ended up with some bitter leaves at the end of the season, you can cook them as you would other greens, either alone or with an assortment of greens.

MARIGOLD or **FRENCH MARIGOLD** (*Tagetes patula*) is a showy annual that is often planted in and around vegetable gardens to attract pollinators. It also repels nematodes, although a few scattered plants will do little to protect your tomatoes and other crops. To truly rid an area of nematodes, you'll need to plant marigolds as a cover crop and plow them under. In addition, marigold flowers are edible.

Regions: EASY, in N, C, S.

Planting: Plant the seeds directly in the garden after last frost. Barely cover the seeds with soil and pat it down.

Growing: Full sun or slight shade. Marigolds continue growing throughout the hot summers in most of the state.

Maintaining: Drought tolerant after the seedling stage.

Harvesting: Pick the newest flower heads or just pull off the ray florets—the ones that look like petals at the edge of the flower head. After flowers dry on the plant, you can harvest the seeds for next year's crop.

Using: The flowers have a citrusy and somewhat bitter flavor. Marigolds can be used in place of saffron to add color to rice pilaf and similar recipes. You can also add marigold flowers sparingly to salads. People who raise chickens or other fowl often include marigold petals in the feed to add color to their meat.

RADICCHIO (*Cichorium intybus*), a perennial grown as a cool-weather annual, is a cultivar of chicory, which forms a head that is red or burgundy with white streaks. Long used in Italy, it has become more popular in this country as new, more reliable cultivars have been developed. Heirloom varieties don't form a head until after the first growth has been cut back to the ground, but new cultivars have eliminated this step. Another cultivar called Belgian endive is grown in the dark from taproots that have been dug from the field after the first flush of growth.

Regions: MODERATE, in N, C, S. The northern part of the state will have a longer growing season. Radicchio bolts in the heat.

Planting: Plant the seeds directly in the garden as soon as the weather starts to cool in the fall. Plant them thinly and just barely cover them with fine soil. Water them thoroughly several times a week at the beginning of the growing cycle. The seeds should sprout in five to seven days. It's important to thin seedlings so that they have adequate room to grow.

Growing: Full sun or slight shade; more shade will heighten the contrast of the white veining against the burgundy leaves.

Maintaining: Deep, once-a-week irrigation works best to encourage its long taproot. Don't let up on the irrigation or the heads will become overly bitter.

Harvesting: You can pull off outer leaves as needed, but most growers wait for the head to form. Some varieties produce come-again growth after the head is cut off.

Using: Mix these bitter greens with other foods or serve them with a sweet balsamic-vinegar dressing. Italian cooks grill the leaves in olive oil, which reduces some of the bitterness. You can use it finely chopped or shredded to spice up and brighten up your salads.

STEVIA or **SWEET LEAF** (*Stevia rebaudiana*) is a frost sensitive short-lived perennial that is widely grown as a sweetener and medicinal herb in South America. It has become more available (both as plants and as a commercially prepared additive) in this country since the Food and Drug Administration (FDA) approved it as a food additive. People who need to reduce their sugar intake may find that stevia tastes sweeter than other no-calorie sweeteners and has a less bitter aftertaste.

It grows well in Florida, especially frost-free areas. Even those who don't need to watch their sugar intake may decide that Stevia deserves a spot in their herb gardens to mix with herbal teas or mint juleps. People describe it as being between ten and three hundred times sweeter than sugar, but it has virtually no calories.

Regions: EASY, in N, C, S.

Planting: Plant the seeds directly in the garden after the last frost or buy seedlings or rooted cuttings. It's easier to start with plants because the seeds have a low germination rate, plus you can test the sweetness before you plant it. A given plant's degree of sweetness is an unknown when you start from seeds.

Growing: Full sun or slight shade; more shade in south Florida in the summer months. Stevia readily reseeds itself in the South.

Maintaining: Provide moderate moisture after the seedling stage; Stevia does not like soggy soil. Cutting back the plant will keep it bushy and encourage new growth. The roots are shallow, so weed removal and mulching are important.

Harvesting: Cut leaves as needed. They can be dried and ground up for use in recipes.

Using: Use bruised or rolled leaves in hot or cold teas and drinks—even water. Use it finely chopped in sweeter salads such as coleslaw or carrot and raisin salad. Some people use it as a sweet garnish. Stevia is often paired with fruit, fruit juices, or other sweeteners.

SUNFLOWERS and **SUNCHOKES** (*Helianthus* spp.) are native to the Americas, but are grown worldwide for their seeds, oil, and tubers, also known as Jerusalem artichokes (*H. tuberosus*). Most sunflowers are annuals, but some, including the sunchoke, are perennial.

Sunflowers of all types are desirable to plant near your crops because they attract pollinators and birds and, because they are allelopathic to many other plants, they keep down the weeds. Keep this in mind when planning your crop rotations—the crop following those sunflowers might be stunted or suffer a low germination rate.

Regions: EASY, in N, C, S.

Planting: Plant the seeds directly in the garden after the last frost. They germinate quickly and grow fast. You could also start the perennial sunchokes from tubers.

Growing: Full sun. Sunflowers will grow and survive in poor soil, but a richer blend will produce larger plants with larger flower heads.

Maintaining: Provide moderate moisture after the seedling stage. Sunflowers do not like soggy soil.

Harvesting: Harvest the seeds after their shells become hard. You can harvest the tubers of the sunchoke at any time, but most people wait until the end of the summer or fall seasons to dig up the plants.

Using: You can slow roast the seeds in their shells after they've been soaked in saltwater overnight. Use the sunchoke tubers as you would potatoes. They are an important crop for people with diabetes because their carbohydrate, inulin, is not digested.

TARRAGON, MEXICAN TARRAGON, (*Tagetes lucida*) is a half-hardy perennial shrub that dies back where there are killing frosts.

It adds a spicier note to the typical anise/vanilla flavor of the classic French and Russian tarragons (*Artemesia dracunculus* and *A. dracunculoides*), but can be used as a tarragon substitute. It is recommended for Florida because it does not require a reliable period of cold weather.

Regions: EASY, in N, C, S.

Planting: Sow the seeds after of the last frost and when the soil has warmed to 65°F. You can also plant rooted cuttings.

Growing: Full sun or slight shade; more shade in south Florida. Use it as a border; trim it to keep it neat.

Maintaining: Keep the flowers trimmed to encourage more blooms.

Harvesting: Cut leaves and flowers as needed once the shrub is well established. The leaves can be dried, but they are definitely better fresh.

Using: Add to soups or sauces at the end of the cooking to retain the most flavor. Use as a rub for grilling fowl or fish. Because the flavor is lost upon drying, it's traditional to preserve tarragon in vinegar. Use the flowers in salads and as a garnish. French tarragon is a main ingredient of fines herbes, but you can certainly add this Mexican native to your herbes de Florida.

Basellaceae

The basella family (Basellaceae) has only one crop that grows well in Florida—Malabar spinach.

MALABAR SPINACH or **CEYLON SPINACH** (*Basella alba*) is a heat-tolerant, vining plant with leaves that taste like spinach. The two available varieties have red or a green stems. The red variety is striking—a true ornamental edible. It's a perennial in frost-free zones and a freely seeding annual in the rest of the state.

Regions: EASY, in N, C, S.

Planting: Soak the seeds overnight and plant them one inch deep after the last frost. You can also plant cuttings from last year's vines. You won't need many of these—each vine puts out an amazing amount of growth.

Growing: Full sun or slight shade. A trellis or fence to support the vine is recommended—this also keeps the leaves clean.

Maintaining: Cut back the vine during the season to stimulate more growth.

Harvesting: Cut leaves as needed once the vine has grown to about three feet. The leaves wilt quickly once separated from the vine—most growers harvest whole sections of vine. Given its aggressive nature, this should not be a problem.

Using: Use as you would spinach—raw or cooked. The mucilaginous texture can be used as a thickener in soups and stews, but is not as thick as okra. Okra-haters may not mind it, and most people don't notice any sliminess when the leaves are mixed with other greens in a salad.

Brassicaceae

The mustard family (Brassicaceae) contains many of our classic vegetables including the cole crops, mustards, and radishes. Most are cool-weather crops.

ARUGULA or **ROCKET** (*Eruca sativa*) is a cool-weather, easy-to-grow annual with spicy leaves.

Regions: EASY, in N, C, S.

Planting: Plant the seeds directly in the garden or start them in flats in the fall and throughout the winter. Plan for a succession of crops. Use the thinnings as spicy micro-greens. You can also use this crop as a quick-growing filler between slower-growing crops.

Growing: Full sun or slight shade.

Maintaining: Mulch around the stems to keep weeds at bay and to hold in moisture.

Harvesting: Cut leaves as needed.

Using: Most cooks use raw arugula to add heat to various types of salads. You can also use it to perk up soups, pasta dishes, salsa, and mixed greens.

BOK CHOY or **PAC CHOY** (*Brassica chinesesis*) is a nonheading cabbage. Its leaves grow close together on long stalks much like a fat celery. It's a cool-weather crop that does not tolerate hard freezes. While sometimes referred to as Chinese cabbage, there is a different cultivar also called Chinese cabbage or napa cabbage (*B. rapa* var. *pekinensis*), which has similar requirements and uses. There seems to be some disagreement about which is the "real" Chinese cabbage. Find a variety that suits your situation, and call it whatever you like. *Regions:* MODERATE, in N, C, S.

The Cole Crops

Some consider any crop in the Brassicaceae family to be a cole crop, while others include every crop in the Brassica genus. Most, however, narrow the classification to only the cultivars of *Brassica oleracea*. And what an array of cultivars they are. Now you know why cabbage salad is called "coleslaw."

Depending on the authority, the cultivars of *B. oleracea* are divided into seven or eight major groups according to their form.

Acephala group—Kale, collard greens, and ornamental cabbages.
Alboglabra group—Chinese broccoli and obscure pot herbs.
Botrytis group—Cauliflower, broccoli, and broccoflower.
Capitata group—The red, green, and Savoy cabbages.
Gemmifera group—Brussels sprouts.
Gongylodes group—Kohlrabi.
Italica group—Italian broccoli, sprouting broccoli, purple cauliflower. This group includes the looser-headed varieties.
Tronchuda group—Tronchuda kale and cabbage, Portuguese kale, braganza.

Many of these crops are obscure now, but don't be surprised if they become more standard American vegetable offerings in the future. Kohlrabi, for instance, a relatively new addition to the American table, has been grown in Europe for centuries.

Planting: Plant the seeds directly in the garden or start them in flats in the fall and throughout the winter, except in north Florida, where you'll skip the colder months or arrange to cover the rows during hard freezes.

Growing: Full sun or slight shade, with more shade in the summer.

Maintaining: Mulch around the stems to keep weeds at bay and to hold in moisture. Irrigate regularly and deeply.

Harvesting: Harvest bok choy when it's twelve to eighteen inches tall.

Using: This mild-tasting crop is great in soups, salads, and stir-fries. The stalks can also be used as a celery substitute. Once you start using it, you'll find that it's quite versatile.

BROCCOLI (*Brassica oleracea* var. *botrytis*), a cole crop in the Botrytis group, is a popular cool-season annual. We normally eat the tightly closed flower heads (called curds), but you can also use the leaves and stems as you would cabbage.

Regions: EASY, in N, C, S.

Planting: Plant the seeds directly in the garden or start them in flats every four weeks or so starting in the fall and continuing throughout the winter. Amend the soil with compost and composted manure for the best growth.

Growing: Full sun or slight shade.

Maintaining: Mulch around the stems to keep weeds at bay and to hold in moisture. Irrigate regularly and deeply. Use row covers to keep bugs from the young plants, but remove them once the plants start producing their curds.

Harvesting: Don't harvest any leaves until after you have harvested the main flower head. If you leave the plants in the ground and continue to irrigate, secondary flower heads and smaller leaves will sprout. You may end up with several rounds of secondary curds and another month or two of production. You may wish to let some of the plants flower to attract pollinators and other beneficial insects.

Using: Broccoli can be used in many ways: finely chopped in tossed salads or pasta salads; as a meatball substitute in spaghetti sauce; in stir fries and soups. You can use the sweet come-again curds as a dipping vegetable. Use the young leaves produced after the main flower head has been harvested in salads, stir-fries, soups, or mixed with other greens.

BROCCOLI RAAB or **RAPINI** (*Brassica rapa* var. *ruva*), a turnip in the ruva group, has become more popular recently as a cool-season green. There are many varieties, and each has different flavor overtones. Some are spicy, while others are nuttier. All are rich in antioxidants, so you'd be nutty not to grow some!

Regions: EASY, in N, C, S.

Planting: Plant the seeds directly in the garden or start them in flats in the fall and throughout the winter. It matures in little more than a month. Amend the soil well with compost and composted manure for the best growth.

Growing: Full sun.

Maintaining: Mulch around the stems to keep weeds at bay and to hold in moisture. Irrigate regularly and deeply.

Harvesting: Chop back one half of the plant as soon as the flowering stalks appear. The flower heads look like small broccoli curds, but the important parts of this crop are the greens and the stalks.

Using: Broccoli raab greens and stalks add some spice to otherwise bland dishes. Use them raw or cooked.

BRUSSELS SPROUTS (*Brassica oleracea* var. *gemmifera*), a cole crop in the Gemmifera group, is a long-season, cool-weather annual. We grow it for the sprouts that form along its rather gangly stem.

Regions: MODERATE, in N, C; NOT RECOMMENDED, in S.

Planting: Plant the seeds directly in the garden or start them in flats early in the fall and grow them through the winter. The sweetest sprouts will come after a couple of frosts.

Growing: Full sun. The stem will become quite long and usually bends over. You can stake it to keep it upright, but most growers don't bother.

Maintaining: Mulch thickly around the stems to keep the weeds at bay and to hold in moisture. The roots are shallow, so the mulch also helps to keep the soil cool throughout the growing season. Irrigate regularly and deeply. Apply some fish or seaweed emulsion during the growing season to supply more nutrients.

Harvesting: Cut the sprouts (little heads) formed at the bottom of the stem when they become firm. Traditionally, the leaf under each sprout is also removed as you harvest. Before using the sprouts, submerge them in water to remove insects.

Using: Brussels sprouts are traditionally steamed or roasted and served with butter, but your fresh-out-of-the-garden sprouts may inspire you to use them in more creative ways. Shred about twenty of them using the slicer on your food processor, thinly slice two apples, add half a cup of crumbled goat cheese, and dress the salad with a sweet oil and vinegar dressing.

CABBAGE (*Brassica oleracea* var. *capitata*), a cole crop in the Capitata group, is a popular cool-season annual. We grow it for its head, but its loose leaves are also delicious. Cabbages are available in several colors, and the leaves may be smooth or ruffled.

Regions: EASY, in N, C, S.

Planting: Plant the seeds directly in the garden or start them in flats in the fall and throughout the winter. If you start them in flats, transplant them carefully to minimize root damage. Plan for a succession of crops. Amend the soil well with compost and composted manure for the best growth.

Growing: Full sun or slight shade, with more shade toward the summer.

Maintaining: Cabbage has shallow roots, so hand weed and mulch around the stems to keep the weeds at bay and to hold in moisture. Irrigate regularly and deeply. Use row covers to ward off bug attacks. Remove cabbageworms as you see them.

Harvesting: Cut the head after it has formed. If you leave the base of the plant with a few outer leaves, most cabbages will send up more leaves. These small come-again leaves are often sweeter than the cabbage itself because of the short growing time. Making a one-half-inch-deep cut down through the surface of the remaining stem may stimulate the plant to form two or more new heads.

Using: Cabbage is used cooked and raw in a variety of dishes, and your fresh-out-of-the-garden cabbages may inspire you to use them in even more creative ways, especially raw.

CAULIFLOWER (*Brassica oleracea* var. *botrytis*), a cole crop in the Botrytis group, is a Goldilocks, cool-season annual—it will grow only when conditions are just right, not too hot and not too cold. We usually eat the tightly closed flower heads, called curds, but unlike broccoli, the curd of most cauliflower cultivars needs to be protected from the sun to keep it white and mild tasting. The newer purple or green varieties may not need this protection. Broccoflower, a cross between cauliflower and broccoli, is grown like cauliflower.

Regions: MODERATE, in N, C, S.

Planting: Plant the seeds directly in the garden or start them in flats early enough in the fall so that the flower heads can be harvested before hard frosts are likely. Later in the winter, you can start another set of cauliflower seedlings after the last of the hard frosts to be harvested before the hot weather sets in. Amend the soil well with compost and composted manure for the best growth.

Growing: Full sun or slight shade. As soon as a curd forms, gather the basal leaves over it and secure them together with a soft tie or rubber band.

Maintaining: Mulch around the stems to keep the weeds at bay and to hold in moisture. Irrigate regularly, and deeply.

Harvesting: Cut the curd with a sharp knife four to six inches below the flower head. If you leave the plants in the ground and continue to irrigate them, secondary flower heads and smaller leaves will sprout, but not to same extent as broccoli.

Using: Cauliflower can be used in many ways: steamed lightly and served with a creamy cheese sauce; chopped up finely in tossed salads or pasta salads; and used in stir fries and soups. You can use the flower heads as a dipping vegetable and the leaves like cabbage.

ETHIOPIAN MUSTARD or **TEXSEL GREENS** (*Brassica carinata*) is a frost-sensitive, heat-tolerant kale that is a natural cross between *B. nigra* and *B. oleracea*. It's a long-season annual with a loose-leaf habit similar to that of collards.

Regions: EASY, in N, C, S.

Planting: Plant the seeds directly in the garden every four to six weeks after the last frost. It prefers a somewhat alkaline soil.

Growing: Full sun or slight shade.

Maintaining: Mulch around the stems to keep the weeds at bay and to hold in moisture. It grows best with regular, deep irrigation.

Harvesting: Cut the young, tender leaves, flower buds, or full-grown leaves.

Using: The leaves and young stems can be eaten raw, mixed with other greens in salads. More mature or full-sized leaves are cooked like collard greens, either alone or in soups. The buds and their stems are best cooked and can be used like broccoli.

KALE or **COLLARDS** (*Brassica oleracea* var. *acephala*), a cole crop in the Acephala group, is a popular, cool-season annual. We grow it for its delicious leaves, but the flowers are also edible. Kale is easy to grow, and attracts fewer pests than some other cole crops. There are a variety of forms and colors, some of which are quite decorative, and many people grow kale as a winter display in their flowerbeds. (Decorative kale is sometimes mistakenly sold as flowering kale, but true flowering kale has a tall stalk with bunches of four-petaled yellow flowers.)

Regions: EASY, in N, C, S.

Planting: Plant the seeds directly in the garden or start them in flats in the fall and throughout the winter. Amend the soil well with compost and composted manure for the best growth.

Growing: Full sun or slight shade, with more shade in the summer.

Maintaining: Mulch around the stems to keep the weeds at bay and to hold in moisture. Irrigate regularly and deeply.

Harvesting: Cut the outside leaves for use as soon as the plant is large enough to withstand the removal. In northern Florida, some cooks wait until after the first frost, when kale leaves become sweeter.

Using: Kale dresses up dinner plates when used as a garnish, but its sweet taste and light texture make it much more useful as an edible. Use it raw in salads, or cooked in many ways. Kale leaves make excellent veggie chips. Kale can be included in a mess of greens to offset the bitterness of many other greens.

KOHLRABI (*Brassica oleracea* var. *gongylodes*), a cole crop in the Gongylodes group, is an unusual, cool-season annual that has recently gained favor through its popularity with farmers markets and local food groups. It is grown for its weird, Sputnik-shaped, enlarged stem-bulb with leaves that stick out at odd angles.

Regions: EASY, in N, C, S.

Planting: Plant the seeds directly in the garden or start them in flats in the fall and throughout the winter. Amend the soil well with compost and composted manure for the best growth.

Growing: Full sun or slight shade, with more shade toward the summer.

Maintaining: Mulch around the stems to keep the weeds at bay and to hold in moisture. Irrigate regularly and deeply.

Harvesting: Cut the stem-bulb when it's two to three inches in diameter. Larger bulbs become tough and woody. Definitely harvest them before the hot weather arrives.

Using: Many people prepare the kohlrabi like turnips, but you may also like them in salads or as dipping vegetables.

MUSTARD GREENS, MIZUNA, or **INDIAN MUSTARD** (*Brassica juncea*), is a spicy, easy-to-grow, cool-weather annual that's eaten raw or cooked, especially when cooked with an assortment of greens. The varieties known as mizuna bear little resemblance to other mustard greens—they are very mild and fast-cooking, and are as often eaten raw in salads. The seed is widely used to make mustard—it's now used more often in brown-mustard formulas than the classic black mustard (*B. nigra*). It has become an aggressive weed in some parts of the country, but not in Florida.

Regions: EASY, in N, C, S.

Planting: Plant the seeds directly in the garden or start them in flats in the fall and throughout the winter. Plan for a succession of crops, as it germinates quickly and reliably and is harvestable in about a month. Thin the seedlings to provide adequate room for the plants; eat the thinnings as micro-greens.

Growing: Full sun or slight shade.

Maintaining: Mulch around the stems to keep the weeds at bay and to hold in moisture. Irrigate regularly and deeply.

Harvesting: If you're more interested in the greens than the seed, begin to harvest leaves as needed as soon as the plant is established—after around 40 days. Otherwise, for the best flower (and seed) production let the plant run its course with its full complement of leaves.

Using: Use the greens raw or cooked. It's often used to add a mild, peppery flavor to various Asian dishes. It's so easy to grow that some growers use it as a cool-weather cover crop and plow it under as green manure. To make mustard, gather the seeds and grind them in a mortar and pestle with enough cold water to make a paste. Chill the paste for several hours and then add vinegar or lemon juice. You can add herbs, other spices for flavor, or honey for sweetness.

RADISH (*Raphanus sativus*) is a spicy, extremely easy-to-grow annual with a short cycle (just thirty days from seed to table). It germinates so quickly that radishes are often used to mark the rows or planting areas of slow-to-germinate species such as parsley and carrots. There are many varieties to try, from the small red globe with the white center to solid white radishes as big as carrots. The larger varieties take somewhat longer to mature. Some radishes are hot, while others are mild.

Regions: EASY, in N, C, S.

Planting: Plant the seeds directly in the garden in the fall and throughout the winter. Plan for a succession of harvests. It germinates quickly and reliably. Thin the seedlings to provide adequate room for the plants.

Growing: Full sun or slight shade.

Maintaining: No special maintenance is necessary, but an adequate water supply will enhance the rate of growth and make the roots sweeter and crisper.

Harvesting: Pull radishes as needed and add the tops to the compost pile. If you leave radishes in the ground for too long, they're likely to become woody and bitter. Also, worms may attack radish roots that are left in the garden.

Using: Usually eaten raw, radishes can also add a surprising zest to stir-fries and soups.

RUTABAGA (*Brassica napus*) is a root crop that is usually grown as a long-season annual because it takes ninety days to reach harvest.

Rutabaga roots look like large, yellow turnips—they are yellow through and through. Unlike turnips, the greens aren't particularly tasty, but they do make good compost or mulch because they are so big. A relatively new variety of rutabaga (*B. napus* var. *oleifera*) is grown for its seeds, which are used to make canola oil. (Haven't you always wondered what the heck a canola was?) Rutabaga probably first occurred in southern European gardens as a hybrid between turnip and kale.

Regions: EASY, in N, C, S.

Planting: Sow the seeds directly in the garden or start them in flats in the fall and throughout the winter. It matures in ninety days, so you may have only one planting in south Florida, maybe two or more in the north. It germinates quickly and reliably. Thin the seedlings to provide adequate room for the fat roots; eat the thinnings as micro-greens.

Growing: Full sun. Extra compost and composted manure will help feed this hungry crop.

Maintaining: Mulch around the stems to keep the weeds at bay and to hold in moisture. Irrigate regularly and deeply.

Harvesting: Pull the crop at ninety to one hundred days no matter its size—any longer will cause the root to become fibrous and woody.

Using: Rutabagas are frequently eaten boiled and mashed, but you can also grate them raw and use them in salads and anywhere you might use grated carrots. You can also create a combination mash with rutabagas, potatoes, and carrots—a monster mash?

TATSOI, SPINACH MUSTARD, SPOON MUSTARD, ROSETTE BOK CHOY, or BROADBEAKED MUSTARD (*Brassica narinosa*) is an easy-to-grow, cool-weather mustard most often grown for its greens. This plant is an important green in Asian cuisine and has become popular in North America. Unlike most mustards, this plant has a rosette of soft, dark-green spoon-shaped leaves with a mild but distinctive flavor. The plant is beautiful enough to be added to an ornamental garden. Commercially produced seeds may be hard to find, but once you grow some, it's easy to save your own seeds for the next season.

Regions: EASY, in N, C, S.

Planting: Plant the seeds directly in the garden or start them in flats in the fall and throughout the winter. It germinates quickly and reliably, and matures in a little less than two months. Thin the seedlings to provide adequate room for the fat roots; eat the thinnings as micro-greens.

Growing: Full sun or slight shade.

Maintaining: Mulch around the stems to keep the weeds at bay and to keep the spreading leaves from touching the soil. Irrigate regularly and deeply—this plant is not drought tolerant.

Harvesting: Cut leaves as needed after about forty days. Once it bolts, the leaves become bitter, so unless you are saving the seeds, pull it out, and get ready for the next crop.

Using: Eat tatsoi raw in salads, or, for a more dramatic effect, cut the whole plant, wash it, and place it in a bowl in center of table for diners to tear off individual leaves and dip into dressing. There are many methods of cooking the tender and quick-cooking greens; they can easily be added to a stir-fry or braised as you would any greens.

TURNIP (*Brassica rapa* var. *rapifera*) is a classic crop in the rapifera group. You might see it served at Thanksgiving, and throughout the winter and into the spring. The greens are also widely used, especially in southern and Cajun cooking.

Regions: EASY, in N, C, S.

Planting: Plant the seeds directly in the garden or start them in flats in the fall and throughout the winter. It germinates quickly and reliably, and matures in a little less than two months. Thin the seedlings to provide adequate room for the fat roots; eat the thinnings as micro-greens.

Growing: Full sun or slight shade.

Maintaining: Mulch around the stems to keep the weeds at bay and to hold in moisture. Irrigate regularly and deeply.

Harvesting: If you're primarily interested in the root crop, refrain from cutting too many of the leaves. For the best flavor, harvest the root when it's relatively small. If you're more interested in the greens, cut leaves as needed. Once the plant bolts, the leaves become bitter and the root will shrink, so pull it out and get ready for the next crop.

Using: Fresh turnip roots are a far cry from those waxed things on the grocery-store shelves. You can cook them in soups or mash them with butter and nutmeg, but they are also good grated raw in salads. There are many methods of cooking the greens. If the greens are on the bitter side, add them to boiling salted water, cook them for a few minutes, and then drain. Then, add some olive oil and roasted sunflower seeds to the pan, put it back on the heat, and stir the greens into the oil until they are covered.

WATERCRESS (*Nasturtium officinale*) is a wetlands perennial that has become invasive in some parts of the country, but not in Florida. There is also a native, endemic Florida watercress (*N. floridanum*) that occurs in all but the panhandle region. Don't confuse watercress with the common name of the garden nasturtium (*Tropaeolum majus*).

Regions: EASY, in N, C, S.

Planting: Plant the seeds in wet, rich soil in the early fall or early spring. Once they have sprouted, watercress need wet soil moistened with nonstagnant water. You can also root cuttings; that way you'll know ahead of time how the leaves taste. If you have a small pond or water feature with a solar-powered pump that circulates the water, you can grow watercress along the edges. Some people grow it in a bucket and change the water every day.

Growing: Shade or partial shade, in water.

Maintaining: Watercress can get rangy, but harvesting it regularly will manage its exuberance and encourage new tender growth.

Harvesting: Cut off whole sections of the stem, but use only the leaves.

Using: Fresh watercress and cream-cheese sandwiches are a classic, but you'll find other uses for its slightly peppery leaves in salads or as a garnish.

Bromeliaceae

The members of the bromeliad family (Bromeliaceae) are widely grown in ornamental gardens for their interesting leaves and spectacular flowers; pineapple is the only commercially important food crop in this family.

PINEAPPLE (*Ananas comosus*) is a tropical fruit that will be damaged in a light frost and killed in a heavy frost or long-term cold snap. The common name "pineapple" is a portmanteau of the Spanish "piña," because people thought it looked like a pinecone, and the English "apple," because it is so sweet. The pineapple "fruit" is not really a fruit at all but a mass of individual berries fused to a central stalk. The leaves on top of the "fruit" are actually attached to the stalk, which has grown beyond where the berries are attached.

Regions: MODERATE, in N, C; EASY, in S. (If you wish to grow pineapples in northern or central Florida, grow them in large containers so that you can move them inside during the cold months.)

Planting: To start a pineapple, choose a fruit in the grocery store or farmers market with nice green leaves. Twist the top off and eat the rest of the fruit. Let the top sit for a few days to dry out. Remove several layers of leaves from the base of the pineapple top. Fill a tall pot with a sandy, bromeliad soil mix and push the base of the pineapple top two to three inches into the soil so that the remaining leaves are upright. Thoroughly moisten the soil and keep the container, with what is essentially a cutting, in a location with shade or filtered light. Keep the soil moist, and in about a month or two you should have a new, rooted pineapple plant. Like most tank bromeliads, it does best if you allow water to sit in the cup formed at the top of the leaves.

Growing: Once your pineapple plant starts growing new leaves, you can move it into a sunnier location and water it about once a week if there is no rain. During the winter, when the days are short and the nights are cool, your plant will bloom if it is mature enough. The bright blue flowers encircle the stem—each lasting only one day. After the plant blooms, the fruit begins to form. It will take three to six months to develop and begin to ripen.

Maintaining: Provide moderate moisture and fertilization. You can leave the mother plant in place for several years. By removing the fruit, you will induce the plant to produce more. When the plant loses vigor, dig it out and start a new plant.

Harvesting: When the compound fruit is golden about halfway up and smells sweet, it's probably ready to be harvested. When unripe, the pineapple is somewhat toxic, and when overripe, it takes on the smell of fermented fruit. Knowing when to cut it off is important. When you cut it, leave a little of the stem at the bottom of the fruit for protection. You can harvest the leaves at the top to start another plant.

Using: This well-known fruit needs no instructions!

Cactaceae

The cactus family (Cactaceae) includes a number of edible cacti, but they can be a little prickly . . .

PRICKLY PEAR (*Opuntia* spp.) is a perennial evergreen with bright yellow flowers. There are a number of species of *opuntia*, and several are native or endemic to Florida. The most common is (*O. humifusa*), which occurs naturally throughout the state and is widely used in Mexican cooking. Talk about a drought-tolerant crop! Plus, its flowers attract native bees and other pollinators, so you may want to locate it near your other crops even if you don't plan to use it for cooking. Be careful of the thorns and the small, barbed hairs known as glochids—they will dig into your skin at the lightest touch. Use thick leather gloves when handling this plant. The pad or *nopal* is an enlarged stem; there are no true leaves.

Regions: EASY, in N, C, S.

Planting: Bury the bottom half of a pad in the soil, and then water it thoroughly. It will become established more quickly if you irrigate it once a week for a month or so in the absence of rain. It does best in well-drained, sandy soil and in hot, sunny microclimates.

Growing: Very little attention is required to grow this plant, and a dense prickly-pear hedge can serve to keep some of the large garden pests at bay.

Maintaining: Trim any yellowing pads or, when plant becomes too large for the space, trim back whole pads to the desired size.

Harvesting: Harvest the fruits (called *tunas*) after they turn a dark rose pink. The pads (*nopales*) may be harvested at any time, but the newer ones are the most succulent.

Using: After skinning and cleaning the *nopales*, cut them into strips and boil them—their flavor resembles that of green beans. Toss them in a salad with diced onion, tomato, cilantro, chile, and lime juice, or add them to scrambled eggs. Grilling *nopales* until they are browned or slightly charred and serving them alongside grilled meats is a Mexican tradition. Slice them into strips, squeeze some lime juice and olive oil onto the *nopalitos*, then toss and serve. *Delicioso!*

Caprifoliaceae

The honeysuckle family (Caprifoliaceae) contains a single edible crop—mâche or corn salad. Mâche or corn salad (*Valerianella* spp.) is a fast-growing, cool-weather vegetable with a mild spinach taste. A European weed, it often grows in wheat fields, and peasants foraged it for their salads. The British sometimes refer to wheat as corn, so it was the salad in the cornfield: hence its name "corn salad." There are a couple of different species. In Florida, it's best to choose those with the greatest tolerance for heat.

Regions: EASY, in N, C; MODERATE, in S.

Planting: Sow the seeds directly in the garden starting in the fall and continue sowing every three weeks or so until a month before it's time to plant your hot-weather vegetables. It usually develops a rosette of leaves before it gains in height.

Growing: Grow it along with spinach and other cool-weather greens.

Maintaining: After thinning, no special maintenance is required.

Harvesting: You can start harvesting as early as fifty days after planting. Cut off the outer leaves as needed or cut the whole plant to the ground. New leaves may grow from the stem. This is an open-pollinated crop, so you can let some of the plants flower and set seed.

Using: Use this mild-flavored crop as you would baby spinach.

Convolvulaceae

The morning glory family (Convolvulaceae) includes sweet potatoes, a hot-weather crop. It also includes water lettuce (*Ipomoea aquatica*), an Asian crop that has become invasive in Florida and should not be planted or grown here; but if you're clearing it from a clean water source, you can eat it.

SWEET POTATO (*Ipomoea batatas*) is a beautiful perennial vine that is treated as a long-season annual during the heat of the summer. While usually grown for its storage roots, the greens are also edible. Two major types of sweet potatoes are grown in Florida: the standard type, with soft, orange flesh, and the drier, white-fleshed type called bonatios or Cuban sweet potatoes. These are not the same as yams, even though supermarkets may label them so. (For true yams, see the Dioscoreaceae family.) Even though yams and sweet potatoes are totally unrelated, they may be prepared and served in the same ways.

Sweet-potato vines do not naturally climb trellises, but rather trail along the ground, leaving new roots in their wake. They are quite decorative until the end of their season.

Regions: EASY, in N, C, S.

Planting: Grow sweet potatoes from purchased slips or cuttings, or start your own cuttings by suspending an organic and untreated sweet potato in a jar of water for about six weeks before the hot weather arrives. When the sprouts are six to eight inches long, twist each one from the mother potato and plant them in a starter pot or flat. When the hot weather arrives, build mounds at least twenty inches across with large indentations in the centers and with lots of rich compost mixed in with your soil. Plant two or three slips in equally spaced holes around the edge of the mound, and keep the mound moist so that the slips do not wilt. It's a good idea to provide afternoon shade for the first week or two until the slips are established.

Growing: The vines will cover the area so allow them plenty of room. If you are short on space, you may be able to trellis some of the vines.

Maintaining: Requires deep irrigation—the indentation in the mound provides a central catchment area. Mulch the area to keep the soil warm, damp, and free of weeds. Let up on the irrigation toward the end of the season.

Harvesting: You may start harvesting the roots whenever they are large enough for your needs, but if you are harvesting them early in the season, be sure to rebuild the mound. When the vines turn yellow, it's time to harvest all of the roots. You can use a garden fork to turn over the soil, but you may find that digging them out by hand works better because the potatoes are prone to bruising at this stage. Use any roots that you nick quickly; don't store damaged roots. Sweet potatoes store best after they've "cured" for several weeks in a hot humid room. Then store them in a cool dark location.

Using: Sweet potatoes are highly nutritious, and are one of nature's "superfoods." They can be cooked in many ways for use as main course dishes, side dishes, or desserts.

Cucurbitaceae

The **SQUASH FAMILY** (Cucurbitaceae) is an important crop family that includes both long-season and short-season annuals such as squashes, cucumbers, melons, pumpkins, zucchinis, and gourds. The flowers are either male or female and require pollination in order to develop a fruit; for pollination to occur, the flowers must be visited by insects eight or nine times. The male flower is borne on a slender stalk, while the female flower sits atop a little fruit. To promote pollination, take measures to attract insects, mainly bees and wasps, to your garden or you may hand-pollinate the female flowers with a small paintbrush. If you are growing several members of this family in close proximity, cross-pollination may occur. This will not affect the quality of the fruit, but it matters if you plan to save the seed to plant the next year. The flowers are edible, but don't harvest them until after they've been pollinated unless you wish to reduce your yield. Most cooks stuff the flowers with a cheese mixture, dip them in a light batter, and fry. You can include squash flowers in a tempura.

While you'll want to attract insects for pollination, many crops in this family are prone to insect damage, and the stems and fruits are

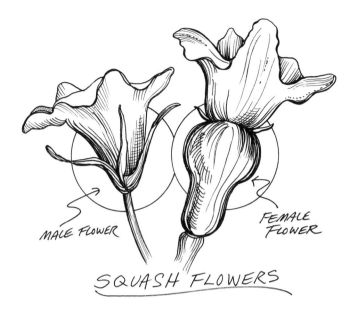

MALE FLOWER

FEMALE FLOWER

SQUASH FLOWERS

especially vulnerable to boring insects. You're unlikely to notice the larvae of stem-boring insects until it's too late, but you may be able to save the vine by slicing the stem lengthwise where you see damage or frass, pulling out the larvae with tweezers, and taping the stem back together. You might be able to reduce infestations by using a translucent row cover when the plants are young to keep the moths and other insects from the crop; remove the cover once both male and female flowers are available for the pollinators. Butternut squash vines seem to resist stem borers, and most zucchinis and summer squash grow so quickly that you can harvest a good-sized crop before the damage from the borers kills the plant.

This family contains seemingly endless varieties and cultivars, but most members have similar cultivation and irrigation requirements. To avoid repetition, the cultivation suggestions for all the squash crops are presented here; for additional suggestions and for harvesting and usage, see the description of each individual crop.

Regions: EASY, in N, C, S.

Planting: Before the hot weather arrives (or in the early fall for fast-maturing crops like zucchini and cucumbers), build mounds at least thirty inches across with lots of rich compost mixed in with your soil and with large indentation in the centers. Some growers set up a circle of trench composting four to six inches under the entire mound and bury kitchen scraps and other rich and easily compostable materials such as waterweeds. This will not only provide your crop with plenty of micronutrients, but will also help the mound to retain moisture.

You should space the mounds twenty to thirty inches apart. If you're using raised beds, you may have room for only one mound in each bed. Your garden will look like a field of volcanoes. Create two or three planting holes equally spaced around the rim of the crater in each mound. The seeds are large and have a high germination rate, but plant two or three of them at the recommended depth in each planting hole and keep the area moist, but not wet, until they germinate. Transplanting seedlings is not recommended

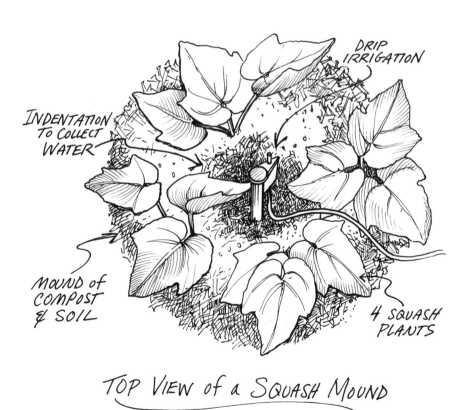

TOP VIEW of a SQUASH MOUND

unless they are grown in a plantable container that will quickly decompose once it's in the soil.

Growing: The seedlings will be fairly large. When there are two sets of true leaves, choose the best seedling for each of the planting holes and cut the others off at the soil level. Continue to keep the area moist. The seedlings will grow quickly; as they get larger, start irrigating in the center of the crater only. This way the water will collect and soak into the ground and won't roll away across the dry soil. This spot irrigation also avoids getting water on the leaves, which reduces your chances of mildew and fungal attacks. In the middle of the growing period, you could add fresh compost or dried fish emulsion to the bottom of the indentation for a mid-season nutrition boost.

Maintaining: All members of this family require deep irrigation—the indentation in the mound provides a central catchment area. Mulch the area to keep the soil warm, damp, and free of weeds. If you are using manual irrigation (either as a supplemental or primary irrigation method), you could place a small bucket or other container with several small holes drilled into its bottom into the bottom of the indentation. When you water, fill the bucket to ensure a deep and slow watering.

For the winter squash crops, cut back on your irrigation toward the end of the season to avoid splitting the fruits and to enhance their flavor. This is not recommended for cucumbers or the summer-squash crops because these fruits are harvested when immature.

Harvesting: Use a sharp knife to cleanly cut the fruit from the vine. Wipe the knife with alcohol regularly so that you don't spread diseases between plants. Handle the fruits with care to avoid bruising or nicking the skin.

CHAYOTE, CHRISTOPHENE, or **VEGETABLE PEAR** (*Sechium edule*) is a vining perennial or long-season annual. This Mexican crop has been grown since the Aztec age and is an important ingredient in Hispanic and Caribbean dishes. While widely grown in south Florida, it can be grown throughout the state. If you wish to grow chayote, you'll need to find a green market or farmers market that sells the fruit—it's unlikely to be sold at your garden center. There are both smooth and ridged, spiny varieties, but in Florida you will probably only find the smooth variety.

Planting: See family planting directions beginning on page 128. The fruit contains one large seed that must be planted while still inside the fruit—don't cut the fleshy part of the fruit away. Most growers store the fruit in a cool, dry environment, and, after the soil has warmed up in the spring, plant only those fruits that have sprouted.

Easy Stuffed Chayote

This recipe is a variation of a Nicaraguan dish called pescozon (pes-co-SONE). Plunge whole chayotes into boiling water, and boil them until they are soft (that is, until you can poke through them with a slender, sharp knife). Remove them from the pot to a small tub of iced water. This will cool them and should make the skins easy to remove. Cut the whole, boiled, peeled chayote in half lengthwise, and remove the seed. Slice off a bit of the rounded outside so that it will lie flat in a pan, inside up. Stuff the seed cavity with grated or crumbled cheese—use a strong or salty cheese like aged provolone, Parmigiano Reggiano, Latin queso blanco, or feta. Then, put the halves back together with the layer of cheese in middle, dredge the chayote in flour, which will cling to the wet surface, and then gently shake off any excess flour. Dip the chayote in egg batter (recipe follows), then panfry it on both sides over medium heat until the cheese is melted and the batter is crispy and golden brown. Enjoy it as a light lunch, or as a main dish with rice and salad or Nicaraguan slaw (shredded, salted cabbage with a bit of onion and carrot tossed in equal parts white vinegar and water and chilled in fridge for a few hours.) One chayote per person.

For the egg batter, mix one medium egg, one teaspoon of flour, and one teaspoon of water per chayote, plus salt and pepper to taste. Beat well with a whisk, fork, or mixer, until frothy.

Sometimes the fruit will sprout while it's still on the vine; in this event, plant the fruit with its new vine in a pot to carry it through the winter months, or, if you live in south Florida, plant it directly in the ground.

Harvesting: The vine will grow to thirty or more feet long and won't start flowering or producing until late in the season—one hundred days or more after planting. If the soil is rich and has been adequately irrigated, each vine could yield between fifty and one hundred fruits. The leaves and roots are also edible. When the days grow short or cold, cut the vine back to the ground and cover the area with four inches of mulch—pine needles or straw are best—more if you need to protect it from frost damage. After two years, you may also harvest some of the underground roots without killing the plant.

Using: Chayote is mild and can be used in place of summer squash. It's great in soups, and is often served with a citrus-based dressing. Be careful when peeling chayote as it will leave a sticky residue on your hands. Wear rubber gloves or boil unpeeled chayote whole, and then, when it's somewhat soft, scoop it out for use. The starchy roots can be prepared like Irish potatoes.

CUCUMBER (*Cucumis sativus*) is a vining annual that is more closely related to melons than to squash. Most growers use a trellis or string system to keep the cucumbers away from soil-borne pests and to increase the air circulation to reduce the risk of fungal infection. The cucumber mounds may not need to be quite as large or as spread out as those for other members of the squash family because of the trellis or cage, but providing good-sized indentation for irrigation is still important.

Planting: See family planting directions beginning on page 128.

Harvesting: You may start harvesting the fruit as soon as it's large enough for your needs. It's best not to let the cucumbers grow too large because they can become bitter and seedy. Also, once the vines sense that some fruit has ripened, they will stop blooming, so keeping picking to promote the largest yield. If you're saving the seeds, wait until the end of the season. Once the inevitable fungus sets in and the leaves and fruit turn yellow, pull out the whole vine and dispose of it in the yard waste or trash—not in your compost pile.

Using: Cucumber is a common vegetable that needs no introduction, but if you haven't tried a cucumber and fresh dill sandwich with thinly sliced sweet onions and a creamy dressing on fried multigrain bread, well, then, you're missing out on a delightful experience. Make the dressing with fresh dill, plain yogurt, brown mustard, olive oil, mayonnaise, grated Parmesan cheese, horseradish, and a few drops of lime juice.

GUADELOUPE CUCUMBER (*Melothria pendula*) is a vigorous native, perennial cucumber vine that occurs throughout Florida. The fruits look like miniature watermelons. There is a lot of misinformation about the edibility of this plant, but as long as you eat only the light-green, immature fruits, you'll be fine. You're unlikely to find seed for sale, but once you have some growing, you can save the seed. In most parts of Florida, the plant will live for several years.

Planting: See family planting directions beginning on page 128. These vines grow quickly and could smother your other crops, so grow them on a fence or extensive trellis system away from everything else. Being native to Florida, the plant needs no special care.

Harvesting: Harvest only the light-green, immature fruits; the dark-green to blackish fruits not only taste bad, but are said to be a strong laxative. It's a good idea to harvest the over-ripe fruit and throw them in trash to prevent this vine from reseeding the area and becoming a weed in your garden.

Using: Use these delicious, cute fruits like cherry tomatoes in salads or as a play watermelon for your daughter's Barbie doll.

LUFFA, **CHINESE OKRA**, **SPONGE GOURD**, or **LUFFA SQUASH** (*Luffa acutangula*) is a hot-weather zucchini substitute and is used in Chinese cooking. There are two types: smooth and ridged. Both are edible. The ripe, dried fruit can also be used as a plant-based sponge or loofah.

Planting: See family planting directions beginning on page 128. These vines grow quickly and will smother your other crops, so grow them on a fence or extensive trellis system away from everything else. Look in Asian grocery stores for the seeds.

Harvesting: Harvest the fruits when they are less than ten inches long for the best eating.

Using: Use it exactly as you would zucchini, but peel the bitter outer skin first. The tender, young fruits are best. Try it in stir-fries, sautéed with other vegetables, or braised with browned butter. It is also good steamed or added to omelets. A classic Hmong dish is stir-fried pork with luffa, garlic, and lemongrass.

MELONS (*Cucumis melo* and *Citrullus lanatus*) grow well in Florida's long hot summers and there are many varieties to grow. From muskmelons with their netted rinds (most folks call them cantaloupes) to watermelons large or small, you're sure to find some that work well for your location. If your edible gardens are small, you may be able to force the melon vines up a strong trellis, but be sure to support the heavy fruit with soft slings tied in place.

If you allow your melons to crawl on the ground among your other vegetables, the vines with their large leaves will make an effective mulch for reducing weeds and cooling the soil. And since they are growing from their own mound, they won't compete with your other crops for water. Some growers like to slide a piece of cardboard or plywood, or some extra straw mulch, under the developing melons in order to keep them clean and away from slugs and other soil-borne pests.

Planting: See family planting directions beginning on page 128.

Harvesting: It's not easy to tell when a melon is ripe, and the widely divergent advice on the subject makes it clear that no one really knows. With some melons, the stem easily detaches or the nearest leaf changes color when ripe, but others varieties do not have such indicators. As you are keeping a garden log, you'll know how many days it's been since you planted your melon seeds and you will have noted from the seed packet the number of days to maturity. So if the rind is firm and the recommended number of days has passed, you're probably safe. When it comes to ripeness, experience is the best teacher.

Using: Sweet melons should be a part of every summer diet. You can add small chunks of melon to your tossed salads, dressing with a light, fruity vinaigrette. And what would the 4th of July be without the traditional watermelon-seed spitting contest?

SQUASH (*Cucurbita* spp.) varieties are divided into two major groups—winter squash and summer squash. Despite their names, both are both harvested in the summer. The winter squashes are harvested when the fruit is mature and the rind is hardened. Winter-squash varieties—hubbard squash, calabaza, pumpkin, butternut squash, watermelon, Seminole pumpkin, spaghetti squash, acorn squash, and gourds—keep well in a cool, dry location. You may even have some left by the time winter arrives. Summer squashes are harvested when the fruit is immature and the rinds are soft and edible, so they don't keep as long as winter-squash varieties. Examples include zucchini, crookneck squash, summer squash, and pattypan squash.

Many **SUMMER SQUASH** varieties are bushy rather than vining, with their leaves and flowers growing close together on the stem. A few plants can produce an amazing amount of fruit in a short time. Plant a small crop each month to even out your supply until it gets too hot, and then start again in early fall.

Planting: See family planting directions beginning on page 128.

Harvesting: Summer squash can be harvested at any time, but earlier is better; once the squash grows longer than twelve inches, it can become tough and bitter. This is especially true for zucchinis, which seem to grow several inches each day once they get started. It's important to walk through your summer squash beds often to keep up with the yield. When a vine begins to deteriorate (e.g., when many of the leaves turn yellow, flowering slows, or the fruit fails to form), yank it out of the garden sooner rather than later to avoid attracting insects and spreading fungus. If you have an active (hot) compost pile, you can compost the spent vines safely, but if your pile is an informal heap, it's better to trash the vines.

Using: Summer squash can be used freshly cut or grated in salads, in stir-fries, or steamed with onions and other vegetables. If your supply is too great, make some zucchini bread instead of foisting the extras on your nongardening neighbors. You could also grate the zucchini and freeze it in a sealed container or zipped freezer bag so that you can make fresh bread during the winter. Summer squash has some of the largest flowers in this family, so be sure to stuff some with a cheese mixture and fry them lightly in olive oil—harvesting the flowers will reduce the fruit yield, which in this case, may be a good thing.

WINTER SQUASH vines can spread thirty or more feet. If you don't keep track of them, they may climb up a nearby tree, making harvesting quite difficult, but mostly they crawl and put down extra roots where they touch the soil. Some gardeners train them to shade the feet of their other crops, which decreases the number of weeds and moderates the temperature of the soil. Quite often, all the fruit ripens at about the same time. Fortunately winter squash stores well, but you may still want to plant a small second crop a month or two after the first to even out your supply or to target maturity dates to coincide with special occasions. You may want pumpkins for Halloween or Thanksgiving, so plan ahead.

Planting: See family planting directions beginning on page 128.

Harvesting: Winter squash is harvested after the rind hardens in the summer. Sometimes the rind will turn color such as when the white spot where watermelons rest on the ground turns creamy or when butternut squash deepens from a whitish color to a buttery tan, but some winter-squash varieties offer no indication other than the size and firmness of the rind.

Using: Winter squash is usually served cooked, and there are so many ways to use it: in soups, breads, and pies, and mashed or diced. Most winter-squash varieties can be prepared either to be eaten directly or precooked for other uses like this: Cut the squash in half lengthwise and remove the seeds and stringy material. Place it cut-side down in a flat-bottomed dish with half an inch of water, cover the dish with a lid or plastic wrap, and cook it in the microwave for eight to ten minutes or in a 350°F oven for thirty to forty minutes. If you wish to eat the squash alone, turn the halves over, place them back in the dish with water, add a dollop of butter and some nutmeg and brown sugar, and then microwave them for another two or three minutes or bake them for ten minutes. Eat the flesh right out of the rind. The seeds are edible, too. To cook the seeds, clean them and place them in a pan, barely covering them with generously salted water, and cook them on medium heat, stirring often until the water is nearly gone. Then spread the seeds on a cookie sheet and dry them in the hot sun or in a 250°F oven.

Spaghetti squash has an interesting property that makes it a good, low-carbohydrate pasta substitute. After cooking it as described above, use a fork to flake out the squash—it will form long, flat strings. Sauté some sweet onions, sweet bell peppers, garlic, and, at the last minute, some diced tomatoes. Toss the noodle-like squash with the sautéed vegetables and some feta cheese. Season with finely chopped fresh basil.

Dioscoreaceae

Members of the yam family (Dioscoreaceae) are often confused with sweet potatoes, but true yams are not related to that look-alike crop. The extremely invasive air potato (*Dioscorea bulbifera*) is a member of this group and should not be planted in Florida. In fact, it should be removed wherever possible, as its vigorous vines have covered entire forests.

YAM (*Dioscorea* spp., principally *D. cayenensis* and *D. rotundata*) requires an eight-to-ten-month growing season to reach maturity, making yams unsuitable for any but the most tropical climates. Historically a nutritious food for subsistence farmers in the tropics, the tropical yam is an easy addition to south Florida gardens.

Regions: NOT RECCOMMENDED, in N; MODERATE, in C; and EASY, in S.

Planting: Yams are propagated chiefly by replanting the top of a harvested root. The trailing vine is usually grown on a trellis, but you could let it crawl along the ground. Most of south Florida is too rocky for this crop, unless you provide deep raised beds that can accommodate its big roots.

Growing: Other than deep soil, it has no special needs.

Maintaining: Keep the vine within the boundaries you've set.

Harvesting: Dig out the root at the end of the season. It can get quite large so be sure to dig deep. Then save the top of the root to plant again the next season. It's best to store the root top in a cool, dark place until you're ready to replant it.

Using: The true yam is starchy and bland. Peel it, cut it into bite-size or large chunks, and then boil or steam for fifteen minutes, or until it is soft but not mushy. Add your favorite flavorful accents like butter, salt, and pepper; or try coconut milk and orange peel for a taste of the tropics. Very adaptable, the yam is complemented by sugars or salts—your choice.

Euphorbiaceae

Members of the spurge family (Euphorbiaceae) have milky sap. Important plants in this family include poinsettias, rubber trees, and the invasive Chinese tallow (*Sapium sebiferum*). The only edible crop is cassava, also called manioc or yuca—yes, it's spelled with one *c*. (*Yucca*, with two *c*'s, is a genus of plant with a tall, white flower spike.)

CASSAVA MANIOC or **YUCA** (*Manihot esculenta*) is a woody shrub grown for its roots as a long-season annual. This tropical plant requires at least an eight-month warm season, but eleven months will yield a better harvest. It can grow to five or more feet in height. There are bitter and sweet varieties, and luckily most of the cuttings you will find from other gardeners are the sweet variety. The bitter variety is not widely planted and contains large amounts of hydrocyanic acid; it must be boiled for 5 minutes, and then boiled again in fresh water, to cook.

Regions: NOT RECCOMMENDED, in N; MODERATE, in C; and EASY, in S.

Planting: Place woody stem cuttings that are six to ten inches long horizontally about an inch deep in the soil as soon as it warms up in the spring. Small, palmate leaves will emerge from the soil within a week if the soil is warm and moisture is plentiful. If it takes longer, don't despair—they will grow very quickly once the weather is hot and the rains are plentiful.

Growing: No special needs—this crop should do fine with average soil and irrigation. It's best to harvest the crop within a single year because the root quality of older plants declines considerably.

Maintaining: It will grow to five feet or more during its long season, so plan for the shade on the north side of this crop.

Harvesting: Keep the crop in the ground until you are ready to use the roots, as they do not store well. Pull the whole plant out at the end of the fall in north and central Florida and anytime between winter and spring in south Florida. Dig carefully around the roots and check their size. If they are at least an inch in diameter, they are big enough to harvest. Be careful to loosen the soil so that the enlarged roots come out in one piece; if they don't, you can still dig them out and use them. Keep the tall woody stem in a shady spot and replant sections when you are ready for next season. They may start to sprout roots and leaves while in storage. Observe the pattern of any growth that has begun, and then cut the yuca into

---

Oven-Baked Yuca Fries

Follow the directions for boiling yuca on page 141. Drain the yucas and allow them to cool slightly.

Preheat the oven to 425°F.

Separate the triangular wedge sections (they look like cottage fries) from the center core, which is a hard string running down center of the yuca root.

Place the yuca wedges on an cookie sheet oiled with, preferably, olive or virgin coconut oil.

Drizzle a bit more oil over the wedges, to your liking.

Bake the wedges in the oven for 10–15 minutes or until they are golden brown.

Turn the wedges over and bake for an additional 10–15 minutes. Remove them from oven, sprinkle with sea salt, and enjoy!

sections to replant, taking care to protect the nodes where sprouts have emerged.

Using: If you are not using the yuca right away, refrigerate them, but for no more than three days. To remove the outer layer, slice a line down the root to pierce the skin, then place a paring knife under the skin and pry it off. The skin should separate readily from the tuber, though it may get stuck where the stringy roots are attached.

Cut the yuca into two to three-inch lengths and place them in boiling, salted water. Cook them for between twelve and twenty minutes, or until they are tender. The pieces will begin to fall apart in triangular sections around the center core. Discard the cooking water.

Fabaceae

The pea family or the legumes family (Fabaceae) include beans, peas, soybeans, and peanuts. Many cover crops also belong to this family. While our atmosphere contains 78 percent nitrogen (N), most plants do not have access to this important nutrient unless it's combined with other elements in the soil—composted manure is one of the most common nitrogen-rich amendments used in organic gardens. Legumes are an exception to this rule because they develop a symbiotic relationship with various *Rhizobia* bacteria, which have the ability to "fix" nitrogen gas from the air and make it available to the plant, a process that happens in the root nodules. When growing legumes, you don't need to add as much nitrogen-rich compost, and indeed, too much nitrogen can reduce the yield. Legumes such as clover and sunn hemp are often used as cover crops because they enrich the soil both while they are growing and especially after they are plowed under. You should plant each section of your edible beds with some legumes every third or fourth year, and preferably just before a heavy feeders like squash or tomatoes.

A word about *Rhizobia* inoculants: You can purchase live cultures of bacteria to inoculate each of your legume crops with the exact bacterial strain it needs to quickly form those productive nitrogen-fixing root nodules. Each legume crop requires a different strain of bacteria, so be sure to purchase the correct strain or purchase pre-inoculated seed. The bacteria can die if you keep it on the shelf for too long or expose it to light or moisture. So if you wish to purchase some, do it just before planting time and don't buy expired stock.

Do you need inoculants? The answer is probably not, if you've grown legumes in this garden space before or if you're a casual home gardener with no fixed harvest requirements. But if you're growing edibles in sterile soil or if you need to maximize your yield as quickly as possible for commercial purposes, inoculants will ensure the quick formation of those handy root nodules. If you're running a certified operation, make sure your inoculant is approved for organic use.

BEANS (bush and pole) (*Phaseolus vulgaris, P. limensis*) are short-season annuals with short production periods, but pole varieties have a somewhat longer season. These are your green beans and your lima beans. Many varieties have been developed over the course of the 5,000 years they've been in cultivation. We used to call them string beans, but the strings have been bred out of most of the varieties grown today. Also, there are many types of shell beans that are grown longer and must be shelled in order to harvest the dried beans, which are used mostly for soups or refried beans.

Regions: EASY, in N, C, S.

Planting: For bush beans, plant the seeds directly in the garden when the soil reaches 60°F. For lima beans wait until the soil reaches 70°F; you may be able to plant lima beans throughout the summer. Plant a new set every ten days to two weeks, until the heat sets in and the days reach the high 80s on a regular basis. Plant pole beans near a trellis at the north side of the beds so they don't shade your other crops. Every three weeks or so, plant more seeds.

Growing: Mulch well and provide regular, deep irrigation.

Maintaining: Because this is a short-term crop, insect damage to the leaves should not affect the yield.

Harvesting: Use a knife or scissors to cut the beans from the plants. You may harvest the young pods or wait for the full-sized beans, which can be eaten raw or cooked as green beans or snap beans. It's best to harvest beans from young plants, so once your next set of beans starts to produce a good crop, pull the old crop even is it's still producing. If you're growing lima beans or other shell beans, let the beans mature until you can clearly see their outlines in the pods. The pods of shell beans may also turn color as they ripen.

Using: These are your standard beans, but if you've never eaten them straight from the garden, you'll hardly recognize them as the same boring, over-cooked vegetable from your childhood.

BROAD BEANS or **FAVA BEANS** (*Vicia faba*) are a long-season, cool-weather crop grown through the winter in north and central Florida. Please note that the horse bean (*V. faba* var. *equina*), as the name suggests, is fed to horses. The broad bean that is suitable for human consumption is *V. faba* var. *major*.

Regions: EASY, in N, C; NOT RECCOMMENDED, in S.

Planting: As soon as the weather begins to cool, plant the seeds in mounds with an irrigation indentation in the top, as you would squash. These beans are bush-type beans, but some tall varieties may need staking to keep the beans off the ground. Beans need a lot of sun, which can be a challenge because they're grown during the short days of winter.

Growing: Mulch well and provide consistent, deep irrigation until shortly before harvest if you are growing the crop for the dry bean.

Maintaining: Because you'll be maintaining this crop for four or five months, be vigilant about insect attacks—either remove the insects by hand or spray them away with water.

Harvesting: You may harvest the young pods for use as a green bean, but most growers plant this crop as a shell bean and harvest its mature beans. The vegetative parts of the plant are sold as a straw in other countries. You could use its dead vegetation as a mulch, or add it to your compost.

Using: To shell the beans, put them in a steamer, lower in the beans into boiling water for five to eight minutes depending on their size, and then plunge steamer into cold water. Then, once the pods have cooled, squeeze out the beans. You can use them in soups and stews or cook them until they are soft and puree them with a little garlic and olive oil for a hummus-like mixture. Parboil the shelled beans and sauté them in olive oil and garlic—this works well as a side dish or sprinkled like nuts in a salad. If you harvest the immature fruit, prepare it as you would a typical green bean. Eat raw beans in moderation—too many may upset your stomach.

CHICKPEAS, GRAM BEANS, or **GARBANZO BEANS** (*Cicer arietinum*) are a tender, long-season annual with feathery leaves and a shrubby habit. It's neither a bean nor a pea, but a legume with a different configuration. A chickpea plant is bushy and attractive, and can be grown in a pot outside the kitchen or near the front door. It's an important crop for Middle Eastern cooking, particularly for making hummus.

Regions: EASY, in N, C, S.

Planting: Plant the seeds (two or three to a planting hole because the germination rate is low) just before the last frost or, in south Florida, at the beginning of winter. The yield per plant is less than most legumes, so plant enough for your needs. Keep the soil moist.

Growing: After the seeds sprout, mulch well and provide regular, but deep irrigation.

Maintaining: This bean is relatively easy to care for, but do mulch to keep the weeds down.

Harvesting: You may cut the young pods for use as a green bean, but most commercial growers wait for the pods to dry before harvesting them. This will take at least three months, but a well-cared-for plant may continue bearing for another few months. You can cut individual pods from the plant or pull the whole plant and dry it flat elsewhere—a hot, dry surface is best. Once they are sufficiently dry, the pods will crack open on their own. If the pods are not dry enough, they are notoriously difficult to crack open—use a rolling pin on a hard surface. Don't waste the nutrient-rich plants; work them back into the soil or add them to your compost.

Using: Why not go out and pick a small handful for a snack? Mature, fresh chickpeas, not dried, but shelled and eaten raw, are delicious and nutritious. Dress them with lime juice and a dash of pepper for added zing. Cook a few with rice for a protein boost. The young green pods may also be cut finely in salads, prepared like green beans, or cooked with a mess of greens. If you harvest the dried beans, they'll keep in a cool, dry location for a year, but you'll find good uses for them before that year goes by.

HYACINTH BEAN (*Lablab purpureus*) is a long-season, heat-loving, drought-tolerant pole bean with attractive flowers and lovely purple beans. Many gardeners plant this bean solely for its beauty and easy care. These cool beans provide many a porch more privacy in the summer when allowed to climb a string trellis and form a beautiful green curtain. The flowers attract butterflies, bees, and hummingbirds.
Regions: EASY, in N, C, S.
Planting: As soon as the weather begins to warm, plant the seeds several inches apart at the foot of a good-sized trellis.
Growing: After the seeds sprout, mulch well and provide regular irrigation until the vine grows to six feet or so, after which you can irrigate less frequently.
Maintaining: This bean is relatively easy to care for. It will reseed on its own.
Harvesting: You may harvest the young pods for use as a green bean, and you may also harvest the flowers. The mature beans may also be harvested, but boil them twice before eating them to reduce their bitterness.
Using: Prepare the immature fruit as you would a normal green bean. They are better cooked than raw, although they lose that gorgeous purple color when cooked. The flowers make lovely mild-flavored garnishes or can be used in salads. Eat the dried beans only if you're desperate—there are so many much tastier choices that don't need to be boiled twice.

JICAMA, YAM BEAN, or **MEXICAN POTATO** (*Pachyrrhizus erosus* and *P. tuberosa*) is a long-season, warm-weather vining crop that needs a nine-month growing season. The tuber is the only edible part of this plant; everything else, including its bean-like fruit, is poisonous.
Regions: MODERATE, in N, C; EASY, in S.
Planting: In north and central Florida, sow the seeds inside six weeks

or more before the last frost to get a good start on that nine-month growing season. It's a vine, so you'll want to provide a trellis to keep it confined. Work the soil well to a depth of at least eight inches so that the tubers can grow freely.

Growing: Full sun or slight shade; more shade in south Florida.

Maintaining: Prune excessive vine growth so that the plant directs more of its energy to tuber formation.

Harvesting: The tubers don't form until after the short days of fall have arrived and well after the flowers have bloomed and the seeds have set. In south Florida, the tubers can become quite large, but smaller tubers (no larger than a softball) are preferred for both flavor and texture.

Using: Peel away the brown skin and use this mild, crisp root raw or cooked. It retains its crispness after cooking and is often used as a substitute for water chestnuts. Although the French call the Irish potato *pomme de terre* or earth apple, it would be a more apt description of this crispy tuber.

The **PEANUT** (*Arachis hypogaea*) is a long-season annual that does best in hot weather. Peanut cultivars can be either bunching or running in habit and have either Virginia or Spanish nut types. Virginia peanuts have large pods that contain one or two large kernels each. Spanish peanuts have smaller pods that contain two or three small kernels each. Of course, peanuts are not true nuts, botanically speaking, but rather a type of hard bean.

Regions: NOT RECOMMENDED, in N,C; MODERATE, in S.

Planting: Purchase certified seed and after the last frost, remove from the shells and plant in wide rows formed with well-worked loose soil. Be sure to leave enough room between plants and to keep the soil level—no growing at the edge of a raised row. The soil must be well drained and must have a good supply of calcium to ensure good shell formation. Test your soil first, and if the calcium level is low add eggs shells, fish emulsion, or bone meal before planting the seeds.

Growing: Keep the rows weeded and the soil around the plants loose and unmulched. After the plant produces its pretty yellow flowers, a sturdy stem called a peg develops at the base of each flowering branch, and the pegs then grow into the ground around the base of the plant. This is why you need the soil around each plant to be loose and level.

Maintaining: After the pegs have grown into the ground, add a layer of straw mulch to keep the weeds down. Continue to irrigate the area along with the rest of your crops, but stop watering when the majority of the leaves turn yellow.

Harvesting: Because the peanuts bloom over a long period and the pods do not all mature at the same time, deciding when to harvest can be tricky. If you are harvesting for green or boiled peanuts, you may choose to do so a little earlier. When the soil is bone dry and there's no chance of rain, slowly lift the entire plant out with a garden fork and turn it upside down in the field. If your soil is loose enough, all the peanuts should remain attached to their pegs. Some growers gather the plants to dry somewhere else, while others leave the plants to dry in the field from several hours to a few days. When the peanut shells are dry, cut them from the pegs.

Wise gardeners will not waste these nutrient-rich spent plants, but work them back into the soil somehow—either by turning them under or adding them to their compost piles.

Using: Most people have trouble fully digesting a lot of raw or green peanuts, so it's best to serve them after they've been roasted or boiled. Peanuts are highly nutritious and contain many trace elements. Peanuts differ from other legumes in that they are high in fat and protein, but low in carbohydrates. So they are more like true nuts, after all.

COOL-WEATHER PEAS (*Pisum sativum*) can be divided into several categories. The standard English pea (*P. sativum* var. *sativum*) is harvested when the pods are fully grown. The peas are "shelled" so you can consume just the peas inside. Closely related are the snow pea (*P. sativum* var. *macrocarpon*) and the sugar-snap pea, both of which have an edible shell and are harvested when young. The snow pea has been used in Asian cooking for centuries. The sugar-snap pea, a hybrid of a snow pea and a shell pea, was introduced in the 1970s. They've become quite popular because they're easy to grow, have a sweet taste, and are versatile in the kitchen.

Regions: EASY, in N, C, S.

Planting: Plant the seeds in the fall. In most of Florida, you can grow them right through the winter; in north Florida, you could plant them through February for an early spring crop. Peas are tolerant of light frosts, but if there are repeated heavy frosts, the flowers will die and the fruit may turn brown. But if the vine is still in good shape, continue to irrigate, and it will start to flower and fruit again as the weather warms up.

Growing: Peas require a trellising system and regular irrigation. Full sun is best for your midwinter crops, but the ones you plant in the early spring will do better with afternoon shade.

Maintaining: Peas have shallow and weak roots, so weed the area by hand to minimize root disturbance.

Harvesting: For the sugar-snap peas and snow peas, cut the pods when they are small and tender. For the English peas, wait to harvest until the pods have hardened. Use a knife or scissors to harvest the pods so that you don't disturb the vine or mangle the pod.

Using: Standard shelled peas need no introduction. What would a tuna noodle casserole be without peas? Peas with edible pods have many uses in the kitchen: they can be eaten raw in salads or used in stir-fries and soups. If you have children helping in the garden, you may find that a great many of these delightful peas won't make it into the kitchen at all.

SUMMER PEAS, SOUTHERN PEAS, BLACK-EYED PEAS, YARD-LONG BEANS and **COWPEAS** (*Vigna unguiculata*) are all fast-growing, heat-loving annual vining varieties. There are several subspecies, and each has a different use, from serving as animal fodder to bringing good luck on New Year's Day. The yard-long bean (*V. unguiculata* subsp. *sesquipedalis*) should probably be called the foot-and-a-half bean. It is essentially a green bean substitute, only longer. The black-eyed pea (*V. unguiculata* subsp. *unguiculata*) is a southern favorite that is harvested when mature as a shell bean. The other crops developed from this species will similarly fall into one of two categories: those that are harvested while immature and the pods are soft and edible and those that are harvested as mature shell beans.

Regions: EASY, in N, C, S.

Planting: Plant the seeds in the spring after the last frost and when the soil has warmed. They will need a trellising system or fence to climb. Choose the sunniest spot you have. Soak the seeds overnight before planting.

Growing: Irrigate liberally when vines are young, but cut back once they've grown to a couple of feet. Summer in Florida is the wet season so they only need moderate irrigation, although good drainage is important.

Maintaining: Keep the weeds down around your plants; other than that, no special care is required.

Harvesting: For the yard-long beans and other immature fruit in this group, harvest early and often to keep the fruit coming. Cut the beans off with a knife or scissors to reduce damage to the bean and the plant. Many growers bundle the beans together with soft ties on both ends of the beans. For the black-eyed peas, allow the pods to develop and then gather the whole pod. You'll need to shell the beans.

Using: Use the yard-long beans as you would a standard green bean—raw or cooked, or preserved as dilly beans. Cook black-eyed peas for your dinner on New Year's Day—the good luck the diners have throughout the year will be proportional to the amount of beans they consume that day. As with most shelled beans, rinse and soak the black-eyed peas before cooking them.

Hemerocallidaceae

The daylily family (Hemerocallidaceae) contains those garden mainstays the daylilies. Each flower lasts only a day, but daylilies produce so many flowers that they make quite a splash in the garden. Some botanists used to include daylilies in the lily family, but enough differences, particularly in the chemistry of the plants, separate them from true lilies, many of which are poisonous. So be sure you have a daylily and not a true lily.

The **DAYLILY** (*Hemerocallis* spp.) is a spreading perennial that produces tubers. There are thousands of cultivars; some are evergreen, while others go dormant in winter. Some of the newer cultivars are ever-blooming, but the classic varieties bloom just once a year. All parts of this classic ornamental plant are edible. It's unlikely that you will find organically grown stock, but after growing the daylily under your care for two or three seasons, it should be safe to consume.

Regions: EASY, in N, C, S.

Planting: While the plants will tolerate poor soil, if you plant them in rich garden soil and keep them moist, they'll thank you with luxurious growth. It's best to plant the tubers in late winter or early spring, but you can plant them more or less successfully at any time of the year. Many gardeners use daylilies as garden borders. They don't do well in standing water; so make sure the soil is well drained.

Growing: Irrigate liberally until they are established. In the central and northern parts of the state, most daylilies will die back in the winter, but not those planted in the south.

Maintaining: Keep the weeds down around your plants; other than that, they require no special care.

Harvesting: Cut off the flowering parts and the leaves any time after plant is established. The best time to harvest tubers is the winter just after they die back. One strategy for planting and harvesting the tubers is to plant them as a long border. After a couple of years, begin digging out the plants at one end of the row, add some new compost, and replant the area with enough tubers to replenish the area. Move down the row as the growing season progresses; by the time you reach the other end, the first plants will be ready to harvest again.

Using: The buds and the flowers are traditionally used in tempura, but you may also stuff the flower with your favorite cheese mixture and fry it lightly in olive oil. The leaves don't have much taste and are tough, but you can add them to cooked greens or to stir-fries. The tubers look like fingerling Irish potatoes, and you may prepare them in the same way. Even vegetable haters will appreciate their slightly nutty flavor.

Lamiaceae

The mint family (Lamiaceae) includes many of our classic culinary herbs. Those from the Mediterranean region include basil, oregano, rosemary, thyme, sage, and of course, the mints. There are also mints native to Florida that you may wish to include in your herb garden.

Most plants in this family have square stems and opposite leaves, but it's actually the bilaterally symmetrical flower that identifies them as members. The odors produced by many members of the mint family make them useful to flavor our cooking, salads, teas, garnishes, and of course, our mint juleps. The odors also make the plants repellent to bugs; so most mints have little trouble with insects. If you start with plants or cuttings, you can shop with your nose to find the one with the best scent.

BASIL or **SWEET BASIL** (*Ocimum basilicum*) is an easy-to-grow mainstay of most herb gardens. Basil is a tender annual that is killed by frost in northern and central Florida. Once the frost has done its damage, the plant tastes terrible, so harvest all of your plants before the frost and place their stems in containers or vases filled with water to keep them fresh. There are hundreds of cultivars, presenting gardeners with a wide choice of flavors, sizes, and textures. They'll do well in Florida's heat, but you may wish to look for varieties that are resistant to fusarium wilt so that your crop will last longer into the summer.

Regions: EASY, in N, C, S.

Planting: Sow the seeds in full sun well after the last frost or in a warm area, or plant rooted cuttings in the soil after the last frost.

Growing: Position tall basils on the north side of shorter plants in the planting bed.

Maintaining: Trim the plant back to induce new leaf growth and to prevent flowering—two new stems will sprout at the node below each cutting. When flowers form, the basil leaves become somewhat bitter. On the other hand, it's a good strategy to let some of the basil go to flower, because the bitter basil is fine for pesto and the flowers attract many beneficial insects. The flowers are also edible and can be used as garnish in salads and other dishes. Basil is susceptible to late summer fungal attacks, but you can take some cuttings early in the season and root them in water or damp sand away from the garden. That way, when your plants out in the garden start to show signs of fungal infection, you can harvest the whole crop and still have healthy cuttings to plant later in the season. Plant these cuttings in a pot or in a different location in the garden, so they won't be in contact with the fungus.

Pseudo-Pesto

This pesto is not as bitter and heavy as a standard pesto because it has a longer ingredients list and produces more of a pesto-like sauce.

6 to 10 stems of basil, with flowers and soft stems

½ medium sweet onion

3 or 4 green onion stalks

¼ cup grated Parmesan cheese

¼ cup mayonnaise

¼ cup roasted sunflower seeds

¼ cup nonfat plain yogurt

1 tablespoon of garlic from a jar or 2 cloves of fresh garlic

1 tablespoon horseradish

1 tablespoon herbes de Florida or herbes de Provence

approximately ¼ cup olive oil

freshly ground pepper, to taste

Add all the ingredients to the blender or food processor. Add enough olive oil to make the mixture creamy but not slimy. If you add the basil after the other ingredients have been pureed, the blender doesn't have to work as hard.

You can use this concoction in many dishes including tuna salad, shrimp pizza, dips, salad dressing, and where you might have used mayonnaise alone. You can also use it as a base for a creamy salad dressing; just add plain yogurt, olive oil, and balsamic vinegar. Freeze the pesto in sealed plastic containers so that you can continue to enjoy your summer harvest in the cool-weather months.

Harvesting: Trim as needed as soon as the plants are a foot or so tall.

Using: Use the fresh leaves in salads, stir fries, or soups for flavor. Use the soft stems and leaves for pesto. Dry or freeze leaves for future use, but when using dried or frozen basil, shred or pulverize it just before you use it to release the odor and flavor.

LEMON BALM (*Melissa officinalis*) is a freely seeding perennial that has become a pest in some states, but not Florida. It's grown for its aromatic leaves, and the oils extracted from the plants have many applications, including perfumes and aroma therapy.

Regions: EASY, in N, C; MODERATE, in S. It requires some cool weather.

Planting: Sow the seeds in your herb garden, or grow the plant from cuttings or divisions. It's not fussy about soil type.

Growing: Full sun or slight shade; more shade in south Florida. Position it on north side of shorter plants because lemon balm can reach two feet tall.

Maintaining: Trim it back to induce new leaf growth and to prevent flowering and self-seeding.

Harvesting: Trim as needed as soon as the plants are established.

Using: Use the leaves in teas, salads, and desserts. You can also use the aromatic leaves and flowers in potpourris.

MINTS (*Mentha* spp.) are spreading herbaceous perennials that are grown worldwide and used for cooking and in teas. There are many distinctive types of mint—you may wish to grow several.

Regions: EASY, in N, C, S.

Planting: Sow the seeds in partial shade in a damp area well after the last frost. The seeds have a low germination rate in the garden, so you may wish to start them in well-tended flats or to root cuttings from known stock. Mint is aggressive once it's established, so it's a good idea to plant mints in containers sunk into the ground to keep them from taking over the whole herb garden, or any other garden for that matter.

Growing: Position mints on the north side of taller plants to make use of the shade.

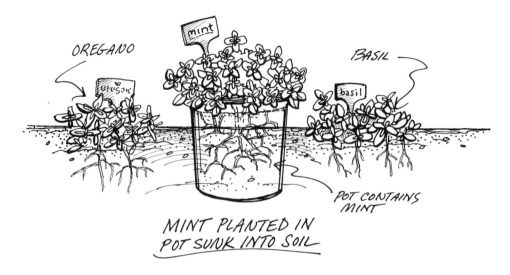

MINT PLANTED IN
POT SUNK INTO SOIL

Maintaining: Trim it back to induce new leaf growth and to prevent flowering—two new stems will sprout at the node below each cutting. Allow some of the mint to flower to attract beneficial insects; plus, the flowers are edible and can be used as garnish in salads and other dishes.

Harvesting: Trim as needed as soon as the plants are established.

Using: Fresh mint leaves are a surprising addition in savory salads. Use them in teas, either alone or to enhance another tea blend; bruise or roll the leaves to release their flavor. Once you have a good stand of mint, you'll wonder how you survived without it.

OREGANOS include several species and many cultivars, and most are perennial herbs. Greek oregano (*Origanum vulgare* var. *hirtum*), Italian oregano (*Origanum × majoricum*), Cuban oregano (*Plectranthus amboinicus*), Mexican oregano (*Lippia graveolens*) (which is actually in the Verbenaceae family, but is covered here for convenience) all have different flavors but a similar pungency that makes them useful in cooking. You should be able to find an oregano that works for you. The Florida native spotted horsemint is also a good substitute: see below.

Regions: EASY, in N, C, S.

Planting: You can grow oregano from seeds, but the flavor and pungency is unpredictable, so be sure to sow enough seed to have your pick of those seedlings with the best odor and flavor. If you start with rooted cuttings, you'll know what you're getting—shop with your nose and your taste buds. You'll probably need only a couple of plants in a family garden.

Growing: Most oreganos prefer neutral or slightly alkaline soil in full sun.

Maintaining: Trim your plants back to induce new leaf growth, but allow some to flower. Oregano flowers attract beneficial insects; plus, the flowers are edible and can be used as garnish in salads and other dishes.

Harvesting: Trim as needed as soon as the plants are well established.

Using: Use fresh leaves to flavor tomato dishes, typically spaghetti sauces, or pizza. Dried, crushed leaves are more pungent than fresh ones, and Mexican oregano is often added to chili powder mixtures.

ROSEMARY (*Rosemarinus officinalis*) is a vigorous easy-to-care-for shrub with a strong piney fragrance. This traditional Mediterranean herb is widely planted in Florida as a drought-tolerant landscape plant. If you'd like to create a formal hedge around your herb garden, rosemary is the perfect choice—it fills out nicely when trimmed. That way you can have your hedge and eat it too.

Regions: EASY, in N, C, S.

Planting: Almost all rosemary is started from cuttings or by layering, where the lower stems are weighted to force them to lie on the ground and root in place.

Growing: Full sun or slight shade. It prefers a slightly alkaline soil.

Maintaining: After rosemary is well established, it needs little care, but if it outgrows your herb garden, chop it back to the ground.

Harvesting: Pick the leaves and flowers as needed. Compost the woody stems.

Using: Use finely chopped rosemary leaves in savory salads and dressings. Add some leaves to your pesto mixtures. Use its blue (sometimes white) flowers as a garnish. Rosemary leaves and flowers are traditional ingredients in herbes de Provence, which is used to flavor stuffings, stews, and soups; in addition, it's used as a grilling rub for meat and fish.

Traditional Mixed-Herb Preparations

All of these mixtures are available for purchase, but as you grow more of your own herbs, you can create your own delicious blends.

Bouquet garni—This is a combination of herbs that are either tied together or enclosed in a cloth bag and cooked along with a soup or stew but removed before serving. A traditional combination includes parsley, thyme, and a bay leaf tied with a leek or onion leaf. Depending on the recipe, the bouquet garni may also include basil, salad burnet, chervil, rosemary, peppercorns, savory, or tarragon. Sometimes the bouquet garni also includes vegetables such as carrots, celery (leaves or stem), celeriac, leeks, or onions, especially when it is being used to make stock.

Herbes de Provence—This traditional, but variable, blend of finely chopped, dried French herbs can be added to soups or stews. It may also be mixed with sea salt, grated citrus rind, and olive oil to make a paste to rub on meat, fish, or vegetables before grilling. You can make your own mixture from your herb garden and call it "herbes de Florida."

Common ingredients include thyme, chervil, rosemary (leaves and flowers), summer savory, lavender (leaves or buds), tarragon, marjoram, oregano, mint, basil, chives (leaves and flowers), bay leaves, and sage. If you have a wax myrtle (*Myrica cerifera*) on your property, you can use the leaves as a substitute for the traditional bay leaves.

SAGE (*Salvia officinalis*) is a traditional herb that has been under cultivation for thousands of years. It is a short-lived perennial, so to keep sage growing in your garden, it's a good idea to root a cutting after two years to start a new plant. While this species is the traditional kitchen herb, there are many other species of Salvia, some of them native to Florida, that make wise additions to your garden to attract pollinators. *Regions:* EASY, in N, C; MODERATE, in S.

Planting: Prefers well-drained soil. You can sow seed in the spring, but most sage is started from cuttings or by layering.

Growing: Full sun or slight shade.

Maintaining: After sage is well established, it needs little care, but keep it cut back to encourage bushy growth. It will live only a few years, usually no more than two in south Florida.

Harvesting: Pick the leaves as needed.

Using: Don't overdo it; a little goes a long way. Use finely chopped sage leaves in stuffings and dressings. Sage is great chopped into browning butter, especially over squash ravioli as a replacement for tomato or cream sauces. Add some leaves to your pesto, or dry them, chop them finely, and add them to your dried herb mixture: herbes de Florida.

SPOTTED HORSEMINT, SPOTTED BEEBALM, or DOTTED HORSEMINT (*Monarda punctata*) is a tall, herbaceous perennial native to Florida that is salt- and drought-tolerant. It attracts pollinators, and while it is not a traditional Mediterranean herb, it does contain thymol, the same oil in thyme and oregano leaves, and deserves a place in or near your edible garden. If you're tired of trying to convince alien herbs to love Florida, this is the plant for you.

Regions: EASY, in N, C, S.

Planting: It is not fussy about soil; indeed, it occurs naturally throughout the state, except for in Dade and Monroe Counties. You can start with seed in the spring, or cuttings and divisions any time.

Growing: Full sun or slight shade. It can reach three or four feet in height, and it will spread and reseed.

Maintaining: After horsemint is well established, it needs little care, but if you supply some irrigation during dry periods or plant it in a damp location, its growth will be more luxurious. Trim it back in mid-spring to control its sprawling habit, if that's important to you.

Harvesting: Pick the leaves as needed.

Using: Use the leaves as a substitute for oregano and thyme or steep bruised leaves to make teas. This Florida native certainly belongs in your dried herb mixture: herbes de Florida. The pink, spotted bracts subtending the small flowers are attractive enough to include in a floral bouquet.

SWEET MARJORAM (*Origanum majorana*) is a creeping perennial that is closely related to the European oreganos, only less pungent.

Regions: EASY, in N, C, S.

Planting: You may grow it from seed, but the flavor and pungency is unpredictable, so sow enough seed to choose those seedlings with the best flavor. If you start with rooted cuttings, you'll know what you're getting—shop with your nose and your taste buds. You'll probably need only a couple of plants in a family garden.

Growing: Prefers neutral or slightly alkaline, well-drained soil in full sun. It's attractive in containers alone or with other herbs.

Maintaining: Trim it back to induce new leaf growth, but allow some to flower. Marjoram's tiny flowers attract beneficial insects; plus, the flowers are edible and can be used as garnish in salads and other dishes.

Harvesting: Trim as needed as soon as the plants are well established.

Using: Use the fresh leaves to flavor tomato dishes such as spaghetti sauce or pizza. The dried, crushed leaves are more pungent than fresh ones. Marjoram is often added to chili powder mixtures.

THYME (*Thymus vulgaris*) is a perennial, spreading ground cover that is often planted between stepping-stones or pavers or as a fragrant lawn substitute. Native to the Mediterranean region, it has been under cultivation for thousands of years and does well in hot, dry climates. There are other aromatic species of *Thymus*, but *Thymus vulgaris* is the species most common in herb gardens. There are many cultivars of *T. vulgaris*, and each has a slightly different aroma and habit. Take some time to grow thyme.

Regions: EASY, in N, C; MODERATE, in S.

Planting: You can grow your plants from seed, but the flavor and pungency is unpredictable, so be sure to sow enough seed to have your pick of those seedlings with the best flavor. If you start with rooted cuttings, you'll know what you're getting—shop with your nose and your taste buds. You will probably need only a couple of plants in a family garden.

Growing: Thyme prefers neutral or slightly alkaline soil in full sun.

Maintaining: Trim it back to induce new leaf growth—two new stems will sprout at the node below each cutting. Thyme flowers attract beneficial insects, plus the flowers are edible and make a pretty garnish in salads and other dishes. After a few years in the garden, thyme will become scraggly, so you'll probably want to start a new set of plants using cuttings from your favorite plant.

Harvesting: Trim as needed as soon as the plants are well established.

Using: Use the fresh leaves in salad dressings or to flavor tomato, meat, and fish dishes. Dried, crushed leaves are more pungent than fresh ones. It's one of the essential ingredients in both bouquet garni and herbes de Provence.

Malvaceae

The mallow family (Malvaceae) includes mallows that have been appreciated for their gorgeous flowers and for their medicinal properties. Those decorative flowers are also edible if you grow them without using poisons. Did you know that marshmallows were originally made from slime extracted from a marsh mallow and whipped like an egg white? This whipped concoction was used as a vehicle for delivering unsavory medicines. Yummy!

OKRA (*Abelmoschus esculentus*) is a classic, southern crop that loves hot weather and also makes a beautiful addition to your edible landscape, with its gorgeous, pale yellow flowers with maroon centers and its unusual seedpods.

Regions: EASY, in N, C, S.

Planting: Plant the seeds directly in the garden in the spring after the soil warms up. Soak the seeds overnight, plant two or three seeds in each planting hole, and choose the strongest plant after your seedlings have grown a few sets of true leaves—allow enough space for their branches to spread out, but not so much that sunlight reaches the soil between the plants as this will encourage weeds. Some varieties of okra can grow to six or more feet in height. Create watering swales in the wide rows between the plants, much like you would

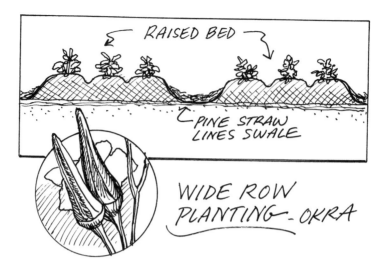

in a squash mound, so that when you irrigate deeply, the water will soak into the soil.

Growing: Full sun or slight shade.

Maintaining: Irrigate regularly and deeply throughout the season to keep the plants blooming.

Harvesting: Harvest the fruit with a knife or scissors when it's three to four inches long. Larger fruit becomes stringy and fibrous. Harvest often so that the flowers keep coming. You may freeze the extras (whole pods with the stem attached) in a sealed plastic bag for use as needed in the off-season.

Using: Like its cousin the marsh mallow, okra becomes slimy when boiled in water and indeed is the thickening agent in traditional jambalaya and Cajun gumbo. You can fry okra using your favorite batter or as part of a stir-fry with onions and tomatoes—frying eliminates the sliminess. Thinly sliced, young, raw okra pods make a good addition to salads. Most people notice only the pleasant crunch because the slime factor doesn't fully develop until the pods are older. Once you begin using okra, you'll wonder why you didn't plant more.

ROSELLE (*Hibiscus sabdariffa*) is a tall, shrubby annual in north and central Florida, but a perennial in frost-free areas. Roselle is a staple

crop in the Caribbean basin, where it is used in fruity tea and jellies—
some compare it to cranberries but without the bitterness. What's really unusual is that the "fruit" is actually the swollen calyx, which becomes a beautiful burgundy color. (The calyx consists of the outermost flower parts, usually the sepals.)

Regions: EASY, in N, C, S.

Planting: Plant the seeds or cuttings directly in the garden in the spring after soil warms up or in the summer. Plant two or three seeds in each planting hole because the germination rate is low. If more than one seedling sprouts, choose the one that is strongest after they've grown at least one set of true leaves; allow each plant enough space for their branches to spread out. Roselle can grow to six or more feet in height. Create watering swales in the wide rows between the plants, much like you would in a squash mound, so that when you irrigate deeply, the water will soak into the soil.

Growing: Full sun. Tolerates wet soil.

Maintaining: Irrigate regularly and deeply throughout the season. Keep the area free of weeds, especially when the plants are small. When the plants fill out, the weeds will be less of a problem. No matter when you plant them, roselle won't begin to bloom until the days become short, in late September or October.

Harvesting: Harvest the calyces with a knife or scissors about ten days after blooming. Harvest often so that the flowers keep coming. Before using the calyces, remove the seedpods in the center of the floral structure.

Using: Steep the calyces in hot water, add sugar to taste, and strain the mixture to make a tea. The leaves and stems can also be eaten raw in salads or cooked with other greens.

Poaceae

The grass family (Poaceae) has provided humans with sustenance for eons. Important crops in this family include corn, wheat, rice, barley, sugarcane, oats, rye, and sorghum. Florida's gardeners and operators of small farms most often grow corn and sugarcane, and maybe some lemon grass in with the herbs.

CORN or **MAIZE** (*Zea mays*) is a nutrient-hungry and water-thirsty annual. The golden tassels on the top of the stalk are the male flowers and release lightweight pollen that is carried by the wind to the female flowers on the cob, which is located farther down the stalk just above a leaf. Each developing kernel is attached to a long, silky strand that protrudes from the end of the husk. After the male pollen has fertilized the kernel, the silk will turn from yellow to brown. Normally, each stalk will produce only one or two ears of corn, so if you decide to plant corn, be sure to grow at least one corn plant for every ear of corn you'd like to harvest.

This traditional American crop has been an important part of Native American civilization and continues to be one of the more important crops on our planet. Native Americans planted corn on hills together with pole beans and squash and called them the Three Sisters. The corn provided a pole for the beans, the squash shaded the soil so that the weeds died out, and the beans fixed nitrogen in the soil. (Actually, beans don't release those nitrogen compounds in significant quantities until they die, but it makes for a good story.) These three vegetables provide a good assortment of nutrients and serve multiple purposes in cooking.

Florida farmers produce a large percentage of the nation's crop, but corn has a reputation of being difficult for smaller growers. To a certain extent this is true, because it needs lots of nutrients, water, and monitoring. Corn borers and fungi attack it, not to mention squirrels and raccoons. If you choose the shorter, faster-growing and heat-tolerant varieties that are resistant to fungal infestations and borer attacks, you may find that you can harvest a decent crop. And when you bite into that ear of fresh corn, you'll find that it was worth the trouble.

Regions: MODERATE, in N, C; DIFFICULT, in S.

Planting: Plant the seeds in rich, well-composted soil early in the spring after the soil reaches 60°F, and then plant a new crop every three weeks to even out your supply. Because corn is wind-pollinated, you'll need to arrange the crop in a compact square or rectangle so that no matter which way the wind blows, some of the corn will be pollinated; long, skinny rows won't work. In traditional farming, corn is planted in ridges, but you could use wide rows with an alternating planting pattern. In drier areas you could create a trench or indentation in the soil so that all the water is absorbed into the soil around the corn. If you are growing more than one variety of super-sweet corn, separate the populations by at least one hundred feet to minimize cross-pollination.

If you are going to grow the Three Sisters, it's best to grow the crops on a mound with a large indentation in the center. Plant three or four corn seeds around the top of the mound and wait until the corn is six to ten inches tall before planting the beans and squash. This combination will require extra irrigation and nutrients, but planting the three crops together does save space in the garden and reduces the weeding chores.

Growing: Full sun.

Maintaining: Irrigate regularly and deeply throughout the season. Keep the area free of weeds, as the roots are shallow. Corn requires a lot of feeding, so supplement your well-composted soil regularly with nitrogen-rich amendments such as fish emulsion or blood meal. Corn doesn't do well in high winds; if some stalks blow over, prop them up promptly with a mound of soil. Sometimes corn produces side stalks; these do not affect the crop yield, so leave them alone.

Harvesting: Harvest the ears when the silk turns brown—about twenty-one days after the silks first emerge from the husk. In corn, freshness counts because the sugar content in the kernels begins to change to starch as soon as the ear is picked. You can slow down the starch formation by keeping the ears cool, but plan to get the corn you pick into the hands of the cook as soon as possible.

Using: There are many ways to use corn and you probably have your favorite, but what would July 4th picnics be without corn on the cob?

LEMONGRASS (*Cymbopogon citratus*) is a perennial, bunching grass. In south Florida, it's evergreen, but in north Florida, it becomes dormant in the winter. It is widely used in Thai cuisine and provides some of the zing in Red Zinger tea. It truly does taste like lemon and contains some of the same chemicals.

Regions: EASY, in N, C, S.

Planting: Plant divisions or nursery-grown plants in moderately rich soil on the north side of your bed or garden—it gets large. You can root sections of the plant that include the bulbous base and then plant them in the garden. The edges of the leaves are sharp, so plant it away from areas that get heavy foot traffic.

Growing: Full sun.

Maintaining: While somewhat drought-tolerant, plants with adequate irrigation will look and taste better.

Harvesting: As it's the swollen base of the leaves that are used, wait until bases are half an inch thick. Wear gloves and long sleeves to protect yourself from the sharp edges. Twist and pull each leaf or use a sharp tool to cut each stem from the bunch close to the soil level.

Using: Crush the base of the leaves by pounding it with the back of your chef's knife, or chop it finely—this is a tough, unchewable grass. Steep leaves to make a refreshing lemony tea.

SUGARCANE (*Saccharum officinarum*) is a short-lived, perennial grass that loves the heat. There are three types of sugarcane: crystal sugarcane, which the sugar industry uses to make granulated sugar; syrup sugarcane, which is used to make syrup; and chewing sugarcane, which is used for . . . guess what? Chewing. So when you acquire your cuttings, pay attention to the type. Most of the U.S. syrup sugarcane crop is grown in north Florida in a band that reaches from Louisiana to Georgia, while the crystal sugarcane is grown in frost-free south Florida.

Regions: EASY, in N, C, S.

Planting: Plant cuttings from known cultivars, because plants grown from seed are highly variable. Each piece of stem should have at least one bud, but five or six buds are better. (The buds emerge at the nodes where leaves were attached.) Dig a six-inch trench in well-composted soil at a site that drains well. Keep in mind that the cane will be tall, so position it where it will not shade the other crops in your garden. Some growers plant a couple of rows of cane to act as a fence and windbreak for the rest of their crops.

In the fall, lay the cuttings horizontally in the bottom of the trench. Most growers lay a double row of cuttings in each trench to prevent skips in the canes where a bud didn't grow. Cover with soil and keep it moist, but not wet. Depending upon the date of planting and your planting zone, some sprouts may emerge from the soil before winter. Pile soil, compost, or mulch around the sprouts to protect them from frost. The real growth will begin after it gets hot the next year.

Many growers interplant shallow-rooted, winter crops such as lettuce or sugar-snap peas near their sugarcane rows. These crops will keep the weeds at bay and will be harvested long before the cane begins to grow.

Growing: Full sun.

Maintaining: Irrigate regularly, but not excessively—sugarcane does not tolerate standing water. Keep the area free of weeds, as the roots are shallow. Most growers continue to mound more soil at the base of the canes to form a ridge. Pile more soil, compost, or mulch over the stubble left after the harvest for the winter. Depending on the type of cane, you may get good growth for three to five years. When the growth becomes sparse, take your cuttings and begin again. Some growers start a new row every second or third year, so that they can count on a reliable harvest.

Harvesting: Cut the canes close to the ground with a machete or garden loppers just before the first frost in north and central Florida. In south Florida, harvest around the first of the year.

Using: Cane, much like maple sap, has been boiled down to make syrup for centuries. Indeed, a traditional cane syrup with no additives is a rare find! In south Florida, a distinctively Caribbean treat is sugar-cane juice (you'll need a heavy-duty juicer) served up cold on ice, either alone or mixed with other fruit juices. Cubans call this sugar-cane juice *guarapo*. If you don't have a fancy machine, peel the outer skin of the sugarcane with a knife and cut the inner woody-yet-juicy flesh into bite-size pieces for chewing.

Rosaceae

The strawberry is the classic crop of the rose family (Rosaceae), but there are some others that you may wish to add to your edible gardens.

ROSES (*Rosa* spp.) are beautiful garden plants, and when you grow them organically without poisons, the petals and the rose hips (fruits) are edible. For the tastiest petals, choose fragrant roses; those without scent are also without flavor. Easy-care, old garden climbing roses or shrub roses are the best choice. Grafted roses should be on "Fortuniana" rootstock for best results.

Regions: MODERATE, in N, C, S.

Planting: You are unlikely to find organic rose stock, but roses that have been growing without synthetic chemicals for two or three years should have purged their systems of any poisons that may have been used. Plant them as directed in rich, well-drained soil.

Growing: Full sun or slight shade; more shade in south Florida.

Maintaining: Irrigate regularly throughout the season. Apply some fish emulsion several times during the year to provide all the micronutrients. Keep the area free of weeds.

Harvesting: Pull the petals from newly opened flowers or leave the flowers alone to let the rose hips ripen to orange or burgundy, and then snip off the fruits.

Using: Use the petals as a garnish plain or sugar them. You can also make rose-petal jelly using a recipe for mint jelly, just skip the green food coloring. If the petals are pink or red, the color will add to the jelly's charm and its delicate taste will recall the scent of the roses. Rose hips make delicious jelly, jam, or syrup.

SALAD BURNET (*Sanguisorba minor*) is an evergreen perennial in northern and central Florida, but it's grown as a cool-weather annual in south Florida. Early colonists brought this plant into the country and often used it as an edging for herb, potager, or kitchen gardens. It has escaped from cultivation in much of the country, but not in Florida. Maybe you'll find room for this attractive plant with leaves that taste like slightly bitter cucumbers. The flowers, borne on long spikes, are attractive.

Regions: EASY, in N, C; MODERATE, in S.

Planting: Plant the seeds in early spring in north and central Florida in moderately rich soil. Plant them in the fall in south Florida and grow the plant through the winter as an annual.

Growing: Full sun or slight shade; more shade in south Florida.

Maintaining: Irrigate regularly throughout the season; salad burnet does not tolerate dry soil. Keep the area free of weeds. Keep the flower heads cut back to promote the best foliage growth.

Harvesting: Cut off the newest leaves.

Using: Use the leaves raw in salads and dressings or as flavoring in vinegars. Use the attractive leaves as a garnish for tomato-based dishes or chop them finely and add them to cream cheese or creamy dressings.

The **STRAWBERRY** (*Fragaria* × *ananassa*) is a short-lived perennial in northern states, but is grown as a winter annual in Florida. It is not usually propagated from seed, but slips (small plants) are readily available. Because you'll be growing them in the winter, make sure you purchase your plants from a local supplier whose cultivars will produce fruit during the short days of winter.

The fruit is not a true berry, botanically speaking, but a swollen receptacle with external seeds. But whatever you call it, the strawberry is a fragile thing and is susceptible to rotting if allowed to touch the bare soil. Traditionally, the plant was heavily mulched with straw to keep the fruit from harm and to keep down the weeds, so people called it a "strawberry."

Even though you can grow the strawberries in the winter in Florida, you will need to protect them from frost. Strawberries are also susceptible to nematodes, slugs, spider mites, and more. In addition, you will probably be sharing your crop with birds, squirrels, and raccoons, but there are ways to plan ahead for the pests, and the rewards are worth it.

Regions: MODERATE, in N, C, S.

Planting: In early fall purchase certified slips or bare-root plants so that you can begin your season with clean stock. For small- or medium-sized operations, you can avoid the soil-borne diseases and weeds by using sterile soil in containers arranged so the stems with the fruit drape over the edges and don't touch the soil. Larger growers create wide rows, alternate the plants down the row, use drip irrigation system, and mulch with plastic. Whichever method you use, the soil should be rich but well drained. Mulch (straw, pine needles, or plastic) is required. After planting, irrigate the new plants every day for at least a week until they are established.

Growing: Full sun or slight shade; more shade in south Florida.

Maintaining: Irrigate with a drip system so that no water gets on the leaves. Irrigate regularly throughout the season because strawberry plants have small root systems and winter is Florida's dry season. Apply some fish or seaweed emulsion several times during the growing season to provide additional micronutrients. Keep the area free of weeds. Once the fruit starts to form, use bird netting and fencing to keep out the larger pests.

Harvesting: Twist the fruits off just before they turn 100 percent red. Handle them with care and use them quickly.

Using: The best strawberries are the ones that are eaten out in the field, but you might want to save some for your favorite strawberry-shortcake recipe or for strawberries and cream.

Solanaceae

The deadly nightshade family (Solanaceae) contains, as its ominous-sounding name suggests, several poisonous members such as the deadly nightshade, tobacco, jimson weed, and mandrake. There are also some poisonous or irritating chemicals in parts of the some of the crop plants. But what a wonderful set of crops! Tomatoes, potatoes, eggplants, tomatillos, and peppers—both sweet bell peppers and hot chiles, which contain one of those irritating chemicals, capsaicin—all belong to this family. And of course, growing your own tomatoes will save you from having to eat those deadly store-bought tomatoes.

The fruits of this family are true berries. Most of the member plants are susceptible to similar pests and diseases. There is no smoking allowed in a nightshade family garden because the smoke can carry tobacco mosaic virus. The tomato hornworm and the Colorado potato beetle larvae will attack any of these crops—pull them off and kill them, but if you see wasp larvae attached to their backs, leave them alone. You want those parasitoid wasps to survive.

EGGPLANT (*Solanum melongena, S. aethiopicum,* and *S. macrocarpon*) is a true, heat-loving perennial from the Mediterranean region that is usually grown as a long-season annual. Originally named for their purple, egg-shaped fruit, the varieties of eggplant offered today come in many shapes and a range of colors including off-white, yellow, and pink. With its neat shrubby growth, fuzzy leaves, purple flowers, and interesting fruits, eggplant is one of the more attractive crops and is suitable for use as a border along a front walkway. Thomas Jefferson is credited for introducing this wonderful crop to our country.

Regions: EASY, in N, C, S.

Planting: Plant eggplant a few weeks after you plant your tomatoes; eggplants will take longer to bear fruit, but will be productive longer into the hot summer months. Even cool weather that doesn't dip below freezing can stunt your eggplant seedlings, so wait until the daily temperature reaches 65°F–70°F before setting them out in the garden. Don't plant too many—once production begins, each plant will yield an abundant crop.

Growing: Grow eggplants in well-drained, rich soil. Because it's a long-season crop, fertilize it with seaweed or fish emulsion two or three times during the season.

Maintaining: Eggplant does not need as much irrigation as tomatoes to produce a good crop, but don't let the soil completely dry out and keep the plants mulched to fend off the weeds. Some of the larger-fruited varieties may need staking. While small-fruited eggplants can produce and carry many fruits, it's a good idea to limit the larger-fruited types to fewer than ten fruits—cut off the extra flowers.

Harvesting: Harvest the fruits with a sharp knife to minimize damage to the plant and to the fruit. You can cut the fruit at any time after it develops good color but before the skin loses its sheen. Fruit that is too mature may turn yellowish. Toss any over-ripe fruit directly onto the compost pile—it will be bitter and seedy.

Using: Eggplant is a prominent ingredient in many standard Mediterranean recipes including eggplant lasagna, eggplant Parmesan, and ratatouille. Eggplant is often used as a meat substitute in vegetarian/vegan recipes; if you add coarsely diced eggplant to your spaghetti sauce, you'll hardly miss the meatballs.

PEPPER or **CHILE PEPPER** (*Capsicum annum* and *C.* spp.) is a perennial crop that's usually grown as a long-season, warm-weather annual. The original, sweet bell peppers were actually an aberration; most peppers contain capsaicin, the irritating chemical that causes spiciness or heat, and that is also used to make pepper spray. The majority of this chemical is contained in the webbing, or the whitish material, around the seeds.

Regions: EASY, in N, C, S.

Planting: Plant your peppers at the same time as or slightly after you plant your spring tomato crop; peppers will take longer to bear fruit, but will be productive right through the hot summer months.

Growing: Grow it in well-drained, rich soil. Because it's a long-season crop, fertilize it with compost, seaweed, or fish emulsion two or three times during the season.

Maintaining: Peppers do not need as much irrigation as tomatoes to produce a good crop, and hot peppers seem to tolerate deficit irrigation better than sweet bell peppers do. Don't let either type of pepper completely dry out, and keep them mulched to fend off the weeds. Many pepper varieties require staking or caging, but there are some small, bushy varieties that are perfect for container gardening.

Harvesting: Harvest the fruit with a sharp knife to minimize damage to the plant and to the fruit. You can cut the fruit off at any stage, but the riper, more colorful fruit will be much sweeter. One pepper plant can provide an amazing number of peppers; continue picking them to keep the plant producing.

Using: Peppers have many uses in the kitchen, including raw in salads and salsas and cooked in stir-fries and soups. If you end up with a peck of peppers to eat, fix some Mediterranean pasta salad or chop the peppers, seal them in a plastic bag, and freeze them for later. Peppers are one of the few vegetables that do not need to be blanched before freezing. However, once they have been frozen, they are best used in cooked foods.

Mediterranean Pasta Salad

1 box macaroni, rotini, ruffles, or shell pasta

2 cups thinly sliced sweet bell peppers, with a small, moderately spicy pepper to taste

1 cup coarsely chopped fresh tomatoes

½ cup finely diced sweet onions

⅓ cup chopped green onion leaves

⅓ cup finely chopped parsley

⅓ cup sliced black olives

⅓ cup roasted sunflower seeds

⅓ cup grated Parmesan cheese

½ cup Feta cheese

Freshly ground pepper, to taste

For the dressing, combine the following ingredients together in a blender or food processor.

1 medium onion, quartered

5 to 8 green onion stalks

⅓ cup chopped basil

¼ cup mayonnaise

⅓ cup plain yogurt

2 teaspoons horseradish

1 part balsamic vinegar and 3 parts olive oil to make the mixture liquid

Boil the pasta for 9 minutes or until cooked but firm (al dente), drain it in a colander, and rinse it with cold water.

Mix all the vegetable ingredients together in a large bowl. Add the cheeses and pasta and, finally, the dressing. Serve immediately, or cover the bowl and store it in the refrigerator. This salad stores well for several days.

The **POTATO** or **IRISH POTATO** (*Solanum tuberosum*) is a tender, vining, cool-weather annual. While native to higher elevations in South America, potatoes are now an important crop worldwide. Americans routinely eat large amounts of potatoes, but when you eat your first freshly dug potato tuber, you'll be surprised at how much flavor they have. Only the tuber is edible; the rest of the plant is poisonous and if the tubers are exposed to light out in the garden, they will turn green and also become poisonous.

Regions: EASY, in N, C, S.

Planting: The seeds are rarely used for propagation, because the potatoes that result are so variable. Use certified seed potatoes, which are disease-free tubers and have not been sprayed with sprout inhibitors like store-bought potatoes have. Unless you purchase them from a local farm-supply store, you may have trouble finding a source for seed potatoes that will ship in time for your Florida crop. Don't depend upon a seed catalog or online company to ship on time—if you receive your seed potatoes in March like the rest of the country, you might as well throw them directly on the compost pile—it's too late to plant them in Florida.

    Because the potato is both a frost-sensitive and a cool-weather crop, you'll need to plant your seed potatoes out in the garden about two weeks before the last frost in north and central Florida, and in fall and through the winter months in south Florida. If a seed potato is small (about the size of a large egg or smaller) don't cut it into pieces. Larger seed potatoes may be cut into smaller pieces, just be sure that each piece has at least one or two "eyes" or growing buds, which are distinct indentations in the tuber. After you cut the seed potatoes into pieces, let the cut edges harden for at least a day before you plant them.

    Plant your seed potatoes about four inches deep in well-prepared soil. After the vines grow about eight or ten inches long, mound soil around each vine so that only the top two or three inches remains exposed. At this point, you may clip off some of the vines to root and plant in order to increase your potato crop. Some growers with raised beds or sandy, well-drained soil dig a trench for the potatoes and fill in soil around the vines until the trench is filled up to the soil level, while other growers build a ridge or a set of mounds as they cover up the vines. You can also use straw for the mound. As the vines grow, continue to mound soil or straw around them. This mounding will keep the tubers under the ground and stimulate more growth of the vines.

Growing: Grow in well-drained, rich soil. Keep soil mounded around the vines.

Maintaining: Irrigate regularly and deeply, but let the ground almost dry out between waterings to discourage fungal diseases.

Harvesting: After the plants flower, you may carefully root around the vines for fingerling potatoes—this is much easier to accomplish if you mound straw around your plants. Removing some of the small tubers should not disturb the plant too much, and it will continue to grow for a while. The final harvest will take place after the vine has died back; some growers leave the potatoes in the soil for at least another two weeks to toughen the skin so that they store better. Some growers use a garden fork to turn over the soil or pull out the whole plant, while others prefer digging by hand so that the tubers are not damaged. This is when you'll be happy that you took the time to deeply prepare the soil at planting time.

Using: Potato: it's what's for dinner, and breakfast, and lunch.

TOMATILLOS (*Physalis philadelphica*), Mexican husk tomatoes (*P. ixocarpa*), husk tomatoes (*P. pubescens*) (a Florida native found throughout the state), and ground cherries or cape gooseberries (*P. peruviana*) are long-season, frost-sensitive annuals that may last for more than one season in south Florida. These species are close relatives of the tomato, but with a papery coating called a husk (modified sepals or the calyx) that forms around the fruit. Once the husk is removed the skin is slightly sticky. The common names are often used interchangeably, but there are real differences in the sweetness of the fruits. The ground cherries are the sweetest and are often used in jams or pies, while the tomatillos (in Spanish, little tomatoes) are tangy and used in salsa verde.

Regions: EASY, in N, C, S.

Planting: Plant these crops when you plant your tomatoes; tomatillos will take longer to produce fruit but they might last through the hot summer months. To produce fruit, the flowers need to be pollinated by a separate, not cloned, plant, so you will need to plant at least two or three plants within twenty feet of each other. Don't plant too many, unless you're in the business of producing salsa verde.

Growing: Grow tomatillos as you would a tomato.

Maintaining: Tomatillos do not need as much irrigation as tomatoes do to produce a good crop, but keep them mulched to fend off the weeds. Tomatillo stems are weaker than tomato stems and are prone to cracking when handled or placed under too much weight, so tie the branches to a trellis with a wide, soft cloth before they get too heavy. Cages may also work.

Harvesting: You can pick the fruit after the husk begins to turn tan. Store the fruit in a cool place with the husk intact.

Using: Remove the husk once you are ready to use the fruit. Tomatillos can be eaten raw in salads, added to stir-fries (at the last minute), cooked in soups, but are most often featured in salsas—with or without tomatoes.

Green Salsa in the Blender

If you desire, add a big handful of cilantro, or a teaspoon of toasted and ground cumin. Make this salsa your own by adjusting the proportions to your liking.

10 tomatillos
½ onion
Juice of 1 lime, or to taste
Sea salt, to taste
Hot peppers, to taste

Blend until relatively smooth. Serve with tortilla chips.

The **TOMATO** (*Solanum lycopersicum*) is a classic crop plant that every gardener wants to grow because store-bought tomatoes are less than delicious. Gardeners transplanted from northern parts of the country may be surprised and disappointed by Florida's pitifully short tomato season.

When the nighttime temperatures remain consistently above 70°F, the fruit stops setting and various fungal wilts and root-knot nematodes weaken the plants, causing the leaves to die; at this point you will have to harvest all the remaining fruit. Trash the plants or set them out with the yard waste—don't add them to your compost pile.

There are hundreds of varieties of tomatoes: the indeterminate varieties require staking or trellising because they are vining and will continue to grow throughout the season, while the determinate types are bushier and may not need support. Look for heat-tolerant varieties with fungus and nematode resistance that have been bred specifically for Florida. Some cherry tomatoes, such as the tiny Everglades tomato, have adjusted to Florida's climate on their own. (Despite the rumors, the Everglades tomato is neither native to Florida nor a separate species.) Some growers have had success producing a grafted tomato seedling, with a desirable heirloom fruiting plant on the top and a sturdy, fungus-resistant rootstock on the bottom. Your goal is to find tomato types that produce a big harvest quickly; this way, you can enjoy the fruits of your labor before the problems set in. Keep good notes on which seeds or seedlings worked best for your garden.

Regions: MODERATE, in N, C, S.

Planting: For a spring crop in north and central Florida, sow your seeds six to eight weeks before the last frost. In south Florida, plant your seeds in the early fall so that they are ready as soon as the weather cools off. If you start your plants in flats, pot them up into larger pots; keep them fertilized with seaweed emulsion, worm castings, or fish emulsion; and keep them in excellent light. This way you'll have healthy seedlings that are ten to twelve inches tall. When you're ready to set them out in the garden, plant them deeper than they were in the pot, burying much of the stem. That said, if you've purchased grafted tomato seedlings, be sure to keep the graft well above the soil line—only the tough rootstock plant should touch the soil. Build an irrigation swale around each plant to let the water soak in. Plan to trellis large or indeterminate types to keep your tomatoes off the ground.

Some small growers plant determinate tomatoes upside down in hanging pots to avoid problems with nematodes, and to reduce maintenance—no weeds and no staking. You'll need a strong support system, a five-gallon bucket with a three-quarter-inch hole in the bottom, a sheet of coconut fiber, and sterile, bagged soil and compost. To maximize your crop space, plant basil in the top of the bucket.

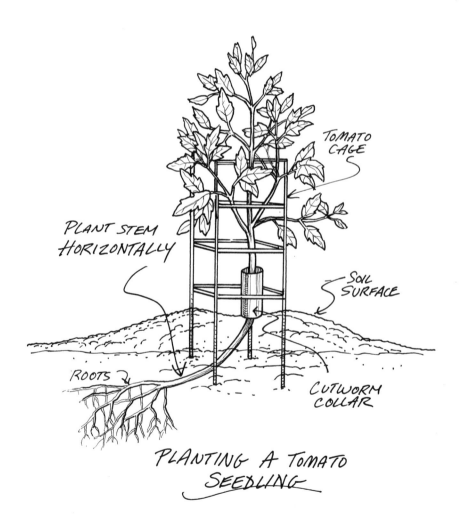

TOMATO CAGE

PLANT STEM HORIZONTALLY

SOIL SURFACE

ROOTS

CUTWORM COLLAR

PLANTING A TOMATO SEEDLING

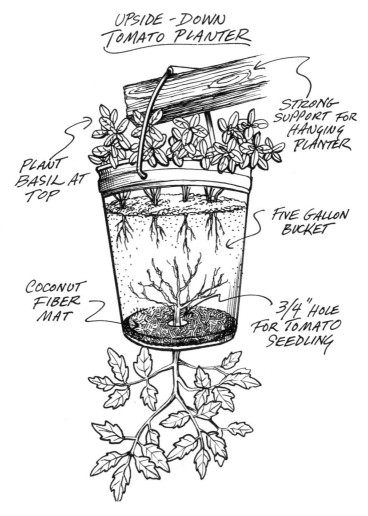

UPSIDE - DOWN
TOMATO PLANTER

STRONG
SUPPORT FOR
HANGING
PLANTER

PLANT
BASIL AT
TOP

FIVE GALLON
BUCKET

COCONUT
FIBER
MAT

3/4" HOLE
FOR TOMATO
SEEDLING

In north and central Florida start the seeds for your fall crop toward the end of the summer. These seedlings will grow faster because of the heat, but time your planting so that the nights are cooler by the time they are ready to bloom. You may be able to have fresh tomatoes for Thanksgiving and Christmas!

Growing: Grow tomatoes in full sun in rich soil with good levels of micronutrients, especially calcium.

Maintaining: Irrigate regularly and deeply, so that you grow well-formed fruit. Either irregular irrigation or a lack of calcium can cause blossom-end rot. Keep the area free of weeds and mulch heavily to keep the soil moist and to moderate the soil temperature. Trim back the bottom leaves and any new shoots or suckers that appear below the first blossom branch; early in the season, you can root the suckers in damp sand if you need more plants. Some people claim that adding some table salt around the tomatoes produces a tastier fruit. Salt stresses the plant and probably causes the fruit to store less water, but this is probably not a good practice because table salt is an herbicide and will build up in the soil. Instead, experiment with less irrigation near harvest time to induce stress without adding salt to the soil.

Harvesting: You can pick the fruit once it's more than half ripe and let it finish ripening inside, but not in the refrigerator. This way, you'll be less likely to share your harvest with the birds and squirrels that are attracted to the red color.

Using: You may end up with a lot of tomatoes to use all at once. The tomatoes you don't use right away can be canned, dried, frozen, or turned into salsa.

Easy Fresh Tomato Salsa

Dice, or process into small pieces using short pulses in the food processor, the following ingredients:

3 large tomatoes, or enough small ones to fill 2 cups
1 medium green pepper
1 medium onion
Hot peppers of your choice, to taste (or omit if you don't like the heat!)
1 finely chopped bunch of cilantro, or to taste
Sea salt, to taste
Juice of 2 fresh limes, or to taste

Allowing the salsa to sit for an hour will meld the flavors, but who can wait? The bright, fresh flavors on crunchy tortilla chips are delicious!

Tropaeolaceae

The nasturtium family (Tropaeolaceae) is closely related to the mustard family. The only crop in this family is the garden nasturtium—not to be confused with watercress (*Nasturtium* spp.).

NASTURTIUM (*Tropaeolum majus*) is an edible garden annual that's widely planted in and around vegetable gardens to attract pollinators and to repel nematodes.

Regions: EASY, in N, C, S.

Planting: Sow the seeds directly in the garden after the last frost and every three or four weeks up until a month before frost sets in again. This way you'll be sure to have a fresh batch of young plants throughout the hot summer. In frost-free zones nasturtiums may be grown as short-lived perennials.

Growing: Grow nasturtiums in full sun or as an understory plant in the shade of taller crops such as tomatoes, peppers, or okra.

Maintaining: Given adequate irrigation, they require no special maintenance—they are easy-care and decorative. If they are grown in a richer soil with above-average irrigation, they'll reward you with larger leaves and more flowers.

Harvesting: You can pick the flowers as soon as they appear, but wait until the plant is well established before you harvest the leaves.

Using: All parts of this peppery plant are edible. Cooks love to use the flowers as garnish, but they can also add a colorful zing to salads and other dishes, or stuffed with a cheese mixture and fried. The leaves can also be added to salads or to cooked greens.

Zingiberaceae

The ginger family (Zingiberaceae) contains a number of popular ornamental and medicinal species, but ginger is the most familiar edible crop in this family. Actually, ginger has also traditionally been used for medicinal purposes—your mother may have given you ginger ale when you were nauseated.

GINGER (*Zingiber officinale*) is a tropical perennial that grows from enlarged rhizomes (underground stems).

Regions: MODERATE, in N, C; EASY, in S.

Planting: Purchase "seed" rhizomes or organic ginger from a market. Make sure the rhizomes are not totally dried out and have some eyes (like potato eyes), which are the growth points. Plant the rhizomes in a partly shady area in rich but well-drained soil. You can divide the seed rhizome as along as each piece has one or two eyes. Plant them about an inch deep, cover them with soil, and then mulch the area.

In south Florida, plant the rhizomes in areas that are mostly shady; some gardeners grow them on the north side of a permanently trellised crop. In frost-prone areas, plant ginger in large, deep containers that can be moved indoors for the winter or grow it as a long-season annual, planting saved rhizomes a couple of weeks before the last frost and harvesting through the late fall until frost sets in again.

Growing: Grow ginger in an out-of-the-way section of your garden where it won't interfere with your crop rotation.

Maintaining: Keep moist, but not wet.

Harvesting: Harvest in the late fall or early winter. Gently dig up the rhizomes, take what you need, and either replant the rest or seal the planting stock in a plastic bag, put it in an opaque container, and store it in the refrigerator for the winter.

Using: Ginger has some kick, although fresh young ginger has a milder flavor than the older rhizomes sold in stores. It is often used in spicy Asian recipes, and you can also finely grate the dry rhizome to make your own ginger for a gingerbread castle.

TURMERIC (*Curcuma longa*) is a tropical perennial grown from enlarged rhizomes. Turmeric rhizomes for planting are not widely sold, but you may purchase them from the produce section of specialty or natural foods markets. Asian stores, especially those offering South Asian foods (i.e., from India, Sri Lanka, Pakistan), often carry them. Make sure the rhizomes are fresh, not dried.

Regions: MODERATE, in N, C; EASY, in S.

Planting: Like ginger, plant turmeric in a partly shady area in rich but well-drained soil. Plant the rhizomes about an inch deep, cover them with soil, and then mulch the area.

In south Florida, plant the rhizomes in semi- to almost-full shade, in an area that has been enriched with compost. The large leaves grow on short stems and are quite attractive. You may get a ginger-like flower. In frost-prone areas, plant turmeric in large, deep containers that can be moved indoors for the winter or grow it as a long-season annual, planting saved rhizomes a couple of weeks before the last frost and harvesting through the late fall until the frost returns.

Growing: Grow turmeric in an out-of-the-way section of your garden where it won't interfere with your crop rotation, perhaps under the shade of tall trees.

Maintaining: Keep moist but not wet.

Harvesting: Harvest turmeric in the late fall or early winter. Gently dig up the rhizomes, take what you need, and either replant the rest or seal the planting stock in a plastic bag, put it in an opaque container, and store it in the refrigerator for the winter.

Using: Turmeric is widely used for its medicinal properties. It can be grated fresh into dishes that call for dried turmeric. The leaves are used for wrapping and steaming Asian foods and in some curries.

Crops Not Recommended for Florida Gardeners

Artichoke (*Cynara scolymus*) requires cool summers and is rarely grown outside of California.

Asparagus (*Asparagus officinalis*) generally requires reliably cold soil for at least six weeks. Florida's erratic winter temperatures do not reliably provide this environment, but, in spite of this, some Florida growers have had success.

Beebalm or bergamot (Monarda didyma) seems to suffer in Florida's heat and humidity and is prone to mildew, but you might try it if you're in north Florida.

Horseradish (*Amoracia rusticana*) only grows as far south as USDA zone 8. It needs a reliable winter so that it can lay dormant.

Lavender (*Lavandula angustifolia*) only grows as far south as USDA zone 8. Most of Florida is too hot for a good lavender crop.

Quinoa (*Chenopodium quinoa*; pronounced keen-wa) can be grown easily in Florida, but the bitter soapy covering on the seeds (saponin) is difficult to remove, so harvesting and using is not easy. (Commercial quinoa has the saponin removed.) If you want to give quinoa a try, follow the directions for amaranth.

Rhubarb (*Rheum rhabarbarum*) requires a deeper cold season than is available in Florida.

Taro (*Colocasia esculenta*) and malanga (*Xanthosoma sagittifolium*) are both members of the arum family (Araceae) and have been widely planted as crops, especially in south Florida, but both have become invasive pest plants. You should remove these plants from your property, but you can harvest the edible corms (bulb-like swollen stems) when you do so. There are plenty of other crops to choose from that are not harmful to Florida's wild spaces.

Resources

For IFAS recommendations for crop varieties that work well for Florida, go to http://edis.ifas.ufl.edu/topic_vegetable_gardening.

For some great ideas for growing vegetables in the heat, see www.tropicalpermaculture.com.

If you're looking for a public seed bank where you can find unusual vegetable seeds, check out www.jlhudsonseeds.net and www.echonet.org.

The Florida Exotic Pest Plant Council lists invasive plants that are harmful to Florida's wild areas. Some of these, such as wild taro, were once widely planted crops. For more information, go to www.fleppc.org.

6

Harvesting, Handling, and Seed Saving

Whether you are growing edibles for your own family, the local soup kitchen, or a farmers market, handling your crops safely is an important step in protecting your harvest from damage and contamination. Chapter 5 offered specific harvesting suggestions for each crop, but this chapter covers some overall best practices for handling your beautiful and bountiful harvest.

Saving seeds is another type of harvest you may wish to consider. To perpetuate the best open-pollinated or self-pollinating crops for your particular location, let the best-looking plants bolt (go to flower) and leave some of the very best fruits that you'd otherwise wish to pick for your seed stock. After three years of saving your own seed, you'll have selected for the best qualities specific to your growing environment and will have become your own seed breeder.

Harvesting Your Crop

This is the best part of organic gardening for many people—enjoying the literal fruits of their labor. It is a gardener's delight to skip the grocery store and instead make a trip to the garden for a meal.

As you survey your daily harvest, you may find yourself planning your meals around the available vegetables rather than a meat course.

They taste so much better right out of the garden. Vegetables—they're what's for dinner, and lunch, and maybe even breakfast!

Let's Talk Tools

There are many specialized tools for harvesting, like lettuce knives, grape hooks, broccoli knives, onion shears, serrated greens knives, field knives, baskets, trugs, hods, broadforks, scythes, machetes, greens harvesters, chamomile forks, potato diggers, tomato shears, and more, but you really only need three basic items for harvesting:

- A sharp knife
- Shears or pruners
- Lightweight, portable container(s) with a smooth interior surface

Unless the fruit or vegetable simply falls into your hands, resist the urge to harvest by pulling something off a vine or stem, as this can cause damage to the plant and the vegetable. Use a knife, garden shears, or pruners to safely separate the crop from the plant.

A knife will be one of your most-used tools. It will cut broccoli or cauliflower heads cleanly, and it is best for bok choy and celery, which need to be cut at the top of the root. Your knife is also the best tool to use for many other crops: lettuce heads, leaf lettuce, arugula, French sorrel, Asian greens like mizuna, and other greens. It may be easier to get into a tight spot between a stem and a fruit like zucchini or cucumbers with a knife than with garden shears. Carry your knife with you into the garden, either in a sheath or inside the harvesting container for safety's sake. Keep it sharpened, and consider cleaning it with alcohol between crops to avoid spreading disease. The easiest way to clean it is to dip it in 70–100 percent alcohol. You'll need a bottle with lid and a washable towel for drying the knife between cuts.

Garden shears or pruners can be used for snipping herbs, cutting kale or collard green leaves, cutting peas from vines, and harvesting eggplants or tomatoes.

When preparing to harvest, it's also best to bring a container with you in order to safely hold your bounty, even if you plan to harvest just one or two items. You may end up harvesting more than you intended when newly ripened produce begs to be cut from the vine. You don't want to be unprepared.

A basket works well for many people who harvest and then go immediately to the kitchen. It can be carried in one hand and will hold your cutting tools. Take care to choose a basket with smooth surfaces that can be easily cleaned. That willow or wicker basket may be attractive, but it might injure the produce you harvested first and that now sits at the bottom of the full basket—think of a tomato skin rubbing against it.

Those colorful, flexible garden trugs, hods, or tubs that gardening suppliers sell are easily cleaned and have carrying handles. You might

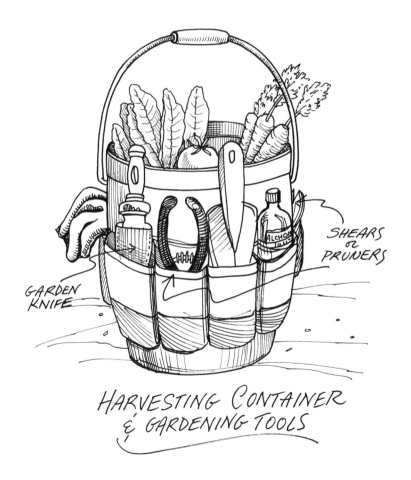

SHEARS
or
PRUNERS

GARDEN
KNIFE

HARVESTING CONTAINER
& GARDENING TOOLS

want to invest in one or more, especially if you will be selling your crops at a farmers market or elsewhere. Farmers use ventilated plastic totes, which can be pricey, but you may find something similar. Whatever you use, keep it lightweight because a few pounds of container added to a few pounds of produce become heavy quickly. Keep it easy and enjoyable, and don't create unnecessary work for yourself.

When to Harvest

To ensure that the vegetables you grow are of the highest quality, you need to harvest them at their peak maturity. This is often slightly before the fruit reaches full coloration or before it gets too large. It can be difficult to determine when vegetables have reached their peak for harvesting. You don't want them to rot on the vine and, usually, you won't want to harvest the vegetable too early. You may make an exception if you're saving what you can before a predicted frost or hurricane. As you gain experience with certain crops, you'll learn to recognize the best time to harvest them.

Vegetables continue their life processes even after they are picked. If your vegetables are fully mature at harvest, you will need to slow their life processes by chilling them. Immature produce such as green tomatoes can be stored at room temperature to enhance the ripening process. Except for reasons of ripening or drying, storage does not improve a vegetable's quality.

Be Nice to Your Veggies

Rough handling can injure your vegetables internally or create an open wound that could serve as an entry point for bacteria and fungi. Internal injury will cause produce to rot quickly. In a tomato study published in *Journal of the American Society for Horticulture Science*, 100 percent of "breaker" tomatoes, green tomatoes just starting to turn red, suffered moderate to severe damage from internal bruising when dropped from a height of only eight inches. Internal bruising is apparent only after the tomato becomes ripe, and causes the fruit to rot quickly.

Decay organisms enter through injuries to the surface of a fruit or vegetable. While the garden is full of hostile bacteria, viruses, fungi, and other microscopic organisms, plants and the edible parts they produce are resistant to most of them. Many beneficial organisms are produced in the garden as well, especially in an organic garden that has a good balance of life forms. Even so, a cut or puncture to a harvested fruit or vegetable is an invitation to decay organisms. The best defense against them is to be gentle with your produce and to avoid damaging it.

Food Safety

Food safety may be the main reason you have chosen to grow some of your own produce. With outbreaks of food-borne illness, caused by *E. coli*, Salmonella, Shigella, and other organisms, it is not surprising that more people want to manage their food from seed (or seedling) to plate.

Once a pathogen has contaminated your produce, it is difficult, if not impossible, to kill or remove it, so taking precautions to prevent this contamination is especially important. Food safety in the garden is much like food safety on a farm. Even very small farms follow Good Agricultural Practices (GAPs), a national program administered by Cornell University that trains farmers and farm workers on food safety. A local inspector may arrive on a farm to conduct a GAPs audit at any time. It is a good idea for gardeners to follow the basics of these practices as well.

Manure Guidelines

Animal and human feces are the largest sources of pathogens on produce, but some basic guidelines will keep them from being a problem. Especially in organic gardening, animal manures from herbivores (cows, horses, rabbits) and fowl are a great source of nutrients and organic matter for soil building and for fertilization, and they can be used safely (manure from meat eaters cannot). In organic production, fresh manure can be composted for use on vegetables within a relatively short time. Composting heats up the manure (and other composted materials) to temperatures between 131°F and 170°F, which, after three to fifteen days at that temperature, kills pathogens that could be harmful to humans. If you apply fresh manure to a crop, organic standards dictate that it must be done no later than 120 days before harvest if the edible part of the crop comes in contact with the soil (roots crops, pumpkins, etc.), and 90 days if the edible part of the plant is above the soil (tomatoes, eggplants, broccoli, etc.). Most organic farms use composted manures as fertilizer to avoid these prolonged times between application and harvest. Sometimes, however, animals will leave their fresh manure in your garden uninvited. As a precaution against this, surround your garden with barriers that keep wild and domestic animals out.

If you regularly work with raw or partially composted manures, designate a pair of boots and a pair of gloves for this purpose and do not wear them when working in and around your planting areas. Also, wash your work clothes after you come into contact with uncomposted manure.

Clean Water

Cleanliness on the farm or in the garden starts with the water you use. Contaminated water is responsible for most cases of food-borne illness that is attributable to produce. The Food and Drug Administration states: "Wherever water comes into contact with fresh produce, its quality dictates the potential for pathogen contamination." You should always use clean water for anything you do in the garden. Both well water and city water should be potable. If it's clean enough to drink, it's clean enough for irrigation, for mixing with seaweed extracts or other organic fertilizers, for washing produce, or for cleaning harvesting tools like baskets or bins. Organic gardeners may wish to use clean but nonchlorinated water such as well water or rain barrel water, as chlorine may kill beneficial organisms in soil. If you do use rain barrel water, have it tested annually to be sure it is safe.

Clean People

Anyone working in a garden or on a farm should practice good hygiene and stay away when sick. Make sure to thoroughly wash your hands after using the bathroom and before going into the garden. Unwashed or inadequately washed hands can carry traces of human feces or pathogens; hands that are not thoroughly washed shouldn't touch the produce. If you have an open wound, either cover it or stay out of the garden until it has healed. Garden gloves can also carry pathogens from compost or soil to produce. Change or remove them if necessary. Teach children good garden hygiene.

Do You Know How to Wash Your Hands?

Don't laugh—most people think they do, but they really don't!

1. Use soap and warm running water. Special antibacterial soaps are not needed!
2. Wet your hands.
3. Apply the soap.
4. Vigorously rub your hands up to your elbows for twenty seconds. Measure twenty seconds by singing the Happy Birthday song twice while rubbing.
5. Rinse your hands well.
6. Turn off the water with a paper towel, not with your bare hands.
7. Dry your hands with a paper towel, or allow them to air dry. Do not share towels.

Cleanliness in the Garden

Harvesting equipment should be thoroughly washed, both before it is used and before it is stored to ensure that it is clean when it is time to use it again—this includes baskets, bins, knives, and shears. Place harvested produce into containers, not on the ground. Remove as much dirt from harvested plants as possible while in the garden. Don't throw rotted produce where it could attract disease carriers like rats. Compost it and follow good composting procedures. When washing your

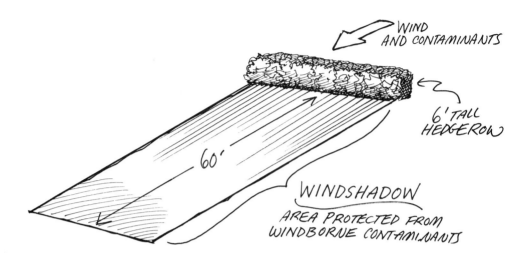

produce, use clean water. If the water gets dirty, change it. Follow the good post-harvest practices described above.

Sometimes pathogens are carried in the dust blowing in the air. Consider the following scenario: A dog poops in an alley a block from your garden. After a few days of cars and trucks running over it, the poop is pulverized. A stiff breeze whips down the alley, carrying the poop powder far and wide—including onto your lovely produce. One way to avoid contamination from your neighborhood is to plant a hedgerow between the alley, or similar source of potential contaminants, and your garden. Its dense foliage will catch most of the windborne dust, which may also include other types of air pollution like pesticides. A ten-foot-tall hedge provides a one-hundred-foot-long wind shadow. Of course, hedgerows are also important to have near your garden because they provide a habitat for the pollinators and predators in the ecosystem in and around your garden.

Cleanliness in the Kitchen

When cutting or cooking your produce, wash your hands before you begin to work. Do the same after going to the bathroom; touching parts of your body; coughing or sneezing; touching a garbage can, the floor, or other potentially contaminated surface; and touching raw meat or eggs. Make sure all work surfaces are clean and sanitized. Use separate cutting boards for meat and produce. These practices will minimize the risk of contamination.

Field Cooling and Storage

Farmers have learned that reducing the heat that crops retain from the field after harvest (known as field heat) preserves their quality and post-harvest life. You can think of this like shelf life, but since vegetables don't typically sit on a shelf, we use "post-harvest" to refer to a vegetable's life from field to fork, which may involve transport and refrigeration at various points. The agriculture industry employs sophisticated methods to meet its standard of removing seven-eighths of the heat left in the crops after harvest. This is called pre-cooling or field cooling, which is different from longer-term refrigeration. Pre-cooling is the first link in the "cold chain," and is followed by refrigeration during transport and storage. Breaking the cold chain shortens a crop's post-harvest life.

The home gardener, who will likely use the crop almost immediately after harvesting it, may not need to worry about this. But gardeners who wish to sell their produce at a farmers market or provide produce to others should know about field cooling. This knowledge can make the difference between your recipient opening a box of wilted veggies and a box of fresh ones.

To understand pre-cooling, let's take a look at what happens on a farm, where vegetables are often packed into boxes right in the field. Take green beans, for example: on an 85°F day, the temperature of the green beans will be 85°F. Pack those beans into a box, and we now have several layers of green beans at 85°F. The box becomes a slow cooker, and unless they are cooled, the green beans will quickly become partially cooked rather than fresh. At least seven-eighths of the field heat must be removed within a few hours of harvest. The final optimum storage temperature for green beans is between 40°F and 45°F. Pre-cooling that box of beans by 40°F within a few hours increases its post-harvest life from one day to nine days. This cooling can be achieved with hydro-cooling, which essentially involves bathing the entire box of beans in potable chilled water until temperature is reduced to about 50°F. After their bath, the beans will continue to cool under refrigeration.

Home gardeners should take care to reduce the amount of field heat in their vegetables after harvest by bringing them into an air-conditioned home or at least into the shade for the few hours between harvest and refrigerator or table. A cold water bath before refrigeration would be beneficial for the following crops, if they aren't harvested for immediate cooking: sweet corn, broccoli, green beans, summer squash, cucumber, kale, collards, and other leafy greens. Leafy greens will actually perk up and be much crisper with a cold-water bath.

Some produce—strawberries, onions, garlic, potatoes, and herbs—should never get wet after harvest. Most herbs should not get wet, but can have their stems cut and placed into a container of water. Basil should never be stored below 50°F because its leaf edges will turn black. Some heartier herbs like rosemary and thyme hold up well without any special attention.

Once your produce is refrigerated, keep it that way until you use it. Temperature fluctuations promote decay and increase shriveling in produce. For example, don't think that you can take a bushel of broccoli out of the refrigerator, display it for sale at a farmers market, and then put the unsold broccoli back in the refrigerator in order to sell it at a market the next day. Your customers will not be happy when their supposedly fresh broccoli turns yellow and then brown the next day. While the broccoli may have been only two days old, the temperature fluctuations hastened its decay. Broccoli is sensitive to increases in temperature, so if you will have it out for sale at a farmers market, put it into a container or cold box, and place a layer of ice directly on top of the broccoli. Humidity levels are important, too, as some crops dry out faster than others, or have a thinner protective layer of cells. The crisper drawer keeps a higher relative humidity than the rest of the refrigerator. Store crops needing high humidity (that is, 95–100 percent humidity) in the crisper; if the crisper is full, put them in a thick zip-lock-type plastic bag.

In summary here are the basic practices for extending the post-harvest life of your vegetables:

- Make sure your hands, and any tools and containers you use, are clean.
- Handle your produce gently.
- Cool your produce soon after harvest if you are not preparing to eat it right away.
- Keep your produce cool and avoid letting it dry out.

Seed Saving

Before the advent of seed companies, farmers and gardeners had only two sources of seed for their next season's crops: their own harvest or another farmer's harvest. Most of our modern-day crops are available due to the hard work of earlier civilizations and their farmers. But now that we do have seed companies—which have spent millions of dollars on developing hybrid seeds with better germination rates, heat resistance, and disease or pest-resistance—you may decide that their specialized seeds are the better choice. On the other hand, you may long for the good taste of an heirloom crop that's available only from seed-saving groups. You might also save some money by saving your own seed.

Keep in mind that you won't be eating the plants from which you harvest seed, so plant some extra and sacrifice some of the prime fruits or plants. Harvesting your own seed may also translate into a lot of extra time in the garden waiting for your edibles to reach the seed stage, particularly for biennials like carrots and parsley.

Please note that some crop varieties, particularly corn and peanuts, are legally protected through plant variety protections and plant patents. For some varieties, growers are permitted to save only enough seed for their own needs; for others, growers are not allowed to save seed even for their own use. If you're growing patented products, know the rules to avoid legal repercussions.

Hybrid vs. Open-Pollinated Crops

Hybrids are the result of deliberately crossing two distinct cultivars. The seed companies promise that their F1 hybrids are more vigorous and uniform than open-pollinated varieties. Because seed from hybrids can be sterile or produce plants that differ dramatically from their parents, the seed producers ensure repeat business. They control the original parent plants and only they can produce this hybrid seed. Many corn varieties and other crops are hybrids. To be sure, check the package to see if it says "F1 hybrid."

Open-pollinated or self-pollinated (i.e., F2) plants are not hybrids, so you may be able to successfully save seed from these plants for later use. But when plants are open-pollinated by insects, they often cross with others within their family. A melon could cross with a cucumber or a broccoli could cross with a cauliflower. Sometimes these crosses have interesting results, like the broccoflower, but sometimes the offspring bear no fruit, have fruit with no seeds, or have unusable fruit. The only way to maintain the original variety is to isolate each type of plant, either by large distances or by hand pollinating and bagging each flower and fruit. Isolation is usually impractical in a home garden unless you plant only one member of a family. But what fun would that be?

Self-pollinated (or mostly self-pollinated) plants—such as those in the bean family (Fabaceae), the nightshade family (Solanaceae), the mallow family (Malvaceae) and the lettuces in the daisy family (Asteraceae)—give you the greatest chances of success in your seed production.

Leave crops from the bean family on the vine until the pod dries; this should occur between four and six weeks after the eating stage. Be sure to harvest the pods before they break and the seed disperses. If frost threatens, pull entire plant, root first, and hang it in a cool, dry location until the pods are brown. A small number of pods can be opened by hand, but for larger amounts, you'll need to lay out the pods and thrash them with a broom or rubber hose, and then either handpick the seeds or sift them to remove the chaff.

For okra in the mallow family, let the pods dry on the plant, taking care to catch them before they drop. Then, air-dry the seeds on absorbent paper for another week or two before packaging.

For lettuces, you can harvest a few of the outside leaves before the plant bolts without harming seed production. Allow the seed heads to dry for at least two weeks after flowering. Often, individual flower heads will ripen at different times. You can shake small amounts of seed into a paper bag from the individual flower heads each day, leaving the unripened seed on the plant until it is ready. For larger amounts, wait until at least half of the flowers on each plant have gone to seed. Cut off the entire top of the plant and allow it to dry upside down in an open paper bag.

Even though peppers, tomatoes, and eggplants normally self-pollinate, it's not at all unusual for insects to carry pollen from one plant to another. The biggest surprise that awaits the seed saver occurs when a hot pepper crosses with a sweet one; you won't be able to tell by eating the pepper or the seeds whether next year's crop will be hot or not. It's best to keep your pepper varieties as least fifty feet apart. To save seeds from peppers, shake or scrape out the seeds from ripened fruits that have turned red or orange. Spread the seeds out on absorbent paper in a dry location for about a week before packaging.

Similarly, harvest seed from tomatoes by cutting across the fruit so that all the seed chambers are opened, and then scrape out the seeds. You can use the rest of the tomato for sauce or you can dry it along with the seeds. Tomato seeds are covered in a gelatinous coating that you will need to remove. Place the seeds along with their jelly into a small jar, add enough water to make the mass liquid, cover the jar (but don't seal it), and then place it in a warm location, for about three days. Stir the mixture once a day.

After two days, a layer of gunk will form on the top of the mixture. The gunk is actually a fungus that feeds on the seed jelly and produces antibiotics that help to prevent seed-borne diseases like bacterial spot, canker, and speck. After three days, fill the seed container with warm water. Let the contents settle and then slowly pour out the water with the fungal growth and any immature seeds floating on top. The viable seeds are heavier and will settle to the bottom of the jar. Add some more clean water and slowly pour the floaters off. When you have only clean seeds left, strain them from the water, spread them out on absorbent paper, and allow them to dry completely (this usually takes a day or two).

Storing Seed

Once your seed is thoroughly dried, gently hand rub it to get rid of any chaff, and then store it in a labeled envelope or a small labeled, sealable plastic bag in a cool, dry, rodent-free place. An opaque container stored in the refrigerator works well. Some serious seed savers invest in a second refrigerator to be used solely for seed and long-term produce storage—it serves as a substitute root cellar.

The seed will germinate best the following year. Thereafter, germination rates decline—by how much depends upon storage conditions, seed type, and original seed quality. If you can, and if it's not too difficult to save a particular type of seed, plant all the seed each year and then repeat the process for next-year's crop.

If you end up with an abundance of seed, you could participate in a seed-saver or exchange program. When you acquire seeds from others through these exchanges, you may find that the quality and germination rates vary wildly, so proceed with your eyes open. If you've handled the seed, you will at least know how it's been treated; when others have handled the seed, you just won't know. Many people have had good experiences with informally saved seed, but it might not be a good idea to bet your entire harvest on these seeds.

Develop Your Own Plant Breeds

After three or more years of selecting for the best seeds grown in your garden under your particular conditions, you will have chosen the varieties that are uniquely yours. Seed companies have highly controlled fields, which probably don't come close to approximating the conditions you are dealing with, especially here in Florida. Perhaps we should start a Florida-only seed-swapping group.

Resources

S. A. Sargent, M. A. Ritenour, J. K. Brecht, and J. A. Bartz, "Handling, Cooling and Sanitation Techniques for Maintaining Postharvest Quality," http://edis.ifas.ufl.edu/pdffiles/CV/CV11500.pdf (2007).

Steven A. Sargent and Danielle Treadwell, "Guide for Maintaining the Quality and Safety of Organic Vegetables and Melons During Harvest and Handling Operations," http://edis.ifas.ufl.edu/hs396 (2009).

Amy Simonne and Danielle Treadwell, "Minimizing Food Safety Hazards for Organic Growers," http://edis.ifas.ufl.edu/document_fy1062 (2009).

For information for organic farmers that readers may also find useful, go to the Florida Small Farms and Alternative Enterprises website at http://smallfarms.ifas.ufl.edu/organic_production/organic_vegetables.html.

For basic food safety information from the FDA, go to http://www.fda.gov/food/guidancecomplianceregulatoryinformation/guidancedocuments/produceandplanproducts/ucm064458.htm.

For Good Agricultural Practices (GAPs), go to http://www.gaps.cornell.edu.

Also check out the International Seed Saving Institute, based in Idaho, http://www.seedsave.org.

And the Seed Savers Exchange, based in Iowa, http://www.seedsavers.org.

Weeds, Crop Rotation, and Cover Crops

What Is a Weed?

A weed is essentially a plant that's growing in an inappropriate place. In a vegetable plot, if it sprouts and you didn't plant it, it's probably a weed. In some cases you may have planted an aggressive perennial plant like mint that later becomes a weed. In most of Florida's habitats, plants—lots of them—will sprout within a few days after the soil is disturbed. Our warm climate provides excellent conditions for maintaining a huge seed bank that can remain viable in the soil for many years. Weeds are pests because they take moisture and nutrients from the soil and crowd out crops. They may also provide a habitat for other pests after your vegetable crops have been harvested. Weeds are also pests because your efforts to eradicate them or prevent their appearance can empty your wallet and strain your back.

Which Ones Are Weeds?

When you plant seeds in your edible garden, how do you know which are your crop seedlings and which are weed seedlings? The larger seedlings like squash and peas are pretty hard to miss; tiny seedlings, on the other hand, are much harder to spot. Here's one way to help learn your weeds. After preparing your garden for seeding (whether it's a wide row, a square foot, a mound, or a container), treat a test plot in the same manner as you would your seeded plots, but don't plant anything in it. When plants start sprouting, compare your unplanted test plot with the area where you've planted crop seeds. The seedlings that grow in the test plot are most likely weeds. Nevertheless, you may still want to bring in an experienced gardener to help you to identify which ones are the weeds, because there may be some desirable volunteers as well. The seedlings in your planted area that match your weeds in the test area are most likely weeds that can be removed.

If you're using a combination of garden soil, compost, and composted manures, you will have to contend with weeds. If you're using a sterilized soil combination in a raised bed, you will likely see very few weed seedlings at first, but some will drop in during the season. Learning to identify weeds at the seedling stage will save you countless hours in the future.

Weed Strategies

As with other pests, your goal is to make your landscape inhospitable to the weeds without compromising the habitat for your desirable plants. If you are sowing seeds directly in the ground or in containers, use a sterilized top-dressing, such as vermiculite or shredded coir, to allow your seeds to sprout without immediate competition from weeds. As the desired seeds sprout, mulch around them, but don't allow the mulch to touch their stems. Remove any weeds that do grow when they are small, and definitely before they bloom or go to seed.

Tough Weeds

First, a word about the really tough weeds. These are the weeds with deep strong roots or tubers such as catbrier, Florida betony, wild taro, nutsedge, and torpedo grass. They can grow through any mulch in a heartbeat. At least you can eat the Florida betony's weird white tubers—they add a radish-like crunch to your salads.

Learn which weeds in your area have deep roots by using your shovel. The plants with taproots may be difficult to remove, but once they're pulled or dug out, they won't grow back again. It's the plants with deep rhizomes (i.e., underground stems) and tubers that are the most difficult to eradicate. They can grow back quickly unless you extract every last piece of root from the soil.

You must remove or block these garden aggressors from the area, including from the pathways between the beds, before you can even think of planting crops there. Blocking them may not be all that helpful; many tough weeds will grow right through weed barrier cloth. The aggressive roots of torpedo grass, taro, and others will travel underneath barriers or even five-foot-wide sidewalks to invade the other side.

If you have identified these weeds, dig up what you can and dispose of them. Wait at least two weeks (four is better) and then check to see what has grown back. If you have time, dig up the new growth and wait again. Treat the next set of new growth with undiluted vinegar, boiling water, or a blowtorch. Wait at least another two weeks before planting your crops. Keep an eye out for any regrowth of these weeds for a year or two, and dig them out as soon as possible so that they don't regain their strength. Yes, it's a lot of work, but it will save you time in the future. Weed control is an investment.

Pre-Emergence Treatments

Before the start of a planting season, growers can use a number of methods to reduce the germination rate of weed seeds. Before using any of these methods, prepare the soil and arrange your planting areas.

Corn Gluten

Corn gluten is a germination inhibitor that reduces the number of seeds that will grow for a period of time. It will also affect the germination rate of your crop seeds, so use it only in areas where you will be planting seedlings or cuttings—not seeds. When it starts to decompose, the gluten adds nitrogen and other slow-acting nutrients to the soil.

Site garden beds away from trees and be aware of the effect of long winter shadows. The plantings in these beds are staggered to ensure a continuous harvest. Photo by Man in Overalls of Tallahassee Food Gardens.

A front-yard garden in Sarasota. Placing bricks under the pots promotes good drainage.

A beautifully planted, tiered raised bed. Its design provides the crops on the top with a greater depth of soil. Photo by Man in Overalls of Tallahassee Food Gardens.

A turf-free backyard in south Florida. Photo by Antonio Guadamuz.

In south Florida, count on enormous collards. Photo by Antonio Guadamuz.

The fiber containers in this archway could have been planted with edible crops. You don't need a huge space to produce a good crop of vegetables.

This easily accessed raised bed with a good crop of cucumbers sits on a metal picnic table. Thanks to Victoria Freeman.

A modified keyhole garden with a compost pile in the middle. Photo by Emilia Contreras.

Above: Kevin Songer holding a luffa squash on Breaking Ground Construction Company's green roof. Installing a green roof is a substantial investment, but if you have access to one, you can grow a lot of shallow-rooted vegetables.

Right: Garlic growing in a board as one of the plantings on a green roof. Photo by Kevin Songer.

A southwest-facing bed with sandy soil needed to be enriched. All the soil was dug out to a depth of eight or nine inches—down to the irrigation pipes. Then, in-ground composting was arranged in layers until it was six inches above the original soil line.

Growing areas mulched with pine needles, and walking areas around the beds mulched with arborist's wood chips.

The next spring the tomatoes and peppers were amazing. This bed will not need the double-digging treatment again, just compost or trench composting between crops.

A thick layer of water hyacinths serve as the bottom layer for two beds prepared on very sandy soil. This layer helps the bed retain more moisture. Layers of soil and compost were added to the beds before planting.

After two sets of crops (chard and cabbage followed by squash), the water hyacinths (*top photo*) were fully composted. Now the bed is cleaned of crop residue and enriched with new composting layers. It will sit for at least a month under a thick layer of mulch before the next round of crops is planted.

To carve out more garden space, the unpoisoned turf was removed and added to the compost pile. The pathway was mulched with arborist's wood-chips and the new garden space was enriched with composted horse manure and compost.

Above: The new bed set up for wide-row planting in mid-fall. The pine-needle mulch between the rows is about six inches deep.

Right: The same bed (from another angle) the next spring, with corn salad and red-stemmed spinach in the middle row and soft-necked garlic in the outside rows.

Square-foot gardening is an easy way to make sure that you plant just enough seeds to ensure that the crops are not crowded and that no prepared soil space is wasted. Photo by Man in Overalls of Tallahassee Food Gardens.

A square-foot garden demonstration during a festival at Fairchild Tropical Gardens in Coral Gables. There are garden fests throughout Florida. Attend a few to pick up new ideas and new plants.

Above: If you want a head start, buy seedlings, but educate yourself on what's appropriate for your climate and purchase from a trusted local source: a nursery, a farmers market, or a garden fest.

Left: Beware of seedlings for sale at big-box stores. They may offer crops that are inappropriate for your section of the state or at the time of year. It seems like all of Florida is stocked with the same plants as Atlanta, which are not always suitable for Florida's planting zones.

Some gardeners plan to have certain recipe ingredients ready all at the same time. This combination of onions and one garlic bulb with their greens, carrots, and a bunch of flat parsley provides a good start for a carrot soup.

Not the best way to plant zucchinis. This bed is inadequately prepared, the plants are too close together, there are way too many plants for a family garden, and most important, there is nowhere for water (from rain or irrigation) to sink into the soil—the bed is rounded so the water will simply run away.

These basil seedlings are too close together and will need to be thinned for best results. You could treat this pot as a seedling nursery, and transplant most of the seedlings to other locations once they grow a few true leaves.

Some seedlings like this squash and the volunteer basil next to it are recognizable by their size and shape even before they grow any true leaves. They both have two seed leaves (cotyledons), so they are dicots.

To give seedlings a head start, you can keep them away from the garden in various flats or containers. These pepper seedlings were started in cardboard tubes that were held upright while the seeds sprouted. The new seedlings will have a built-in collar to protect them from cutworms.

Planting more than one seed per hole is a good idea for plants with low germination rates, like okra. If more than one seed sprouts, cut all but one off at the soil line.

Seeds are not the only method of propagation. These basil cuttings were rooted in water and are being planted in late summer for a fall/winter crop.

Kitchen scraps including eggshells are laid in a thick layer in the trench between the new rows. Then the scraps are covered with an inch or two of soil and pine needles. By the time the roots of the new crops reach this area, it will be full of rich, dark soil.

A trowel marks the top of the trench between the two wide rows. To the left of the trench are three bell pepper plants next to the parsley. On the right, okra will be planted. Toward the bottom, a bunch of nasturtiums will grow under the okra shade.

Right: These sweet, short-day onion plants don't look like much when you start in the fall, but plant them four inches apart in a wide row and they'll surprise you.

Below: Well into spring, here are about half of those onions plants in a twenty-four-inch wide row between broccoli and carrots. About a third of the leaves have fallen over. When the soil is bone dry and when more than half of the leaves have fallen over, they will be ready to harvest.

Don't wash the onions upon harvest; just brush away the soil and dry them in a garage or dry shed for several weeks. Hang them by their leaves—either braided or knotted—over a rope or wooden rack. This promotes good air circulation during the drying process.

After drying onions (or garlic), cut off the roots and leaves with clean, sharp scissors. Store the bulbs in a paper bag and keep them in a dark, dry, cool location. Go through your stored vegetables every six weeks or so to remove any that have begun to rot or sprout.

Perennial onions like these Egyptian walking onions do best with regular weeding, an annual topdressing of compost, and a layer of mulch to preserve moisture.

Once you have established a stand of perennial bunching onions, you won't need to purchase them again because you can multiply your crop by dividing each plant. Replant enough separated bulbs to sustain the population.

Meadow garlic, a Florida native, bears both bulblets and a few white flowers on its flowering scape, while the chives bear only flowers. These perennial members of the onion family deserve a spot in your herb garden. All parts of the plants are edible.

The carrot family (Apiaceae) includes carrots, celery, cilantro (coriander), dill, fennel, and parsley.

There are many types of carrots. You're sure to find a few that you and your family like. Make sure your soil is lump-free because when a carrot root comes to a lump in the soil, it forks or bends.

Do you see the celery watcher? (A green anole the same color as the leaves.) When you use organic methods, you'll have Mother Nature on your side.

This flat-leafed parsley is flowering and attracts beneficial insects. The gardener is not the only one with this information—a green anole lizard (the same species as the celery watcher on the previous page) has found a bug to eat. It's upside down on the stem in the center of the photo.

Majestic dill flower heads can reach fourteen inches across. They attract pollinators, and more important, the small parasitoid wasps that prey on tomato worms and other pests.

The daisy family (Asteraceae) includes stevia, marigolds, sunflowers, and the many lettuces.

Right: There are several types of lettuce, but the leaf lettuce is easiest to grow and is generally more heat-tolerant. This decorative chef's mixture would not be out of place in the front yard or in a container garden on a deck.

Left: Sunflowers can be grown simply to attract pollinators and birds, but you can also save the seed to roast. Sunflowers exude a chemical that poisons other plants around it, so you can use sunflowers as a weed-resistant border near your vegetables but not with them.

Right: Marigolds belong to the daisy family and you should plant them in and around your edible beds. But if you have trouble with nematodes, use them as a cover crop. Here they are planted at the base of a Malabar spinach vine, the only crop in the basella family (Basellaceae).

Many important crops belong to the mustard family (Brassicaceae). All parts of the plants in this family are edible.

Cabbage and broccoli grow well right through Florida's winters. If you leave the roots in place after the initial harvest, new growth will produce a "come-again" crop.

The four-petaled turnip flowers inspired another name for the family—Cruciferae, which means cross bearing.

If you have room and time in your crop rotation scheme, allow some of the mustard family crops to bloom. They attract many pollinators and other beneficial insects to your garden. Plus you can eat the flowers.

Zucchini flowers are gorgeous, but like all members of this family, each flower must be visited by a pollinator eight or nine times to ensure good fruit production. Make sure you plant lots of flowers in and around the vegetable garden.

A summer harvest: squash flowers, onion greens, a butternut squash, and bell peppers. One problem some home growers have is an abundant crop of squash that ripens all at once. You can stem the flow by eating some of the flowers. Before stuffing the flowers with a cheese mixture, remove the stamens from the center, then dip the stuffed flowers in a beer batter, and fry. Yummy.

To grow the best cucumbers, provide them with a trellis or cage. Pick them early and often to keep the vine producing. They are more closely related to melons than to squash.

Volunteer butternut squashes come in various sizes and shapes. If you have a glut, you can split them lengthwise, dig out the seeds, and bake or microwave them in pans filled with about half an inch of water. Scoop the cooked squash from the rinds and serve it right away mashed with nutmeg and butter. You can also use some of the mashed squash to make bread or pie and freeze the rest.

The Pea Family or the legumes (Fabaceae) includes beans, peas, and peanuts. Because the plants in this family fix nitrogen from the air, many of them also serve as cover crops that enrich the soil.

Right: Sugar-snap peas are the hybrid of a snow pea and a shell pea—they were first introduced in the 1970s.

Left: The rambunctious but beautiful hyacinth bean needs a trellis to climb on.

Right: Cassava manioc in the spurge family (Euphorbiaceae) and sweet potato vines in the morning glory family (Convolvulaceae) share a raised bed in south Florida. You can grow sweet potatoes in all of Florida, but the cassava needs the tropical climate of south Florida.

The mallow family (Malvaceae) is best known for its native and exotic hibiscus flowering shrubs, but it's the two heat-loving crops in this family that are important for Florida's vegetable gardeners—okra and roselle.

If you grow flowering hibiscus without poisons, the edible petals can really dress up a drab salad. Keep hibiscus flowers fresh in a bowl of water until you're ready to make your salad.

The beautiful okra flower is pale yellow with a dark maroon center.

Harvest the okra pods early and often to keep the plants producing. Remove them with a sharp knife to avoid damaging the plant or the pod. Okra does best with consistent, deep irrigation and in really rich soil that is augmented during the season. Then get ready for jambalaya.

Above: Roselle is an unusual crop because we harvest the cranberry-colored calyx, that is, the sepals and bracts below the flower. They are used for jellies and teas, and guess what? They taste like cranberries.

Right: Sugarcane, in the grass family (Poaceae), creates an effective, tall border to keep dust (and all that it carries) out of your edible garden.

The nightshade family (Solanaceae) includes some of our most important crops, such as tomatoes, potatoes, and peppers. Unlike the onion family, some parts of the plants, such as the flowers, are poisonous.

Left: Peppers can be harvested while they are green, but why would you do that when ripe peppers taste so much better?

Below: Is there anything better than a tomato eaten right off the vine? These early girl tomatoes produce a lot of fruit in a short time—an important attribute for Florida gardeners.

Right: The appearance of potato flowers signals the first opportunity to carefully dig for some fingerling potatoes, but the full-sized potatoes will not be ready until the vines die back. These purple flowers are produced by a blue potato cultivar.

Below: Keep the area around potato vines mounded with soil or straw because potatoes exposed to the light while growing will turn green and become poisonous. Don't wash potatoes after you harvest them; just brush off the soil. Wash them well when preparing to cook them.

Right: Potato and onion soup is good hot or cold. This serving is adorned with cherry tomatoes and fresh dill from the garden. It's okay to play with your food to make it more interesting.

Left: When starting a raised bed, you can lay cardboard down to kill the grass and other weed seeds. Lay in all new soil on top of the cardboard, which will eventually rot. Photo by Man in Overalls of Tallahassee Food Gardens.

Below: Torpedo grass and wild taro roots will find their way into your bed—even through cracks in weed-barrier cloth. Be sure to remove any deep-rooted weeds before you plant.

Right: Torpedo grass and dollar weed invade the root space of a pepper plant through mulch. You can cut these weeds back to the soil, but digging them out will have to wait until the pepper plant is pulled at the end of the season.

Below: To figure out which seedlings are weeds, prepare an extra area as you would those you intend to plant. The plants that sprout here are from the soil's seed bank and are mostly weeds. Ragweed, Virginia creeper, Chinese tallow, oxalis, blue-eyed grass, and various grasses have sprouted in this unplanted bed.

Left: Florida betony is a beautiful native mint that attracts pollinators, but . . .

Below: . . . it has aggressive roots with these weird tubers that give them their other common name, rattlesnake root. One bonus is that the roots are edible—they add a radishy crunch to your salads or stir-fries.

To provide the optimum growing conditions, you will need to plan for irrigation when siting your vegetable plots. If it's too much of a chore to irrigate and you fail to keep up the flow, most vegetables will slow their growth and produce tough or woody roots or smaller fruits.

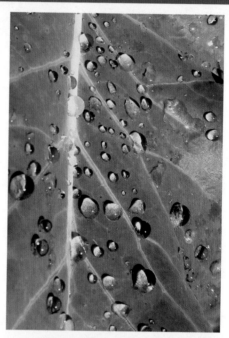

Right: Water tends to hang together, which is why it is beading up on this waxy broccoli leaf. You need to keep this in mind as you irrigate or design irrigation systems for your crops. But, contrary to old gardeners' tales, there is no danger of these water drops damaging the plant in bright sun.

Below: If your soil is dry, it may take several irrigation sessions for the water to sink into the soil. In this photo the soil is still dry below the top quarter inch where the water clings together. Test for moisture while irrigating so that you can soak the soil and thereby encourage roots to grow deeply.

This drip irrigation system is directed into each of these raised beds. Drip irrigation wastes the least amount of water because it is released only at the roots of your crops so very little is lost through evaporation.

A drip irrigation emitter in a large container garden.

Micro-sprayers in a raised bed garden in Homestead newly planted with winter crops and mulched with hay. The carrots are too thickly planted and will need thinning within the next week or so to allow room for growth.

If it's impossible to arrange for automatic irrigation, you may find that a sprayer attached to a forty-gallon bag in a cart is a convenient delivery system. Photo by TuffTech Bags and Ursa Wagon.

Ecosystem gardening encourages you to treat your edible gardens as part of the larger neighborhood. This happens when you provide food and habitat for pollinators and for predators of the pests in your garden. You can use many methods to accomplish this goal. Making sure that there is always something blooming in and around the gardens is an important piece of this strategy.

Right: Nasturtiums provide color and attract pollinators. As a bonus, both the flowers and leaves are edible and add a peppery flourish to salads.

Left: Spotted horsemint, a tall mint native to Florida, with a beautifully complex tower of flowers attracts pollinators. You can use it instead of thyme and oregano in your cooking—it contains the same oil as those Mediterranean herbs do. It's drought-tolerant, salt-tolerant, and will grow in very sandy soil. In other words, it grows well in Florida.

Right: Wildflowers native to Florida like back-eyed susans are easy-to-care-for, pollinator-attracting additions to the landscape near your edible gardens.

Besides flowers, it's good to have a water feature near your gardens to attract various types of predators. Some, like dragonflies and frogs, require water to complete their lifecycles, while others simply appreciate a drink of water.

Dragonflies are voracious predators, both in their underwater naiad stage and as adults. These mating green darner dragonflies are depositing eggs in the water.

Tadpoles mature into insect-eating frogs. One can never have too many frogs in an ecosystem.

You can protect seedlings from soil-dwelling cutworms that come out at night and cut down your small seedlings. A used paper cup with its bottom cut out serves the purpose.

Grafted tomatoes combine a tough nematode- and fungus-resistant rootstock with tastier heirloom tomatoes on the upper portion of the plant. Keep the graft site above the soil level and remove any sprouts from the rootstock.

Learn early on to identify the pests in your garden. The golden rule of integrated pest management: take action unto the pests before they do it unto your crops.

Young, flightless lubber grasshoppers are called devil's horses at this stage. They don't move very fast, so if you see a herd, you can pop a clear plastic bag over the leaf, and scrape them off and squash them.

If you don't kill them when they're young, you'll end up with some six-inch beasts like this one. Notice the chomped vegetation on this banana pepper plant.

Does your swiss chard look like swiss cheese? Cut off the affected leaves, rinse them carefully to remove any left-over chewers, and then cook them as a mess of greens or use them in place of spinach in a quiche.

Remove plants from the garden, keeping as much of their taproot intact as possible (but no soil), and plant them in a pot with all new soil and compost.

A few weeks later you'll be able to harvest more of the crop. Holey leaves may not be marketable, but they certainly are edible. The next batch of leaves looks great.

Far left: Plant a spare row of parsley or dill away from the rest of your crops. When you spot the beautiful black swallowtail caterpillars on your crop plants, move them to your "for-the-bugs" garden so that you can support these beautiful butter-flies and eat your parsley, too.

Left: This rosy wolfsnail is not the one eating the plants. It's a carnivore and eats other snails and slugs. Learn who is naughty and who is nice to have in your garden before you take action.

Two different stages of leaf-footed bugs are after this tomato. They scatter quickly, so catch them by surprise by throwing a clear plastic bag around the fruit. These are true bugs and will suck out the plant's juices.

The dreaded root-knot nematodes have attacked this parsley plant. Once you find such damage, you can let the bed go fallow for a season, solarize it, or plant a cover crop of marigolds to turn into the soil. It might be best to make the following crop a legume.

The damage to this squash vine was probably caused by a bacterial infection. Cleanliness in the garden may prevent some infections but not all.

Squash-boring insects can burrow either into the stem and shorten the life of the squash plant or, like this pickleworm, into the fruits, making them unmarketable but not inedible. You'll rarely see the worm on the outside of the plant, but the frass, the whitish stuff on the left side of the squash, is a telltale sign. The worm will probably still be inside the plant, but you can cut out around the damaged parts and eat the rest of the squash. Stem borers also produce a similar buildup of frass. Use Bt, a bacterium poisonous only to worm or caterpillar larvae, to treat such an infestation.

Cut the vine back to below the visible damage—note the leaf starting to wilt. Do not compost the damaged vine and be sure to sterilize your pruners or shears with an alcohol rub to avoid spreading the infection. Watch for further damage—you may need to cut it back again.

A fence of this height will keep out armadillos, dogs and maybe cats, deer, and wild hogs but not squirrels or raccoons. Photo by Man in Overalls of Tallahassee Food Gardens.

A temporary fence set up around the vegetable beds will also keep out chickens. You don't want them scratching up your seedlings or depositing fresh manure too close to harvest time. Learn how to manage your beds to ensure food safety. Photo by Sarva Deslauriers.

A tall fence will keep out people and deer, but the wide gaps in the fencing may allow rabbits and other small animals to enter. A smaller gauge fencing added around the bottom would create a more complete barrier, but at what cost?

If you make the transition from home gardener to semiprofessional grower, farmers markets are one type of venue for selling your produce. You'll do best if you can offer items that other growers aren't—either unusual crops or the standard fare earlier or later than average in the season.

Your display can be wonderfully chaotic like this batch of eggplants and peppers . . . Photo by Nell Foster.

. . . or a more orderly arrangement sorted by shape and color.

Left: Kohlrabi and leeks are some of the more unusual crops you might offer at a farmers market.

Below: If you sell unusual or odd-looking crops, like heirloom tomatoes, a tasting table may entice more people to purchase. Also note the information sign about the farmer. Tell your story well.

Above: Using large cold boxes as your display case may make all the difference in how your tender crops fare throughout the long day at the farmers market.

Left: When you end up with some small fruits, find a way to capitalize on their size. These little boxes of "Baby 'Looms" make a perfect sampler.

Right: These micro-greens can be sold as an edible or as starter plants.

Left: If your operation is certified organic, be sure to let people know.

Right: If you end up with forked turnips or ugly carrots, you could set up a bargain bin for customers who may not have the money to purchase your prime produce.

Below: Capitalize on your seed-starting capabilities by selling extra seedlings at farmers markets. This type of inventory can carry over for several weeks as is, and any remainders can be potted up to pricier stock.

Right: These kids' square-foot gardens take their size into consideration and are only three feet across. Think of the math lessons you can incorporate into figuring out the spacing. Photo courtesy of Man in Overalls of Tallahassee Food Gardens.

Below: Getting kids involved in growing vegetables is important for their future health and for increasing their awareness of where their food comes from. This way you can avoid the question, "Eeew, why did you bury the carrots in the dirt?"

Below: A new cinderblock garden bed is an exciting project for kids. This is one of the Urban Oasis Project's installments in a Miami neighborhood. Photo by Cesar V. Contreras.

Flaming

Larger growers who follow organic principles can purchase a propane-flaming attachment for their farm tractors to run over their fields. Smaller gardeners could use a blowtorch to accomplish the same effect. An alternative is to burn a dried cover crop, but make sure it's allowed in your neighborhood.

Solarization

The summer, when parts of your vegetable plot may lie fallow, is the time to solarize. First, remove all plant material and loosen the top layer of soil. Next, water it thoroughly; the water in the soil helps to cook it. Cover your prepared beds with heavy-duty, clear plastic sheets and weigh down all the edges of the plastic with soil, boards, or bricks. Make sure it won't come loose in a thunderstorm. Leave it in place for four to six weeks.

* * *

Soil solarization, burning, or flaming will kill everything in the top two or three inches of soil. These methods will kill the surface weed seeds, nematodes, worms, and any other living organisms. They will also melt your drip irrigation system and possibly damage other irrigation systems as well. Accordingly, it's a good idea to remove the hardware near the surface and use caution. Once you start planting, weeding, and tending your crops after burning or solarization, the organisms and weed seeds that lay four or more inches deep could be exposed again. Neither flaming nor solarization will kill deep-rooted weeds.

Robbing the Seed Bank

If you double-dig your beds and bring in compost and composted manure to first establish your vegetable gardens, many weeds will sprout from that beautiful, loosened soil. Arrange the wide rows or mounds ahead of time, with the mulch between the rows, and let the prepared soil sit for a week or two. When the unwanted seedlings emerge from the seed bank, pull out all of them and then plant your crop seeds or seedlings. The theory behind this action is that reducing the weed population at the start of the growing season will decrease the number of weeds that would compete with the crops later on. After you have planted your crops, pull out any weed seedlings when they are small in order to minimize the disturbance to the soil. Once your crops emerge, get mulch down between your plantings right away to prevent more weed seeds from sprouting.

Mulch, Mulch, Mulch

The liberal application of organic mulches is the most recommended treatment for preventing weeds. In addition to keeping weeds at bay, organic mulch moderates the temperature fluctuations in the soil, preserves moisture, reduces erosion (from both water and wind), and eventually enriches the soil. Organic mulch provides both a physical and a light barrier to keep seeds in the soil from sprouting, but it is not foolproof—new seeds will sprout from the top, and deep-rooted or fast-growing weeds with aggressive rhizomes will spread in from surrounding areas.

Because a vegetable plot involves ongoing planting and transplanting, use a mulch that hangs together when raked, such as pine needles or straw—not woodchips, sawdust, or other particulate mulches. Lay down a thick layer between your wide rows so that the mulch is level with the planting area. After you plant your seedlings or after your crops sprout in the soil, lay down an inch or so of mulch around, but not touching, the plants. When weeding the area during the growing season, scrape the mulch away from around the crops; pull the weeds, shaking the soil from their roots; and then replace and refresh the mulch. Store the mulch on a tarp while you're working on the weeds, and when you're ready to put it back around your crops, be sure to lift it from the tarp such that the soil, the smallest pieces, and partially decomposed mulch are left behind—add these leftovers to your compost pile. This sifting of the mulch keeps soil from mixing in with it, and makes it less attractive for new weeds to sprout and grow.

Larger growers often use plastic sheets as a type of mulch, but certified organic operations may not be allowed to do this. The plastic sheeting will not absorb water, so these growers will have to use a drip irrigation system for their crops. Plastic offers excellent protection from weeds, but it does little to moderate the temperature fluctuations in the soil, and of course will not provide any enrichment. Other growers use weed-barrier cloth instead of plastic; this cloth does absorb water and may actually last longer than plastic in Florida's hot climate. A third strategy for widely spaced rows is to use a tough, low-growing cover crop as "living mulch" between the rows. Legumes are good for this because they also add nitrogen to the soil.

Hand Pulling

Ultimately, there is no substitute for pulling weeds by hand, especially those very close to your crop plants. To hand pull weeds successfully, you must do it early and often—you don't want to give the weeds a chance to become so large and so well established that pulling them out will disturb the crops. And be sure to pull them before they set seed—you certainly don't want to cause an escalating weed infestation. When you pull a weed, look at its roots—they will give you some clues about the state of your soil. Also look for bugs in the roots or the leaves. The weeds are a reflection of your garden's environment.

If there are only a few weeds growing in a mulched area, rather than remove the whole layer of mulch, place one hand flat on the mulch with the weed between two of your fingers. Slowly pull out the weed, while your hand holds the mulch in place—this reduces the amount of soil that gets mixed in with the mulch.

While you're out in the garden pulling weeds, you can also harvest some of your crops, scout for pest damage, and maybe pluck some of the pests themselves. So take along a garden cart or wheelbarrow with a bag reserved for diseased plants, a large bucket or container for weeds headed to the compost pile, a jar of soapy water for the pests, a knife or pair of shears, and a basket, hod, or colander for your harvest. Also take a clean rag and a bottle of alcohol for wiping your knife or shears after using them to trim away diseased plants. Most Florida gardeners do this in the morning before it gets too hot, but it's a good idea to wait until most of the dew has dried so that you don't spread fungal diseases from plant to plant. Wear a hat and bring a drink. Enhance your tea or water with a few rolled mint or stevia leaves—you deserve it.

Cultivation—Weeding with Tools

In small gardens with intense planting methods, such as wide row or keyhole arrangements, you may be able to keep up with the weeds by hand pulling alone, especially if you've done a good job of mulching. In larger operations, however, you may need to weed with tools—specifically hoes or stirrup hoes. If weeds are growing through the mulch, first rake it away, and then gently pull the hoe over the soil to drag out the weeds. This is best done when the soil is dry because the weeds will be less likely to grow back from the roots left in the soil. Be extra careful around crops with shallow roots; careless hoeing could do them more harm than good. After you've removed the weeds, replace the mulch between the rows and around the plants. The right tool can save you time, and can save your back.

If you are a large grower with a tractor, you can purchase specific attachments for weeding. Installing plastic or weed-barrier-cloth mulch between rows makes those weeding trips through the fields unnecessary or at least limits them to the narrow growing areas only.

Intercropping

As discussed in chapter 2, certain crops with differing time lines or space requirements can be grown together. This does not eliminate the need for mulching and weed vigilance, but it might reduce the weed population. Instead of leaving big open spaces between newly planted crops, you could fill them with smaller, short-term crops while waiting for the main crop to grow. These smaller crops will shade the soil, keeping out most of the weeds, while the larger crop fills in. For example, during the transition from cool-weather crops to warm-weather crops, you could plant your new tomatoes or peppers in the midst of small, shallow-rooted crops such as lettuce, spinach, or mâche. The small, cool-weather crops will benefit from the shade of the taller warm-weather crops. The cool-weather crops will be harvested before the warm-weather crops really get going. Upon their final harvest, cut the cool-weather greens off at or just below the soil line and mulch the area well. (Pulling out the roots would probably unduly disrupt your warm-weather crop.)

Treatments for Adjacent Pathways

Weeds can also grow in the pathways adjacent to your vegetable beds, raised beds, or containers, and may spread into your edibles, so plan for weed control from the start.

Even with the thick layer of mulch and stepping-stones, weeds will grow from seeds newly sown on top of the mulch, or work their way up from deeper in the soil. Plan for a yearly renewal of the pathway mulch. Lightly rake the top to pull away any weeds, add a one-inch layer of chips, and then replace the pavers. Gravel rarely stops weeds in Florida because dead leaves, soil, and other material settles in between the gravel; if you decide to use gravel, keep it clean.

If deep-rooted weeds attack, you'll need to go to greater lengths than a light raking, but keeping after those aggressive weeds will save you time in the long run. Using boiling water or vinegar in your pathways may be necessary to subdue an out-of-control weed infestation.

Crop-Rotation and Cover-Crop Strategies

When you first plant edibles in a garden, you won't believe your luck—you'll have almost no problems with bugs, nematodes, or fungal wilts. You may have a few tomato worms, but considering everything you'll wonder what the garden gurus are whining about. But just you wait—after a year or two, you'll know!

So prepare for trouble with wise crop rotations. Make sure to keep a record of the crops you've planted in each of your beds in your gardener's logbook—you may think you'll remember what you planted where, but you won't. Assign numbers or letters to each identifiable location within your edible beds. Raised beds and other intensive gardening arrangements make it easy to track the rotations—label each section with a small sign.

Crop rotation is not that complex: don't plant the same or similar crops in one location year after year. Planting your beds with crops with different needs in the successive seasons confounds the pests and balances the nutrient uptake from the soil. Grouping plants according to their nutrient and irrigation needs is also an important part of crop rotation.

Pay attention to the botanical family of each of your crops; they are arranged by family in this book to help you become more aware of these relationships. The reason to be aware of which families your crops belong to is that bugs and other pests often prefer to suck, burrow, or chew on members of one plant family over others. While this book covers more than twenty plant families, most crops fall into a few main groups.

- The tomato group includes three families of heavy feeders: Solanaceae (tomatoes, potatoes, eggplant, and peppers—sweet bell and chile); Malvaceae (okra and roselle); Poaceae (corn—most of the other grass crops are perennials).
- The squash group includes one important family of heavy feeders: Cucurbitaceae (the melons, cucumbers, and squash). Members of this group are prone to root-knot nematodes and squash borers. Crop rotation does not help with the second problem.
- The mustard group includes Brassicaceae (cabbage, broccoli, cauliflower, mustard greens, collards, radishes, brussels sprouts, and more) and Asteraceae (the many forms of lettuce). Most are prone to chewing pests.
- The carrot group includes four families: Apiaceae (carrots, dill, parsley, fennel, and more); Alliaceae (onions, chives, and garlic); Convolvulaceae (sweet potatoes); and Amaranthaceae (spinach, beets, and swiss chard). Many of these crops are grown for their roots and can be attacked by soil-borne pests that tunnel into them.

- The legume group includes only one family: Fabaceae (beans, peas, peanuts, and a number of cover crops). Because these crops fix their own nitrogen from the air with the help of bacteria in their roots, they do best in leaner soil with less added nitrogen. At the end of the season, after many of their roots die off, they leave a nitrogen-rich residue in the soil. This factor makes the legume group important to making your crop rotation work well.

The perennials do not come into play in your crop rotations; you'll need to find an out-of-the-way site where they can thrive with only weeding, mulching, and seasonal top dressings of compost. Your herb garden is a good example, having a fair number of perennials such as mint, oregano, thyme, chives, and rosemary. Annual herbs such as dill, basil, or parsley could be rotated in other parts of your garden.

Fallow Fields

If you have the space, it's a good idea to let some of your garden areas lay fallow for a season, particularly after a heavy infestation of pests. This will confound the generalist, soil-borne pests that attack anything that grows.

A small or medium grower can prepare a field to lie fallow by clearing out all the plant materials, smoothing out the wide rows or removing the square-foot markers, and then adding a four-to-six-inch layer of easily raked mulch—either pine needles or straw. If weeds attack in mid-season anyway, remove the mulch, hand-pull or hoe the weeds, and then replace the soil-free mulch, adding some new mulch to refresh your layer.

You could also take this opportunity to set up trench composting in the whole bed. Remove four to six inches of soil; add in a three-to-six-inch layer of kitchen scraps, coffee grounds, water weeds, or fresh manure; cover this layer with the soil you removed; and then cover all that with mulch. This in-the-ground composting will be finished in six to eight weeks. It's a good idea to time trench composting for just before or just after a heavy-feeding crop.

Cover Crops

Cover crops can help to enrich the soil, keep weeds at bay, prevent erosion (from both wind and water), and may also reduce soil-borne pests such as nematodes. The idea is to cover the soil quickly with fast-growing crops that are either sown thickly as seed or planted more sparsely so that they will spread like a groundcover. Some ground covers, like summer peas, yield a harvestable product at the end of the period, but mostly cover crops are used as green manure and are turned under at the end of the season and again six to eight weeks before the next crop is to be planted. Cover crops that bloom throughout their cycle in the crop rotation also play an important part in your ecosystem gardening by attracting beneficial insects and pollinators.

Some larger growers use cover crops as living mulches between the rows of their main crops, but mostly cover crops are planted to cover an entire bed or field as part of a crop rotation strategy. In Florida, the most productive seasons for growing vegetables are the fall, winter, and early spring, so we usually grow cover crops during the summer when our choices of crops, as well as our energy levels, are limited by heat. Because summer is also our rainy season, when we can receive two or more inches of rain in a single day, cover crops will also serve to minimize water erosion. You may want to arrange your beds like a rain garden with a swale in the middle, giving the rainwater a better chance to soak in.

Some good choices for fast-growing, heat-loving, annual cover crops include legumes such as cowpeas, sunn hemp, alyce clover, deer vetch, or hairy indigo; grasses such as millet or sorghum-Sudan grass; and marigolds, which help to reduce nematode populations. Some good choices for winter cover crops include crimson clover, rye, wheat, or vetch.

No Plant Is an Island

Plants, be they weeds or desirable crops, exist in a complex web of relationships that include the soil, with its millions of organisms, and other plants. As growers, we try to manipulate their environment to maximize the growth of our crops and to eradicate weeds. Sometimes we're successful.

Resources

For more on buying and sourcing cover crop seed for organic farming systems, go to http://www.extension.org/pages/18654/buying-and-sourcing-cover-crop-seed-for-organic-farming-systems.

For an article on increasing your yields of organic corn with more complex crop rotations, see http://www.sciencedaily.com/releases/2008/05/080528102904.htm.

The National Sustainable Agriculture Information Service offers an overview of cover crops: https://attra.ncat.org/attra-pub/covercrop.html.

The Florida Exotic Pest Plant Council maintains a list of plants that are invasive in Florida at http://www.fleppc.org.

For the University of Florida IFAS articles on cover crops, go to http://edis.ifas.ufl.edu/topic_vegetable_cover_crops.

Also check out the Weed Science Society of America at www.wssa.net.

8

Irrigation

Most of our vegetable crops can be described as nicely packaged water—broccoli, carrots, tomatoes, and cucumbers are all, by volume, more than 90 percent water. Supplying crops with regular moisture is critical for growing well-formed, tender, and good-tasting produce, but Florida's best growing season—the cooler months (late fall, winter, and early spring)—also coincides with the dry season. Irrigation is the answer.

We need to supply our plants with enough water when Mother Nature does not. And we need to do so with an irrigation system—be it manual or automated—that encourages deep root growth. Frequent, light irrigation is called for when seedlings are just sprouting, but mature plants grow better on a regimen of less-frequent, more-thorough irrigation. Such a regimen encourages even naturally shallow-rooted crops to grow their roots deeper and become more drought tolerant.

You also need to plan for too much rain, which can erode your carefully composted and mulched soil. While gardeners have a lot to think about, irrigation is more controllable than other environmental factors that are required to produce a good crop.

The Water Cycle in Plants

To be successful gardeners, we need to know how water behaves inside a plant.

Water's Unique Properties

A water molecule is made up of two hydrogen atoms and one oxygen atom, giving it the familiar chemical formula of H_2O. The hydrogen atoms attach themselves to one side of the oxygen, covering about one-third of its circle, so that the molecule resembles the head of Mickey Mouse. The side of the molecule with the hydrogen atoms has a slight positive charge, while the oxygen side is slightly negative. Water molecules act like little magnets and are attracted to each other, forming weak bonds called hydrogen bonds. You can observe this self-attraction, called cohesion, when water beads up into droplets on waxy leaf surfaces.

Water drops act like little magnifying lenses or prisms, and if you look closely you can often see rainbows in the drops. They are beautiful, and contrary to the old gardeners' tale, water drops on leaves in full sun will not burn the leaf tissue. So you may irrigate without fear of harming the plant in the middle of the day if your plants—particularly your seedlings—are wilting in the Florida heat.

Water's polarity also makes it a good solvent for breaking apart, absorbing, and carrying organic materials such as sugars, other carbohydrates, and nutrients.

Osmosis and Root Hairs

At the bottom of the plant, near the tip of the roots, thousands of single-cell extensions on the root's surface, called root hairs, absorb water from the soil. Root-hair cells have a semipermeable cell membrane that allows water and some materials that are dissolved in water, such as nutrients, to flow into the cell. Everything else is blocked from entering the plant. It is the nature of water pressure to equalize over an area, and when there is less water in the root-hair cells than in the surrounding soil, water will flow across the cell membrane to equalize that pressure. Once water fills the root-hair cells, it moves into neighboring cells, building pressure that pushes the water up into the plant; this action is called root pressure. Then the process of transpiration, as discussed later, takes over, sucking the water the rest of the way through the plant.

Root hairs don't last long—from a few hours to a few days—before they are sloughed off into the soil. To develop new root hairs, a root must be growing. Plants and their roots grow in spurts in response to a range of factors, but mostly to wet and dry cycles. After a heavy rain or deep irrigation, the air pockets in poor soil are eliminated and the root hairs die. So while deep irrigation is normally recommended, it may cause a delay in the generation of new root growth. As the soil becomes less saturated, the root hairs start growing vigorously again; they continue to grow until the soil becomes too dry, upon which they die off and the cycle repeats. Humus and organic matter in your garden soil moderate these wet and dry cycles by maintaining those all-important air pockets and holding more moisture.

When a plant is transplanted, most of its delicate root hairs are rubbed off as soil falls away from roots. As a result, transplanted crops need a lot of water in the planting hole and frequent irrigation until new root growth begins and the plant regains its network of root hairs. Not surprisingly, larger plants require a longer period of additional irrigation to become fully established. Close attention and adequate irrigation during a plant's establishment period greatly increases its chances survival and overall vigor. Once you see new growth forming above ground, you can assume that the plant is established and no longer needs intensive irrigation.

Transpiration

After water enters the root tissues, the root pressure begins to push the water higher in the plant. However, without the suction effect of evaporation through the stomata (the pores in the leaves), water would not go very far up the tubular, water-carrying cells in plants, the xylem.

More than 90 percent of the water that enters a plant runs straight through it and evaporates into the air. A full-grown oak tree could

TRANSPIRATION

transpire more than 400 gallons of water on a summer day—obviously our vegetable crops have a much lower volume of transpiration. The larger the plant's biomass, the more water it transpires.

Less than 10 percent of the water is absorbed into the plant's cells, where it serves several purposes: carrying nutrients, keeping the cells turgid, and allowing photosynthesis. When the soil dries out, transpiration slows down. The guard cells around each stomate are highly sensitive to water supply, and when they become flaccid, the stomate closes up, slowing the evaporation of water to protect the plant against severe wilting. Gardeners need to pay attention to the wilting of plants—especially seedlings—and irrigate before permanent damage is done to the plant's tissue.

Most people recommend irrigating in the morning because it allows the plants to dry before nightfall, making them less vulnerable to fungal attacks and to water loss owing to evaporation in the heat of the day. These are valid reasons, but perhaps the most compelling reason not to irrigate in the evening is that, by the time evaporation begins again and the plant restarts the transpiration cycle the next day, much of the water will have descended through the layers of soil and may be out of reach of the roots, especially if you have sandy soil.

The combination of transpiration from plants and evaporation from soil and bodies of water is called evapotranspiration. The Florida Automated Weather Network (F.A.W.N.) website provides daily readings for your local evapotranspiration rate. This information will help you to make wise irrigation decisions.

Photosynthesis

In this magical process, green plants combine carbon dioxide (CO_2) and water (H_2O) with energy from sunlight to form sugar ($C_6H_{12}O_6$) and oxygen gas (O_2). Most vascular plants use water, supplied via transpiration, carbon dioxide, absorbed from the air through the open stomata in the leaves, and sunlight, absorbed by chlorophyll, to photosynthesize. Respiration is the equal and opposite chemical reaction to photosynthesis, and all organisms, including plants, respire in order to gain energy to live.

When it gets too hot, plants close their stomata to preserve water. Most plants cannot continue photosynthesizing because they don't have ready access to water and carbon dioxide while the stomata are closed. Some heat-loving plants, such as corn, sugarcane, and crabgrass, have adapted by using a different chemical pathway in order to photosynthesize more efficiently in the heat.

Wilting

The main symptom of a plant not having access to enough moisture in the soil is wilting. Curiously, the main symptom of a plant having too much water iin the soil is also wilting. While this may seem like a paradox, the fact is that roots are stressed in both wet and dry conditions. Too much moisture causes a lack of oxygen and, eventually, root rot.

To test whether the soil is too wet or too dry, stick your finger two or three inches into the soil near your wilting plant. If it's dry, irrigate deeply. If it's wet, don't—unfortunately, there is no fast remedy for soaked soils; build in a good drainage system in advance to reduce this problem.

Humus-Rich Soil and Irrigation

The wet and dry cycles in your garden soil, caused by rain or irrigation and the lack thereof, will be less abrupt if you've worked in plenty of compost, composted manures, and other humus-rich materials. Humus acts as a sponge, and each piece is able to absorb several times its weight in water. The humus particles hold the water until the demands from plant roots, natural evaporation, or drainage down through the soil decrease the moisture content in the surrounding soil particles. Water from the surface will move downward through the soil horizon. First it will sink out of reach of shallow-rooted plants and later even the deep-rooted plants won't be able to reach the moisture. If your soil surface is well mulched, once water soaks into the soil, very little water will evaporate.

Planting Surfaces and Irrigation

If you're planting your edibles in intensive wide-row, square-foot, or keyhole arrangements, your planting surfaces will be relatively flat. If you make these surfaces slightly concave, water from rain or above ground irrigation will tend to gather in the swales and soak into the soil rather than roll away.

For large crop plants, such as cabbage, tomatoes, peppers, or okra, consider creating a swale around the base of each plant. Some growers create a swale down the middle of each wide row so that the whole row acts as a receptor for water. Squash, cucumber, and melons are thirstier than most other crops, and growing them on mounds is one way to provide them with an even larger containment area for water. Some growers place buckets or other containers with small holes drilled in the bottom in the center of the squash mounds, and then fill the bucket with water to ensure deep, slow irrigation.

Once you have the shape of your soil surface primed to receive water, you need to mulch the entire planting area. The trenches between the wide rows in these intensive planting arrangements will need a much deeper layer of mulch.

On the other hand, during Florida's wet season, your garden could receive two or three inches of rain in a single day. This is where you'll appreciate those well-mulched trenches. After the swales on the planting surfaces fill with rain, excess water overflows into the trenches. The trenches should be arranged to safely carry this excess water to a low spot or dry well away from the gardens. Raised beds with hard sides work well in torrential rains because the soil is held in place, but be sure that excess water can escape easily and without carrying too much soil with it.

Irrigation Types

Getting enough water to your crops can be as simple as using a watering can or a watering wand on a garden hose, or as complex as installing and maintaining a highly automated sprinkler or drip irrigation system. Most growers use some combination of manual and automated watering. Automated systems can conserve water quite effectively, if we use some common sense. "Automated" doesn't mean "set it and forget it." You can and should use automated systems, if you can arrange it, but the best water-use practices require careful planning, observation, and human intervention.

Whatever the design of your irrigation system, you must adjust the frequency and duration of irrigation during rainy periods so the sum of precipitation and irrigation supplies the right amount of water to keep your crops healthy during the growing season. This amount will vary depending upon the crop and its stage of growth. A newly emerged seedling doesn't use much water but must have consistent moisture, while a corn plant uses the most water when it's forming its tassel, ears, and silks. For many crops, like carrots and tomatoes, it's a good idea to cut back on irrigation as the harvest time approaches in order to reduce the splitting of fruit or root. Your tomatoes might taste better, too.

Use a rain gauge to determine how much rain you actually receive within a set period, say, a week. Do not rely on weather services for your rainfall totals—rainfall is highly local, especially in Florida. Keep a record of your rainfall and establish your irrigation times and amounts accordingly. To accomplish this, you will also need to calibrate your irrigation patterns so that you know how long it takes to apply one inch of water. If your irrigation method is a spray sprinkler system that shoots water into the air across the landscape, this is a fairly straightforward exercise: place a number of containers with vertical sides in random spots within a given sprinkler's range. Then, turn on the system or sprinkler for fifteen minutes and measure the amount of water each container collects. If the water measures one-third of an inch, on average, then a forty-five-minute session will approximate one inch of rainfall.

If you irrigate your garden manually, one inch of water is approximately one half gallon per square foot. In other words, a three-gallon watering can will supply an inch of water to six square feet or a two-by-three-foot bed.

Drip or soaker systems are more difficult to gauge. The rule of thumb here is that you get the equivalent of an inch of rainwater by running a one-gallon-per-hour emitter for an hour. The distance between your emitters is a big variable, though.

Ultimately, you may have to let your plants tell you how much water they need and test the soil for moisture by sticking your finger into the soil near a crop row to see how deep the moisture reaches. For a more accurate gauge of moisture, invest in either a manual moisture meter or an automated soil moisture sensor that ties into your irrigation system.

Rain Sensors

Since 1991, Florida has required all permanent irrigation systems to have an automatic shut-off device or rain sensor. This device hooks into your timer or controller and will turn off the irrigation after a certain amount of rain has fallen. To operate correctly, it must be mounted in the open where the rainfall is unobstructed and where the irrigation sprinklers will not hit it. The most commonly used devices rely on absorbent pads or disks. When they have absorbed enough rainwater, the pads expand, shutting off a pressure switch.

You can also place a soil moisture sensor in the soil near the root zone in order to automate irrigation based on actual soil conditions. When the sensor detects dry conditions, it allows the next scheduled watering cycle to proceed. When the sensor detects that the soil's moisture level is above the threshold, it suspends the irrigation cycle. Using a soil or rain sensor turns your "dumb" irrigation system into a smarter one that reacts to the actual weather and soil conditions.

Water Sources

Your first consideration when installing an irrigation system is the water source. If your garden areas are subject to an irrigation permit process, you'll probably be required to use the lowest-quality water available. The potable water that municipalities provided is treated for human consumption and is normally used as a last resort for irrigation.

There are several nonpotable, lower-quality water sources that are suitable for irrigating the landscape, but not necessarily for irrigating edibles unless they are filtered or treated. Starting with the most sustainable water source:

Gray water—This is the lowest-quality water source and is useful for your nonedible landscape. It, however, is not recommended for irrigating crops unless it has been treated or filtered.

This water is collected from a building's sink and shower drains and all of its water-using appliances with the exception of the toilet (which produces "black water") and is retained in a storage tank. It can be used for general landscape irrigation and other functions that don't require a potable water source, such as the flushing of toilets. Many green developments and communities are now planned with gray water systems, and using this reclaimed water reduces the volume sent to sewer and septic systems. Using gray water for general irrigation greatly reduces the strain on Florida's delicate water resources.

If you have a gray water system, be sure to use "gray water safe" soaps and detergents. (Note: If you are washing diapers on a regular basis do not use washing machine water for your edibles, even if it is filtered—it must be treated as black water.) If gray water is readily available, you can install a range of filtration systems between the gray-water holding tank and your crops. You could, for example, use a typical swimming-pool filtration setup (without the chlorine and other pool chemicals) or you could set up a solar-powered pump that runs the

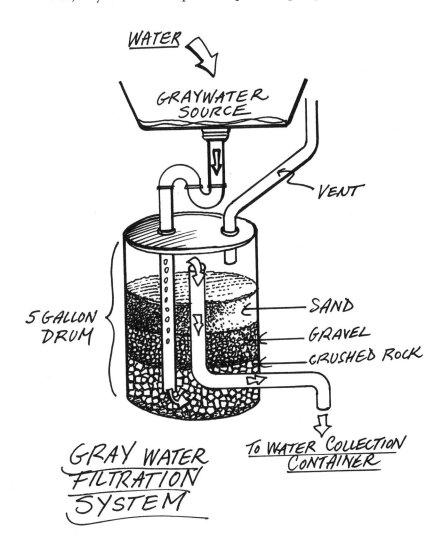

WATER

GRAYWATER SOURCE

VENT

5 GALLON DRUM

SAND

GRAVEL

CRUSHED ROCK

GRAY WATER FILTRATION SYSTEM

To WATER COLLECTION CONTAINER

gray water through a series of sand-filled basins where the water is released in the bottom of each basin. The water must flow upward through the gravel and sand before spilling into the next basin, and eventually into a cistern or a large lined pond inhabited by plants, frogs, and fish. You could also add harvested rainwater to this filtered gray water to further dilute any detergents and other residues.

Harvested rainwater—To meet the irrigation needs of your edible crops through the dry season will require a fairly large cistern. On a smaller scale, harvested rainwater collected in several rain barrels could certainly be used to supplement other water systems or may provide enough water to irrigate a small vegetable garden. (See "Harvesting Rainwater" beginning on page 225 for more details.)

Surface water—If your property backs up to or includes a body of fresh water with a fairly reliable water level, such as a spring-fed lake, a pond, a storm-water retention pond, a river, or a canal, surface water could be your source for irrigation. To drive a system like this, you will need a pump to move the water through the system. Be sure to have the water quality tested before you use it on your edibles.

Shallow well water—A well dug into a surficial aquifer or ground-water works well as a source of irrigation. Such heavy use of a well, however, impacts Florida's water resources more than the water sources listed above.

Residential or commercial water supply—This potable water is certainly safe for your edibles, but it's the most expensive water supply—both in terms of cost and of the ecological impact on Florida's resources. If you use your household water for irrigation, be sure to bypass any water-softener systems—those salts are harmful to plants.

Irrigation Design Considerations

Whether you use manual irrigation methods or have an in-ground automated system, different sections of your landscape will have different irrigation needs, and you should treat each section appropriately. To the extent that it is possible, divide your landscape into zones and tailor your irrigation system to the unique needs of each zone.

There are many types of irrigation systems: a hose and sprinkler; a garden cart with a built-in water tank and hand-pumped sprayer; a do-it-yourself drip system with tubing and emitters on a timer; or a sophisticated and somewhat expensive in-ground computerized system. The system that is most suitable for you and your garden will depend upon your budget and your garden space—both its size and character. It will also depend upon how much energy you have to dedicate to the care of your garden.

In-the-Ground, Computerized Sprayer System

This pressurized system operates with a pump that is set to turn on whenever there is a drop in the system's internal pressure. When the computer opens the valves to water a particular zone, the pressure lowers and the pump turns on to activate the sprayers in that zone. Some sprayers pop up in response to the water pressure, while others remain stationary. They spray either in a settable rotating pattern or a constant spray. When the computer closes the valves, the sprayers shut off and sink back into the ground. Individual zones can be programmed for different lengths of time and may have a different type of sprayer depending upon the need. Some sprayers may sit up on permanent poles to gain more height.

Normally installed by a professional or specialist, computerized in-ground systems are widely used in residential and commercial properties in Florida. The biggest advantage to this system is that once it's installed and calibrated, it's easy to use. Ongoing maintenance is limited to checking the spray nozzles once each season and checking for leaks by watching the pressure gauge on the pump when the system is not turned on.

One big disadvantage is that a lot of water evaporates as it's being sprayed. Another problem is that wet foliage creates a favorable environment for fungal infestations. To reduce these problems, it's best to use a sprayer system in the early morning hours before the temperature rises and when the winds are, normally, at their lowest. This way, the leaves will have all day to dry out.

If you are siting your edible gardens in a landscape that already has one of these systems, first determine where each zone of the system irrigates, and then locate your beds or containers so that they are serviced by one or two zones. As you transition from the general landscape to your edible beds, you have two options for customizing your system to meet your garden's needs:

(1) Keep the overhead spray-type fixtures and adjust the timing so your crops receive adequate irrigation on the days allowed under water restrictions. You'll need to supplement with either hand watering or by setting up a system with soaker tapes using harvested rainwater or other water source. Most of Florida's five water-management districts permit irrigation twice a week during daylight savings time, but only once a week during standard time—Florida's best crop-growing season. During a severe drought all irrigation may be halted. Irrigation of crops may be exempted from these restrictions.

(2) Switch the whole zone from overhead sprayers to micro-irrigation outlets—this works best for systems that include a pressure tank. Because the flow of water in micro-irrigation emitters is so much less than in overhead sprayers, water management districts generally don't restrict you to certain days and times. For your crops, you'll probably want drip emitters or drip tube tape, but there are other types of micro emitters, such as bubblers and micro-sprays. It's best to convert the whole zone to low-pressure emitters. You'll need a pressure regulator to reduce the force of water to the flow recommended for your new devices. Also, for any water source with the exception of municipal, you will probably need to install a filter between the water source and the drip tubing or tape.

Drip Systems

In a drip irrigation system, water is applied to the soil via soaker hoses, tubes with emitters, or porous pipes. Florida's agriculture industry leads the nation in the use of drip systems. These systems have a number of advantages: little water is lost to evaporation; no trenching is necessary for installation; water can be delivered to the root zone, so the foliage does not get wet; fewer weeds grow because the surface outside of the root zone is not irrigated; and property owners can design and install their own drip systems.

The simplest of the drip systems is a soaker hose, which usually is a flat section of hose with many tiny holes along its length. This can be used with any water source that has a standard outdoor water spigot. Usually, you'll run a regular, solid garden hose from the spigot to the planted area, where you'll connect it to the soaker hose, which you can arrange around the plants you wish to water. If you use a soaker hose with an elevated rain barrel, remember to turn it off or you could drain your whole barrel in one session. You might wish to insert a mechanical timer at the spigot in order to avoid this problem.

Many kits and parts for drip systems are available at retail stores. These systems are versatile, and can be set up for one set of circumstances and then reconfigured to better serve a new set of crops. No special tools are required, and if you accidentally cut a line or wish to reuse your line with a different configuration next season, you can repair it with a connector or a "goof" plug. Containers serviced by a drip system are usually set up with spur hoses that, depending upon the size of the container, have two or three emitters that empty into the pot.

Usually, the tubes are laid directly on the soil along a planted row or in the swale of squash-type mounds and are pinned down with U-shaped staples or held in position with special stakes. After testing for leaks and making sure that all the emitters are working, cover the tubing with mulch to protect the drip-system parts from the sun and abrupt fluctuations in temperature.

In addition to the tubing and the emitters, you will need a back-flow preventer in order to avoid contaminating your main water supply; a pressure regulator, because this is a low pressure system; and a filter to trap any particles from your water supply and to prevent the drip-irrigation system from becoming clogged. Most systems also require a timer; some are programmable like the computer in a sprayer system, while others are simple mechanical timers that you set when you turn on the water.

The low-pressure nature of drip systems makes them susceptible to becoming clogged, either with soil that has leaked into the tubes or with a buildup of slime from fungi or hard-water salts. You must flush your system regularly and uncover the tubes to check them for leaks. Because you can't see how it's working, regularly scheduled maintenance is crucial to maintaining the effectiveness of your drip system. In most cases you'll time your system check to correspond with planting times or crop turnovers. To best preserve the tubing and emitters, remove the drip system before solarization and before letting a bed lay fallow.

Manual Systems

Even if you have an automated irrigation system, you'll still need to augment it with a manual method when irrigating new seedlings, newly transplanted plants, and water-hungry vegetables such as squash or melons. Connecting a hose to a rain barrel or household faucet for hand watering a section of a garden or setting up a sprinkler in the yard are traditional watering methods; they have the added advantage of getting you out in the landscape, where you can best monitor your garden's condition.

Because manual systems depend entirely upon your time, energy, and monitoring, there is a tendency to under-water with the hose and over-water with a sprinkler. You can better regulate the amount you irrigate by hand by using a series of jugs or pails, each with a three-to-five-gallon capacity. Drill several small holes in the bottom of each container and place them where the need for water is greatest, such as in the middle of a squash mound. Then, when you make your rounds with the hose or watering cart, fill each container to capacity, allowing the water to slowly dribble into the soil. This way, the soil will receive a thorough soaking, but you don't have to stand there the whole time. It's a good idea to sink the containers at least a few inches into the soil so that they don't blow away.

Hauling watering cans to the outer reaches of your property is good exercise, but if it's simply too difficult, then maybe it's time to move your vegetable beds closer to the water source. If long distance watering is unavoidable, you might consider purchasing a watering wagon to reduce the strain. You can use your rain-barrel water for any type of hauling system.

Self-irrigating containers fall into a manual category because you must refill the water reservoirs on a regular basis. Another way to set up self-irrigation in container gardens is to arrange the pots on a slightly tilted tray covered with old towels and with an overflow to the next tray. You can then use a solar-powered fountain pump to move a steady trickle of water from a reservoir container to the highest tray.

Harvesting Rainwater

Harvesting rainwater is nothing new—the earliest civilizations practiced this form of water conservation. These days, most people harvest rainwater using a series of rain barrels or cisterns situated to catch water runoff from the gutters and downspouts of roofs or other impervious surfaces.

Cisterns can store enough water to irrigate your vegetable garden year-round, if you plan ahead and have enough roof space or other collection areas. You can harvest 300 gallons of water from a one-inch rainfall on a 500-square-foot surface, regardless of its slope. With Florida's annual rainfall averaging fifty inches, that 500-square-foot roof will collect an average of 15,000 gallons of water each year. You won't need to store that annual total because you'll be using the water for irrigation throughout the year, but you will want enough storage so that you don't run out during the seven-month dry season when your garden's need for water is at its highest.

If your garden is near a building with gutters, you have a ready-made collection area. If your beds are quite a distance from buildings, you'll have to be more creative in order to harvest rainwater for your garden. There are stand-alone rain barrels with collection tops that look like upside down umbrellas. You could also install a shed, a shade shelter/greenhouse with a solid or translucent roof surface, or a pergola with a slanted roof. These structures or stand-alone collection devices won't provide the surface area to harvest enough water to run

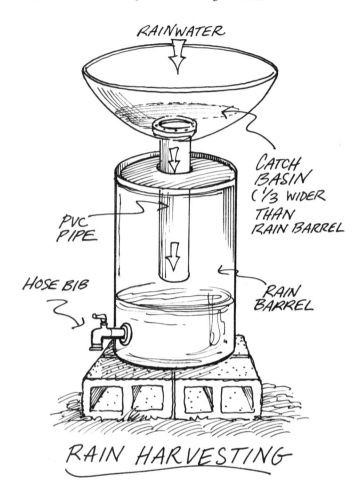

RAIN HARVESTING

your entire irrigation system, but they could certainly provide a source of water for your manual irrigation.

When you gather water from roofs or other structures, plan to filter out tree debris such as twigs, leaves, and needles. You can do so by installing some type of screen between the gutter and the stored water. You could, for example, affix a screen over an opening on the rain barrel or cistern, or on the end of a collection pipe that carries the water to the barrel or cistern. By preventing this organic matter from entering your system, your barrels will stay cleaner. The screen will also keep out bugs and frogs.

Collection Surface Evaluation

In addition to the area of your collection surface, you need to consider its characteristics. Here are some characteristics of the most common roof types:

Metal roofs get hot and the first raindrops will evaporate, but other than that, a metal roof is probably the most efficient surface for harvesting water. It's smooth and the vertical channels form protected pathways that keep the rain from blowing off the roof when there is a crosswind. If your metal roof contains lead-based solders and flashing, the water will not be potable, but it should be diluted enough to be perfectly usable within the landscape, even for your edible garden.

Tile roofs have a lot of surface area per square foot, and once the rain flows into the channels, they are quite efficient. Tile does not deteriorate and should provide good, clean rainwater for the long run.

Asphalt roofs are not smooth, which reduces the flow of water to some degree. They may also leach out small amounts of contaminants and small pieces may break off of older roofs. Asphalt is a petroleum product, so this rainwater would not be potable, but it would be good enough for plants—even vegetables. Running your rainwater through a fine screen before it reaches the rain barrel will filter out any small mineral granules.

Cedar-shake roofs are usually treated with antifungal and antimoss herbicides to help them last longer. Rainwater from a new cedar roof is not going to be good for your plants; an older roof may emit a smaller amount of pesticide. It's probably not a good idea to use this water directly on your vegetables, but you could run it through a sand filter (as described above for gray water) to a pond where it will be diluted. You could then use this pond water to irrigate your edibles.

Zinc strips are sometimes added to roofs to help reduce the amount of moss and algae growing there. They release zinc leachates with each rain. This amount of zinc is harmful to fish and other wildlife, and obviously it's harmful to plants. Be sure to remove any zinc strips before you install a rain barrel or cistern.

To be extra safe, you could install a first-flush roof washer to divert dust, pollen, bird poop, and other contaminants away from your main tanks. A roof washer will capture the first few gallons of water in a separate container or wide collection tube with a float that stops the water flow once this diversion tank is full.

Rain Barrels

You can purchase ready-made rain barrels. Or, you could attend a rain-barrel workshop sponsored by one of Florida's county extension agents and learn how to make one yourself. You'll take home the one you made in class as an added bonus. You can also find detailed instructions from various resources and create a rain barrel system suited to your specific needs. There is no one right way to harvest rain—any way is better than letting it all run away.

Plastic drums, often fifty-five gallons, that have contained food products also make good rain barrels. Barrels that have previously held some type of cleaning product could be used, but you will need to thoroughly scrub them first. Do not use barrels that have been filled with petroleum or toxic chemicals. Finding barrels to use may take some sleuthing, but often bottling plants, restaurants, or food-processing companies have food-grade barrels left over. If you have a choice, get ones that are opaque because white or light-colored barrels will let in enough light to allow algae to grow in the barrel.

Cisterns

Cisterns have been used to harvest larger amounts of rain water for centuries, especially in rural areas that lack municipal water systems or where wells cannot be drilled. Any way you look at it, if you need the water that falls from the sky, it makes perfect sense to capture as much of it as you can. Various types of tanks can be used as cisterns:

Galvanized steel is probably the most common material used for cisterns. Off-the-shelf farm tanks are available up in sizes that carry up to about 3,000 gallons.

Concrete tanks are generally built onsite with forms, but smaller pre-cast tanks are also available. To hold water, be sure to use high-strength concrete (e.g., with a strength of 7,000 psi).

Ferrocement tanks are made by spraying or plastering a cement mortar over a wire-mesh form. Depending upon the thickness of the walls, cracks can develop, necessitating some periodic maintenance and repairs.

Plastic tanks are available in sizes that can hold up to several thousand gallons. Some are rigid, while others are flexible. They are lightweight, easily moved, and can be used above or below ground (tanks designed for underground burial will need to be stronger and may be more expensive).

Durable, untreated wood, such as cedar, redwood, or cypress, can be used for tanks. If they are properly built, such tanks could last many years. Make sure the cypress comes from a sustainable tree farm.

Wrapping a polyethylene liner over a frame provides a low-cost cistern option. To hold water, liners for cisterns must be 20 to 30 mils thick. As with all cisterns and rain barrels, arrange for some durable screening over the top to keep out mosquitoes, children, and debris.

Deficit Irrigation: How Much Is Enough?

Our goal, as growers, is to provide the best possible environment for our crops so that they can grow quickly. Doing so produces better-tasting vegetables and reduces our likelihood of encountering significant pest problems. Knowing the right amount of irrigation to supply to our humus-rich soil is the most important factor in creating this optimum growth.

Insufficient moisture during critical stages of growth, such as when seedlings are newly germinated or plants newly transplanted, will stall growth dramatically, resulting in a poor harvest no matter how much irrigation you apply later. Cutting back on irrigation by one half or more once a plant is established is known as deficit irrigation and has its uses.

When you use deficit irrigation throughout the season (but after your plants have been established), you will probably experience a decrease in yield yet save on the costs associated with irrigation. On the other hand, some researchers have found that providing more space between long-season crop plants can make up for deficit irrigation because the roots have a larger volume of soil from which to absorb moisture with less competition from neighboring crops. This is a lesson gleaned from desert habitats, where the plants are widely spaced and have huge root systems.

To know when to apply deficit irrigation, you will want to weigh the cost of irrigation—both the direct cost of water and your personal labor costs—against the quantity and quality of your harvest. For some crops, such as corn, sugarcane, sunflower, sugar beets, carrots, and potatoes, a drier soil as harvest time approaches yields a better-quality crop with less cracking or splitting. The variable conditions of your soil, natural precipitation, and crop pests make it difficult to come up with an exact formula.

Only you can decide how much of a decrease in yield is tolerable. You may find that if you need to save money on irrigation costs, planting less acreage and providing the recommended irrigation (with the resulting better-quality crop) is a better choice.

Irrigation Is Critical for Yields of High Quality and Quantity

Providing the right amount of water for your crops is not easy, but it is the one factor over which you have the most control. And providing the ideal moisture at the right time can mean the difference between a bountiful harvest and a mediocre one.

Resources

For IFAS topics on vegetable irrigation, go to http://edis.ifas.ufl.edu/topic_vegetable_irrigation.

Documents of interest include "Vegetable Production Handbook," http://web.me.com/mathewslparet/Extension/Tutor_files/VPHandbook.pdf; "Fertigation in micro-irrigated horticultural crops: vegetables," http://www.ipipotash.org/udocs/11_Locascio_Fertigation_in_Micro-irrigated_Horticultural_Crops-Vegetables_p146-155.pdf; and "Drip-irrigation systems for small conventional vegetable farms and organic vegetable farms," http://edis.ifas.ufl.edu/hs388.

For directions on using soil moisture sensors, go to http://www.sjrwmd.com/floridawaterstar/pdfs/SMS_field_guide.pdf.

For the Florida Automated Weather Network, see http://fawn.ifas.ufl.edu/.

For more details on harvesting rainwater, see Ginny Stibolt, *Sustainable Gardening for Florida* (Gainesville: University Press of Florida, 2009).

9

Ecosystem Gardening

Edible gardens don't exist in a vacuum; they are part of the larger community of your yard or farm and the surrounding neighborhood. This community is your garden's ecosystem, and actions taken within the ecosystem affect your edibles. Positive actions include attracting butterflies and bees with native plants and planting thick hedgerows to provide cover for birds. Negative actions include maintaining a huge lawn with poisons and artificial fertilizers and running a bug zapper day and night.

It's easy to get into a mindset where you label all the nonhuman visitors to your edible gardens, such as insects, mites, snails, slugs, rabbits, nematodes, squirrels, deer, birds, and raccoons, as pests that need to be repelled or killed. But that mindset is shortsighted because many of those insects would have pollinated your crop flowers or preyed upon the damaging pests. In addition, an insect population is necessary for supporting the birds, bats, insects, frogs, toads, and spiders that are the voracious predators of pesky garden pests. It's best to work with Mother Nature and to take advantage of her weapons of pest destruction.

Scientists call the latter approach Integrated Pest Management (IPM). When growing edible crops, your best IPM strategy is to encourage the beneficial organisms, to discourage the pests, and to grow vigorous crops that resist attack. When problems inevitably arise, the next step in an IPM program is to determine whether the pest is causing enough damage to warrant taking further more drastic steps. Evaluating the pest damage also helps you determine which of the many possible controls is likely to be most effective and appropriate for your particular situation. When you've practiced crop rotations, handpicked as many pests as you can, added physical barriers or traps, cleaned up old crop debris promptly, mulched carefully, and irrigated consistently, sometimes the best solution may be to get rid of the problem crop and plant something else.

A note on terminology: Entomologists classify true bugs as those belonging to the Hemiptera Order, which have sucking mouthparts; an aphid is a good example. With apologies to the entomologists, this book uses the term "bug" informally to refer to various members of the arthropod phylum (i.e., animals with exoskeletons), which includes six-legged insects; eight-legged spiders and mites; some crustaceans such as sowbugs and pillbugs; and the many-legged centipedes and millipedes.

Poisons: Organic or Not

Whether a pesticide or an herbicide is organic or not, a poison is a poison, and some are more devastating to your garden's ecosystem than others. Organic poisons are derived from living things. In some cases, the organism itself is the poison; such is the case with the bacterium *Bacillus thuringiensis* (Bt), which sickens caterpillars or mosquitoes depending on how it's formulated. Organic poisons can also be chemicals produced by living organisms; the pyrethrins made from chrysanthemum seed cases are a good example. Synthetic poisons such as dichlorodiphenyltrichloroethane (DDT) are manufactured from substances that have never been alive. While organic poisons tend to degrade into harmless chemicals more quickly than synthetic ones, all poisons can throw an entire ecosystem out of balance. Some organic poisons are approved for certified organic operations, but even so, they should be used only as the very last resort. If you do use them, follow the directions carefully and use the smallest possible amount that will be effective. (Read "Using Pesticides" beginning on page 251.)

In a balanced ecosystem, predators are in the minority. In such an ecosystem, a huge number of prey—including aphids, white flies, cabbageworms, leaf miners, mole crickets, spider mites, and many more—may be eating your crops, while the predator populations will be much smaller. Predator bugs include praying mantids, spiders, or assassin bugs, and other animal predators include lizards, toads, birds, and bats.

Let's consider what happens when you attempt to poison pests. A general insecticide (organic or not) will kill the majority of bugs in an area, but more than ninety percent of them will have been either beneficial or benign. Predators such as bats, frogs, lizards, and birds will go elsewhere to feed, and even the microbes in your soil may die. As your landscape recovers from the poisoning, bugs will begin to multiply again, but because you've killed off the beneficial insects that helped keep them under control and driven the birds, bats, lizards, and toads that survived the poisoning to move away, there will be even fewer natural predators to counteract the bad bugs. Many harmful bugs, possibly including new pests that were previously controlled, will recover in even greater numbers than before. Faced with another bug problem, you spray again and the process repeats itself, with the most damaging pests recovering in ever increasing numbers each time. Repeated poisonings often foster a resistance to that pesticide in the bugs you targeted, at which point many people switch to an even stronger poison in a higher concentration. You can avoid the cycle of poison escalation and manage your landscape as a complete ecosystem according to the principles of Integrated Pest Management (IPM).

Relying on insect predators and other eco-friendly strategies to control your pests is not a matter of sitting back and doing nothing. As with any other effective gardening method, IPM requires awareness, education, experimentation, effort, and patience. While it's easy to recognize the larger pest predators, identifying the good, the bad, and the ugly bugs is more challenging. And yet it's a vital step toward ecosystem gardening.

Encourage the Beneficials

The beneficials include birds, bats, frogs, toads, parasitoid insects, snakes, spiders, centipedes, predatory insects, and lizards (but not the larger plant-eating lizards, like iguanas). Encouraging beneficials to visit or live in your garden is an important part of your IPM program and ecosystem management. There are a number of excellent advantages to this method of pest control:

- Your crops will not have any pesticide residues.
- The predators will do much of the work and will wax and wane in step with your pest populations.
- Your pests will be less likely to develop a resistance to pesticides.
- You are not contributing to environmental pollution.

If you're planting vegetables where none have been grown before, very few pests will plague your crops the first year. They will eventually find your garden with its yummy edibles, so plan for ways to attract the beneficials from the start.

There are several types of beneficial organisms and various strategies for encouraging them to live in and around your garden.

Predators of Bugs

Predators hunt and eat bugs or feed them to their young. Most predators are generalists and will devour any insect within range. A bat, for example, will consume thousands of flying insects every night; purple martins, fly catchers, and tree swallows take over during the day depending upon the time of year. Bluebirds and blue jays will dive-bomb your yard, and wrens will pick through your container gardens looking for insects to eat. Frogs, toads, and lizards are all excellent insect predators. While most snails will eat your crops' foliage and are pests along with the slugs, there are also predatory snails that prey on other snails and slugs. Armadillos and moles can smell grubs, snails, and other ground-dwelling pests. While they might make a mess as they dig their prey from the soil, you should cheer for insect predators in ecosystem gardening.

Predatory bugs come in many sizes and shapes:

- Dragonfly larvae (naiads) have a voracious appetite for mosquito larvae in the water; the adults continue to eat mosquitoes and other flying insects.
- Assassin bugs, pirate bugs, and big-eyed bugs have a specialized mouthpart that can pierce through the hard exoskeleton of insects and suck out their insides.
- Ladybug (a.k.a. lady beetle or ladybird beetle) larvae and adults eat aphids and other sucking insects—the alligator-shaped larvae look nothing like the adult beetles. Ladybugs are just one of many predatory beetles.
- Lacewing larvae are avid predators of aphids but will also consume mites, scale insects, and small caterpillars.
- Hoverfly larvae feed upon greenflies, aphids, mealybugs, leafhoppers, scale, spider mites, and small caterpillars. The adults resemble bees.
- Praying mantids are highly efficient predators and are fascinating to watch as they prowl around your garden and grab insects large and small with their wickedly barbed forearms.
- Centipedes are fierce predators with big, poison-injecting jaws. They feed on a variety of creatures. Their relatives the millipedes are mainly scavengers that dine on dead stuff—a good predator to have in your compost pile.
- There many carnivorous wasps, including yellow jackets, that prey on a variety of bugs—either for themselves or to feed their young.
- Solitary bees are excellent pollinators and dine on pollen and nectar as adults, but many types also capture bugs for their young. (Others build pollen balls to feed to their young.) Usually the females dig tunnels in uncultivated soils or drill into dead wood, place the dead bug (or pollen ball) at the end of the tunnel, and then lay an egg on the bug, which serves as the larva's food source. Be sure to leave some dead wood and uncultivated and unmulched soil for these important bees.

- Spiders do much more for your garden than decorate it with lovely dew-catching webs; they are efficient bug catchers—with and without webs.

Parasitoid insects kill their hosts by laying their eggs on or in them and letting their larvae do the dirty work, but they are not considered predators. Most parasitoids are tiny wasps. The adult parasitoid female lays her eggs in or on the host. When the eggs hatch, the larvae consume the host gradually, leaving the vital organs until last, which keeps the host alive until the parasitoid larvae pupate and are able to survive on their own. Parasitoids tend to be host-specific. Best known are the braconid wasps that infest tomato hornworms, resulting in their rice-sized larvae protruding from the worm's back. The chalcid and ichneumonid wasps parasitize mealybugs, aphids, and other insect larvae. Adult parasitoid wasps are tiny (ranging from 1/100 to 3/4 inch long), so provide some plants with tiny florets in a broad flower head, like members of the carrot or daisy families, near your edible garden areas.

The parasitoid tachinid flies are less specific and will devour almost any bug (pest or not), including stinkbugs, beetles, caterpillars, cutworms, and armyworms. If the female fly doesn't lay her eggs soon enough, the eggs will hatch inside her body and the larvae will go to work on her. Talk about a ticking biological clock! The adult flies also require a nectar source, but if flowers are not available they can also feed on aphid honeydew.

Predators of Slugs and Snails

The predators of slugs and snails include toads, frogs, lizards, snakes, some large beetles, and even a predatory snail called a rosy wolfsnail, which is native to Florida. Some of the larger bug-eating birds such as crows, blue jays, and mocking birds will also dine on slugs and snails. You, too, could become a predator and harvest your own escargot directly from the garden. Some people let their chickens roam the garden in search of slugs and bugs. Chickens might uproot tender seedlings as they scratch around, so monitor their activities; also, keep them from the garden when it's within ninety days of harvest time to minimize the risk of contamination from their manure. Chickens should not be allowed in beds of crops that touch the soil such as radishes. You may decide to let your chickens into the garden beds only after the harvest.

Attracting and Keeping Pest Killers

To draw both bugs and their predators to your garden, you'll need to provide them with good habitat—some have called this practice "farmscaping." You'll want to encourage a large bug population to keep the predators supplied with plenty of food. This may seem counterintuitive, given that you're trying to get rid of pests, but your goal as an ecosystem gardener is to allow the populations to reach a balance or equilibrium. You can purchase ladybugs and other predatory insects, but adding too many predators at once rarely works, because if there are too many predators in the ecosystem, they won't have enough food. And of course the ladybugs will "fly away home," or at least to some other place. Perhaps you could share predators with another gardener in your neighborhood.

It's a good idea to keep a variety of flowers with different colors and structures blooming year-round in or near your edible gardens. This way you provide nectar and pollen for both the adult predatory insects and the important pollinators. Create different layers of vegetation near your edible gardens by planting native hedgerows with leaves that reach from the ground to the high shrubbery level to provide good shelter—hedgerows make a good windbreak, as well.

Some plant types are especially good at attracting beneficials:

- Low-growing creepers provide cover for ground beetles.
- Small florets arranged in a flat flower head are a good food source for the adult phase of those tiny parasitoid wasps. It's a good idea to plant an extra "for-the-bugs" garden, where you allow the parsley or dill to flower. That way, you'll also have a place to deposit the black swallowtail caterpillars that you pick from your for-humans-only herb garden.
- Flowers in the daisy family (Asteraceae), such as asters, mist flowers, coreopsis, black-eyed susans, marigolds, zinnias, and

goldenrod, are easy on the gardener's eye and provide nectar, pollen, and seeds for insects and birds.

- Flowers of the mint family (Lamiaceae), such as basil, monarda, salvia, scarlet sage, and various mints, attract hummingbirds, predatory wasps, hover flies, and robber flies.

In addition to maintaining a large bug population, you can encourage carnivorous birds and bats to live on your property by supplying them with appropriately designed bird and bat houses and other shelter such as snags and brush piles. Hummingbirds eat insects when they are raising their young, so keep them coming to your property by growing red or orange tubular flowers and maybe installing a few hummingbird feeders. Install an apartment-style birdhouse for purple martins in an open area near a body of water. Maintain some of your property as an open meadow that is mowed once or twice a year to attract the bluebirds and other ground-feeders. If you garden in a small urban plot, on a balcony, or in a raised bed built with cinder blocks, you could plant butterfly- and insect-attracting plants nearby, in containers near the front door, in a hanging basket under the eaves, or even at the local community center, school, or church. This way, your whole neighborhood will become a functioning ecosystem.

Leave some out-of-the-way places uncultivated, with no weed barrier and no mulch, and provide a log or a pile of brush where critters can make their nests in the ground. Create permanent toad shelters in and around your gardens; toads will return the favor by dining on your slugs and bugs. A toad shelter can be as simple as a piece of clay pot or a flat rock with a small crevice under it.

To provide habitat for frogs and dragonflies, you will need a pond or a water feature so they can complete their life cycles. It doesn't have to be large—a half-barrel or pre-formed, hard-plastic pond sunk in the ground will do—but it should include a variety of plant materials, fish, snails, and both shallow and deep water. If your pond has a beach or mud flats, the butterflies will also enjoy it. If you are raising watercress (*Nasturtium* spp.), you will need a circulating water feature such as a multilevel fountain with a solar-powered pump. You can also tailor this fountain to frogs, birds, and bugs by providing a relatively still section where the overflow collects.

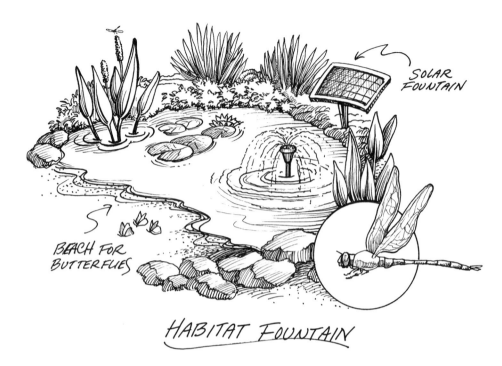

SOLAR FOUNTAIN

BEACH FOR BUTTERFLIES

HABITAT FOUNTAIN

Best Practices in the Garden

While providing good habitat on your property and in your neighborhood for insects and their predators will help to establish balance, there will always be some of those sucking, boring, and chewing pests in your garden. Some important garden practices that will reduce problems with known pests. First of all, you can reduce the impact of the pest attacks by choosing disease- and pest-resistant plant varieties, and by buying good-quality seed, roots, and pest-free seedlings. Paying a little extra for better quality plants is well worth it. Keep good records on where you bought your plants or seeds, when you planted them, and on any other actions you took in your garden log for future reference.

Bugs and other pests often look for a specific type of plant to infest at a specific time. Growing a variety of plants can make it more difficult for species-specific pests to find their food source. In the vegetable garden, intermix crops and rotate them. Do the same with your ornamentals in other parts of the landscape. Fill your decorative container gardens, borders, hedgerows, beds, and other landscape features with a variety of mostly native plants that are attractive to pollinators.

When pests do attack your crops, make it difficult for them to survive. Several times a week during your most active growing seasons, look for pests under the leaves and stems or branches of each plant; this is when it's important to know which are the good bugs and which are not. Remove larger pest bugs by handpicking them or knocking them into a container of soapy water. You could also rinse sucking pests off of your plants with water, just be sure to spray or wash both sides of the leaves. Remove badly infested plants or plant parts, as well as old, sick, or dying plants because they're more susceptible to pests. Don't throw the sick or stressed plants onto your compost pile; rather, throw them away with the trash or yard waste to reduce your chances of a reinfestation.

Whatever controls you use, they will be more effective if you catch the infestations early. Once extensive damage occurs, it is often too late to save the plants or preserve their marketability. You might consider using traps as another form of inspecting for pests. Colored, sticky traps, pheromone traps, pitfall traps, and light traps work well with some pests. Beer traps (i.e., tuna cans or bowls containing an inch or so of beer sunk into the soil to their rims) will attract snails and slugs, as will boards laid flat in the garden (the snails and slugs will collect under them). You can trap whiteflies and aphids on the sticky surface of bright yellow, sticky cards, whose color attracts them. Keep in mind that some of your beneficials may also be attracted to these cards.

If your crops have been plagued with a particular pest, experiment with the timing of your planting. Perhaps you can plant the seedlings earlier or later (Florida's warm climate sometimes provides a good deal of latitude in planting times). Or, skip a year or two and plant something else less vulnerable to that pest. You could install translucent row covers that allow plants to absorb the light they need, but keep out flying insects. This way the airborne bugs won't have easy access to their usual food supply. Be sure to remove the cover in time for pollination. Plants are most vulnerable when they are small; once they grow past the seedling stage, damage from pests may not be as harmful.

Pest Types

The Bugs

Sucking Pests

Sucking pests, such as aphids, scale, mealybugs, whiteflies, stinkbug larvae, leaf-footed bugs, and spider mites, have specially designed piercing mouth parts that can enter tender, young cells in areas of new growth on the plants. Over-fertilized plants, with their flush of new growth, are particularly susceptible to such damage. After piercing the cell wall, the pests suck out and ingest the liquid from the cells near the surface of the plant. An attack by sucking pests will have little effect on a strong, healthy plant, but the loss of liquid and of its outer stem cells could be damaging to a plant already weakened by water stress or a root pest.

Often, ants will assist aphids and scale by protecting them from predators in return for some of the sweet honeydew that the insects exude when prodded. The ants then take the sugary mix back to their nests. The ants actually become farmers and will move the pests to the locations that cause them to produce the most output. You can interrupt this cycle by applying Tanglefoot, Stickem, or other sticky substance to the base of the plants' stems, thereby blocking the ants' pathway to their nest.

A plant that has been under attack by sucking pests will be covered in a coating of sugary ooze even after the bugs have moved on. This coating will attract a sooty mold—a type of black or dark gray fungus. Not only is it ugly, but its dark coating also compromises the plant's ability to perform photosynthesis. If you find such evidence, carefully wipe the sucking pests, along with the sugary ooze and the sooty mold residues, from the stems and leaves with a soft cloth dampened with alcohol. You can also rinse the plant with a stream of water to knock off the bugs and dilute the sugary ooze. The pests are not likely to climb back up to the top of the plant of their own accord, but their ant farmers may pick them up and reposition them there.

Boring Insects

Boring insects often take the gardener by surprise because their initial points of entry into the plants are so small.

Squash borers pupate in the soil and, after they emerge in the spring, the adult female moths lay their eggs on squash vines—usually near the base. The larvae bore into the stems and will do great damage to the vine as they hollow out the stem. Bt is not usually effective against these pests because the larvae are in a protected environment. Crop rotation doesn't help either because the moths will fly some distance to find their favorite stems to lay their eggs. In addition to mulching well and keeping a clean garden (i.e., removing infested plants quickly), there are several ways to deal with squash borers:

- Accept that the borers will attack your plants and that your plants will have a shortened life. Either bury the stem in several places so that it can develop new roots above the infestation or plant new squash seeds every two or three weeks so that you have a continuing supply of new young plants.
- Try to prevent the moth from laying her eggs by wrapping the stem with aluminum foil or duct tape or coating it with Tanglefoot or Stickem.
- Once you notice frass (brown debris) around some holes in the stem, make a lengthwise cut along the stem, remove the larvae, and then tape the stem back together. This strategy is probably not going to save your plant, but it might give you another few weeks of production and it will interrupt the pests' life cycles. Be sure to throw out infested plants with the trash or yard waste; do not add them to your compost pile or allow them to sit around the garden.

Another borer, called the pickleworm, may attack the fruit of your squash plant later in the season. The frass may be the first indication of the infestation. Bt is your best defense.

Corn borers are another problem for the small grower, but usually borers damage only a small part of the ear and you can break that part off and still enjoy the rest of the corn. Borers are a bigger problem for medium and larger growers because their damage makes the corn unmarketable. Some people suggest that applying a few drops of mineral oil to the corn silk as soon as it appears will deter borers, while others rely on Bt. Again, Bt could be ineffective if you apply it at the wrong time because the larvae hide inside the corn husk for most of that stage in their life cycle.

Mining Insects

These tiny larvae live between the upper and lower surfaces of leaves. As they eat their way through the leaf, they leave pale trails in their wake. Miners will not impair the host plant very much if it is otherwise healthy, but their damage can reduce the marketability of leaf crops. Once a leaf is infested, pick it off and throw it away to interrupt the life cycle. Floating row covers are your best defense.

Browsing or Chewing Pests

Browsing or chewing pests will eat holes in your foliage and maybe even your fruit. Chewers include caterpillars, grasshoppers, weevils, beetles, slugs, snails, and sometimes ants and bees. As a group, chewers inflict the most damage to crops. Be prepared to handpick them every time you go into the garden—bring a jar filled with some soapy water and drop them in. There is no substitute for your vigilance.

If the chewers are ground-based and are inflicting more damage than you can tolerate, supplement your handpicking program with diatomaceous earth spread around each plant. (Buy garden-grade diatomaceous earth, not the type sold for use in pools.) The sharp skeletons of these old sea creatures will rip open the undersides of snails, slugs, caterpillars, and worms. Reapply after a hard rain. This method will work on all caterpillars, though, so be sure to use the diatomaceous earth only where needed. Bt will also work to eliminate all caterpillars in the area. You can also trap slugs and snails in the garden with a beer trap—a shallow dish sunk in the soil up to its rim and filled with an inch of beer. Slugs and snail will also be attracted to a flat board, upside-down grapefruit halves, or outer cabbage leaves laid in the garden. Check your traps when you visit the garden and remove your catch.

You can reduce problems with flying or hopping chewers with the timely application of floating row covers. If your crop requires pollination, you'll need to remove the covers as soon as female flowers emerge.

Soil Dwellers

While good garden soil teems with life and organic gardeners work hard to increase its vitality, there are some soil-based bugs that will harm your crops. These include cutworms, wire worms, weevils, and grubs, most of which are beetle larvae. Some stay underground and gnaw on the roots, while others, such as cutworms, emerge at night to do their damage to the leaves and stems of your crops. Organic material in the soil and a good mulching system are your best defenses.

Usually, you won't know that you have browsing cutworms or armyworms until it's too late—these nighttime larvae cut off your new seedlings at the soil level. In the morning you'll find all your carefully planted seedlings clear cut by these miniature lumberjacks. Happily, prevention is easy (if somewhat labor intensive) and cheap. Cut empty toilet paper rolls in half (or paper towel rolls in four-inch sections) and sink them into the soil around each seedling. This cardboard collar will act as an insurmountable wall for the cutworms and also keep the mulch from touching the stem as the seedling grows, which will reduce the chances of a fungal attack later in the growing season.

Mosquitoes

While mosquitoes are not directly harmful to your crops, a gardener's comfort is important. We all know not to leave water standing for more than three days—mosquitoes can breed in surprisingly little water. Scout every nook and cranny in your landscape for items that could hold water. The saucers for your container gardens should be deep enough to hold some water for half a day or so after you water, but the soil in the container should soak it up after that. During rainy periods, turn the saucers upside down under the pots so that excess water can flow away. Cover the water reservoir of rain barrels and self-watering container systems with screens. Empty any birdbaths or small water features with no circulation pump and no flora and fauna every third day. To be most effective, make mosquito prevention a neighborhood-wide or community-garden-wide program.

Fire Ants

The red imported fire ant, an apparently accidental introduction from Brazil in the 1930s, is definitely a pest in Florida gardens. Worker ants aggressively defend their nest and will bite and sting intruders—they bite with their pincer mouthparts and then inject venom with their stingers.

The best poison-free method for treating anthills in your garden is to slowly pour at least a gallon of boiling water onto the hill. To eradicate the colony, the hot water has to reach the queen(s), which are usually deep in the hill. The hot water will also cook nearby plant roots, though, so proceed with care. Another method is to pour a gallon or more of cold water deep into the nest every day for three or four days. Water treatments and other disruptions such as raking or digging will cause the colony to move. Repeat this process for each mound until the ants have relocated to areas where you can tolerate their presence. Unfortunately, we will never be rid of them, but we can keep them out of our way with water treatments. There are old gardeners' tales about sprinkling grits or rice on the mound, but these methods have proven unreliable. Maybe one day we'll have access to a fire-ant bait that is approved for organic gardens.

Not by Bugs Alone

Bugs are only one of many potential causes of unhealthy plants. Fungus, bacteria, or virus-caused diseases, nematodes, water stress, and nutritional imbalance can also be damaging. Often, plants weakened by one problem become targets for another. So while you may be able to see the aphids sucking on a stem, you can't assume that they are the only problem. Correctly identifying the main problem can be tricky, but it's worth the effort. That way, you can either remedy the problem or at least know what you're up against. As with bug pests, defensive gardening is essential. It could be that some of the bugs are also spreading the fungus or virus.

When you identify a sick plant, inspect its entire environment for clues to the problem. Too much or too little moisture, wind, humidity, salt-spray, and sunlight may stress plants, causing them to become susceptible to damage from pests and diseases. Record weather conditions along with your planting dates and other treatments in your garden log; this record could provide clues to the growth patterns and problems you encounter from year to year.

Fungi

You probably won't be aware that a fungus has invaded your plants until it's too late. Fungi are everywhere, of course, and like bugs most of them are beneficial. For instance, they play a significant role as decomposers in your compost pile, and some fungi help plant roots to absorb more water from the soil. Some of the most common problems associated with fungi include powdery mildew, the damping off of seedlings, downy mildew, rusts, leaf spots, root rots, and wilt.

Fungal diseases spread via spores that are too small to see individually, but masses of them on a leaf surface look like a furry or powdery growth. Once the spore lands on the plant, if conditions are favorable (for the fungus, not for the plant), it will germinate and penetrate the tissue where it will grow inside the plant. Once it is inside the leaf or root tissue, the fungus becomes much more difficult to control, so prevention or early control options are your best options for halting or reducing the infection. The good news is that a healthy plant has some of its own defenses against fungal attack, and this innate resistance prevents most of the spores that come in contact with plant tissue from germinating.

Your best defenses against persistent fungus problems in the landscape, especially in the vegetable garden, are purchasing cultivars that are resistant to that fungus, promoting good air circulation between plants by giving each plenty of room, and irrigating only in the morning so that the leaves dry out during the day or irrigating only the soil. Clean up infested plants and dispose of them in the trash or with your yard waste—not in the compost pile. In the vegetable garden, use a long crop rotation (three years or more) so that you are not supplying specialized fungi in the soil with the perfect host each year. Wait until the plants are dry before working in the garden because moisture may contain fungi or bacteria, and you could spread it to other plants.

One homemade remedy for fungi is a solution of baking soda dissolved in water: add one teaspoon of vegetable oil, one teaspoon of baking soda, and one teaspoon of dishwashing liquid to one cup of water, and shake well. Also shake frequently while applying the solution to your plant, and make sure you spray both sides of the leaves, as thorough coverage is necessary for defeating the pest. Be sure to water the plant well the day before you spray it. Leave the solution on the plant for a few hours, and then wash it off with the garden hose. Do not spray your plants during the heat of the day. This mixture also acts as an insecticide, so use it with care.

Bacteria and Viruses

Bacterial and viral infections are usually less evident, and there is less you can do about them. Bacteria usually enter a plant through a wound, such as those that might be created during staking, pruning, and harvesting, so handle your plants as little as possible, and when you do touch them, handle them with care. Sterilize your pruning and harvesting tools with an alcohol rub after working on plants, whether or not the plants appear diseased. It's important to use a sharp knife or sharp pair of shears for pruning and harvesting to minimize the damage to the plants. Preventive gardening strategies are the best defense.

Nematodes

Nematodes are tiny worms that live in the film of water that surrounds soil granules. They abound in soils and while most are benign, some are harmful to your plants, and still others are beneficial. Root-knot nematodes invade the roots of susceptible peppers, squash, okra, and other crops in your edible garden and hamper their growth. You might suspect that you have a nematode infestation when an otherwise healthy plant wilts too quickly, but you won't know for certain until you pull the plants at the end of the season. Do not compost nematode-infested plants, and remove them from the garden area as soon as possible to interrupt the life cycle of these tiny worms.

Your best defenses against nematodes are purchasing nematode-resistant crop varieties and providing such a good growing environment that the plants can survive with fewer functioning roots. If you have done your job in building good, healthy soil that's rich in organic matter and has good tilth, nematodes may be less of a problem.

Crop rotation combats some of the problems associated with crop-specific nematodes—essentially if their favorite plants are not there the next season, they'll die out. If you have known nematode problems, you can purchase predatory nematodes, solarize your soil, or plant a cover crop of marigolds, cow peas, or sunn hemp in the summer.

Larger Pests

Depending upon your location, your garden could be host to a menagerie of landscape browsers. The most sustainable deterrents against these animals are physical barriers. Rabbits, squirrels, raccoons, iguanas, opossums, voles, pocket gophers, and wild hogs all have the potential to be a problem in your vegetable garden, but keep in mind that some of them may actually be after your fat grubs and not your crops. Tall raised beds will deter some of these pests, and hot pepper residue (as either a spray or a powder) will repel many mammals. Just be sure to reapply it after rainstorms.

You can keep burrowing animals from eating your root vegetables by affixing a mesh hardware cloth to the bottoms of your raised beds. The best defense against most of these animals is a fence partially buried in the ground. To keep out hogs, you will have to construct a fence out of heavy metal—concrete rebar works well. Unfortunately, there is no fence or raised bed that will stop squirrels and raccoons. A wire cage built to cover the tops of your plants and to sink into the ground might work. Some growers build screened enclosures for their vegetables. Doing so also makes it easy to add shade panels that can extend the season for cool-weather crops, but remember to find a way for pollinators to access the crops.

Some of these invasive animals, such as wild hogs and iguanas, can and should be trapped. It's illegal to release them somewhere else, but you may be able to find a market for their meat. At least one U.S. website sells farm-raised iguana meat for $60.00 a pound! More and more people are interested in sampling exotic meats. If you have an extensive problem with pest animals, you might consider hiring a professional trapping service to reduce the local population.

If you grow food in visible locations like your front yard or a community garden, you may have problems with people stealing your vegetables. A border of brambly berries, prickly pear, or thorny pineapples may discourage human thieves, but fences with gates and locks are probably the only way to effectively deal with this problem. Neighborhood vigilance and a public offering of some of your excess harvest might help as well.

No one likes talking about them, but rats can be a problem anywhere—in the city, the suburb, or the country. The best solutions are building a sturdy fence around the garden; not leaving pet food, including birdseed, in the area; and keeping the compost area free of rat food such as kitchen scraps. In this case, use only deep trench composting within the fenced area.

You can discourage deer from visiting your garden by laying poultry netting (a.k.a. chicken wire) over the mowed areas near your beds and tacking it down with garden staples. Their split hooves will get stuck in the wire, and they should back off. In the meantime, you can walk on it and mow over it without a problem. Each season, lift it up, rake the vegetation underneath, and then replace it. This is an easier and less expensive solution than installing an eight-foot-tall electric fence around your property, and it works better than blood, hair, or bobcat urine (although it's not nearly as much fun to tell your neighbors about).

To keep birds from eating your strawberries or pecking at your tomatoes, cover your plants with fine netting—just make sure that the holes are small enough that birds can't become tangled in the net. You can use the same material you use to cover your rows at a different point in the season.

Scarecrows and things that move and clang in the breeze are traditional deterrents, and they may work for a while, but birds will eventually figure out that they mean no harm. After all, scarecrows have no brains, and birds do, even if they are "bird-brains." Happily, newer scarecrows have a rudimentary sort of brain in the form of a motion detector attached to a water squirter. They are more effective than the traditional scarecrow because anything that moves gets a squirt.

If you see scavengers around your garden, scare them away any way you can. It's all part of making your landscape inhospitable for the pests.

Using Pesticides

An organic pesticide may sound like an oxymoron, but organic growers are allowed to use some pesticides. Some extreme pest problems call for more aggressive controls than manipulating cultural practices in the plant environment or using biological control agents. In these cases, pesticides are a last resort. (Please do not apply pesticides as a preventive measure or "just in case"; they should be used only when all other methods have failed. Read "Poisons: Organic or Not" beginning on page 234.) Before applying any pesticide treatment in your landscape, contact your local extension agent. He or she can help you to identify the root of the problem and the best strategy for tackling it in your local area. Like any pesticides, organic pesticides are subject to the law, and in this case the label is the law. Always read the label and follow the directions. Make sure the product is listed with the Organic Materials Review Institute. The majority of pests are most easily controlled at a particular stage of their life cycle, usually earlier in their development.

If a pesticide is called for, select the one that is most specific to the pest you wish to target, least toxic to nontarget organisms, and least persistent in the environment. There are some organic pesticides that are approved for certified growers. That said, a chemical derived from a biological source isn't necessarily any safer than an artificially produced chemical. Read the labels on all pesticides completely and thoroughly. To minimize disruption to your ecosystem, spot treat the problem area instead of applying blanket or wall-to-wall preventive treatments.

Bt (*Bacillus thuringiensis*)

Bt is a bacterium that can be formulated to target specific insects. Bt causes digestive failure in the insect and does not persist in the landscape. One strain of Bt is designed to target caterpillars for a few days, while another targets mosquitoes. Use Bt with caution; even though it is not supposed to be toxic to animals other than the targeted species, it does upset the natural balance between predator and prey.

Insecticidal Soaps or Neem Oil

Soaps and oils repel foliage feeders and fungi, break down within days of application, but they are toxic to fish. Both soaps and oils can damage plants if applied when the plants are water stressed, when temperatures are above 90°F, or if high humidity prevents rapid drying. Some plants are sensitive to oil sprays. Perform a test on a small area before making a wider application. If you're working on organic certification, pay close attention to the guidelines for approved products.

Develop a Tolerance for Some Pest Damage

As organic gardeners, we may need to tolerate a certain amount of insect harm in return for pesticide-free produce. Healthy, naturally fertilized, and sensibly watered plants growing in soil alive with microbes can sustain some damage without too many ill effects. A more naturally balanced ecosystem is much less likely to suffer from severe pest infestations.

Should an infestation arise, nature has an extensive arsenal of predators that will feast on your peskiest pests. The populations of these predators will expand and contract with those of the pests.

Resources

For the University of Florida Extension Service's website on Integrated Pest Management, go to http://ipm.ifas.ufl.edu; and http://schoolipm. ifas.ufl.edu.

For the National Science Foundation's website on Integrated Pest Management, see http://cipm.ncsu.edu.

The University of North Carolina maintains the Southern IPM Center at http://www.sripmc.org.

Clemson University's Extension website features numerous articles on pest control; for organic growers, these are useful mostly for their identification of pests and the damage they cause: http://hgic.clemson. edu.

For information about wild hogs and more, go to the Florida Fish and Wildlife Conservation Commission website at http://myfwc.com.

The University of Florida maintains numerous reference sheets that gardeners will find useful. For various bug types that affect vegetable crops, go to http://edis.ifas.ufl.edu/pdffiles/CV/CV11100.pdf. For more information on nematodes, go to http://edis.ifas.ufl.edu/ng047; for "Organic Management of Vegetable Diseases, Part I: Soilborne Pathogens," go to http://edis.ifas.ufl.edu/pp169; for "Organic Management of Vegetable Diseases, Part II: Foliar Pathogens," go to http://edis.ifas. ufl.edu/pp170; and for Vegetable Best Management by Crop, go to http://edis.ifas.ufl.edu/topic_vegetable_ipm_by_crop.

The National Sustainable Agriculture Information Service (AT-TRA) has some publications on Integrated Pest Management at https://attra.ncat.org.

Also check the Organic Materials Review Institute (OMRI) at http://www.omri.org.

Two useful books are Sydney Park Brown and Eileen Buss, *Helpful, Harmful, and Harmless* (Gainesville: University of Florida/IFAS, 2010); and Eric Grissell, *Insects and Gardens: In Pursuit of a Garden Ecology* (Portland, OR: Timber Press, 2001).

10

Trends in Edible Gardening

As an organic gardener, you already care about where your food comes from and recognize that you are part of your local food system. This chapter covers some of the bigger-picture food-system concepts and some of your options should you decide to take your gardening to the next level. By replacing more lawn acreage, brownfields, and blighted urban areas (but not natural or pristine areas, which our wildlife very much need) with edible gardens, we are making better and more productive use of Florida's resources. Plus, growing vegetables locally just might make a dent in Florida's unemployment rate.

Local or Organic?

While there is debate over which is the better choice, the realms of both organic food and local food belong to people who make conscious eating choices. As omnivores, humans can eat just about anything, but as conscious eaters, many of us don't want to eat just anything. "So what should I eat?" Americans have long made food choices for personal diets, but recent conversations about food, like those furthered by Michael Pollan in his book *The Omnivore's Dilemma*, have brought community and environmental health aspects into the equation. Where *organic* asked "how was my food grown?," *local* asks "where was my food grown—and how many miles and semi-trucks did it have to travel to reach me?" As people learn how what they put in their mouths affects the wider world around them, many are beginning to see the value of incorporating both organic and local foods into their eating practices. Eating locally supports the local economy, including our small, neighborhood farmers who earn a living from their land, and reduces the impact of fossil fuel–based transportation on the environment. And there is no food more local than what grows a few steps from your own door.

Urban Agriculture

The twentieth century divided American rural and urban populations more than any other time in history, in large part by separating the producers of crops from their consumers. Separated from food production, some economically struggling urban areas are now becoming "food deserts"; swaths of city blocks where residents can easily buy cigarettes, packaged (highly processed) foods, and liquor but cannot find a fresh tomato. Fortunately, a focus on incorporating gardening into city life can positively affect this situation.

Urban agriculture, whether through urban farms, community gardens, or home gardens, can serve as important source of fresh, healthy produce. Many are staking their hopes for future healthy communities on urban agriculture by creating garden spaces in former food deserts and involving residents and younger citizens in the food production process. It is possible to create new agricultural opportunities in urban areas with all the attendant benefits.

The value of urban agriculture has been firmly grasped by federal and local agencies. The Centers for Disease Control and Prevention (CDC) and local health foundations across the nation have provided grants to organizations working toward healthy communities through urban agriculture, community gardens, farmers markets, and corner stores that offer healthy choices. Experienced gardeners are in demand; organic gardeners can find volunteer and job opportunities with local nonprofit organizations, after-school programs, churches, senior and community centers, and public schools to help teach citizens to how garden organically.

Green Jobs, Micro-Enterprise, and Community Involvement

Enthusiastic organic gardeners can create their own green jobs by starting an urban agriculture program by training at-risk youth to garden or by helping a city, college, hospital, or other entity start an organic garden and then maintaining it. Trainees can then find their own green jobs, and in this way the community will grow. Adult education programs and community colleges offer organic gardening courses for adult learners. The need for experienced teachers presents organic gardeners with another opportunity to translate their experience into a career.

There are many ways that micro-enterprise opportunities can support organic gardening, from baking herb biscuits with homegrown herbs to sourcing and delivering organic soil amendments like compost and horse manure to other gardeners. If you know how to build raised beds, you might find paying customers for your services. Or, offer your services as a "migrant farmer" and set up and tend organic vegetable gardens in other people's yards—some people have a good garden site but are too busy to plant and maintain their own gardens. Maybe you could be flexible with payment for your services and consider a combination of money and a portion of the produce from those gardens that you could sell at a local farmers market.

While the Master Gardener program at your local county extension office does not focus exclusively on organic gardening, becoming a Master Gardener does provide significant benefits: you receive good training, gain credibility, and meet like-minded people. Many volunteer jobs provide opportunities for additional learning and experience; sometimes volunteer jobs turn into paid positions.

School Gardens

Many schools want a food garden these days, and why not? School gardens are a great way to teach math and science skills. They also inspire creativity, hard work, patience, and good nutrition. When kids grow vegetables, they are more likely to try new foods and to participate in food preparation. The secret to a successful school garden is a passionate leader and an enthusiastic group of supportive adults such as teachers, parents, local volunteers, and Master Gardeners.

Your county extension office probably gets at least one call a week from someone looking to create or work with a school garden. A good Master Gardener coordinator can assist organic gardeners in this effort. Or, call the principal of a school you would like to "adopt" to help with an organic food garden. If the school is already gardening or thinking about it, the school administrators will welcome your help; if not, your phone call may be all they need to get started.

Inspired by Chef Alice Waters's edible schoolyard project in Berkeley, California, Slow Food USA has been involved with school gardens since 2001. Slow Food USA is a national movement, but local chapters have accomplished a great deal. For instance, in the past four years Slow Food Miami has installed a total of 140 school garden beds and has provided dozens of mini-grants to cover gardening costs.

Grants for materials and teacher education may be available for your school, and schools may be eligible for additional assistance. Be sure to plan for the summer months when school is not in session. Maybe the students could help set up the beds for solarization until the following school year.

K-12 schools aren't the only ones interested in organic gardening. Gardens at colleges and universities are integral parts of various curricula. Students learn in the classroom, and sometimes that classroom is the garden. Agroecology students build their skills as they apply what they are learning; culinary students taste real, fresh produce and unusual crops they couldn't order from a food-service supplier; geography students get to explore the relationships between people and the land through foodways and horticulture students practice the art and science of growing plants.

Gardens located on campuses, from elementary schools to colleges and universities, provide with many possibilities.

Gardens for Residents

Creative ideas and partnerships also bring gardens into urban areas. The nonprofit organization Urban Oasis Project in Miami has helped many people create raised-bed food gardens at their homes. Urban Oasis also runs farmers markets in food desert communities, where access to fresh, healthy fruits and vegetables had been limited. With the national partner Wholesome Wave, Urban Oasis provides a dollar-for-dollar matching grant to SNAP (formerly known as food stamps) users to purchase produce or seedlings from farmers markets. This effort increases the consumption of healthy vegetables by residents of these neighborhoods, who either purchase more from local farmers or grow their own vegetables.

Community Gardens

Too often we forget the role of the "community" in a community garden. These gardens are relatively easy to start, but without a dedicated community they are hard to maintain in the long run. A person or organization, no matter how well intentioned, is likely to fail if the community that could benefit from the garden is indifferent or is not willing to maintain it. The community must come first; and when it really wants an edible garden, the garden will be successful.

There are many types of communities that might be interested in a community garden, including the following:

- Church congregations interested in turning some of their lawn into a garden to feed themselves and the hungry
- Youth group organizations, such as 4-H clubs, boy or girl scouts, big brother and sister groups, PTAs, or YM/YWCAs, that want to invest in their community
- Adult groups, such as garden clubs, homeowners associations, or other community organizations that want to gather around a shared project
- Municipalities with open space on public land; some even provide irrigation, compost, and other supplies

It is encouraging to see a diverse group of gardeners socializing as they work on their plots, introducing each other to the crops associated with their ethnic and cultural heritage, and literally finding common ground.

A community garden might be a great place to site your garden, or you could share your gardening experience and create one. If you were to create a community garden, would the garden be a collection of individually maintained plots, or one big shared garden space? Both are community gardens, but the maintenance and governance involved with each would be different.

Other things to consider when organizing a community garden include the following:

- Who owns the land and approximately how long will it be available for gardening?
- Is there access to water?
- Will you allow only organic gardening? This is an important question because the synthetic chemicals (either fertilizers or pesticides) applied to one plot can affect others.
- Who owns the hardware? This includes the raised beds, pots, fencing, hoses, tools, sheds, and so on.
- How will you divvy up ongoing shared expenses—compost, manure, water?
- What happens when someone stops maintaining his or her plot?
- If there is a charge for a plot, who will maintain the records of payment?
- Who will manage the waiting lists for plots and other governance issues?

These questions are not new, and the American Community Gardening Association has resources to assist community gardens with all of these issues.

If you're planning a community garden, it's a good idea to contact other community gardens in your area. Not all of them will be listed in online, so ask around, especially within your local green or gardeners groups, local food groups, Community Supported Agriculture groups, and at farmers markets. Good intentions will not make a community garden successful, but good planning, governance, and communication, coupled with hard work and community support, will.

Community Supported Agriculture

The Community Supported Agriculture (CSA) model began in Japan in 1971 and was called "teikei," or "putting the farmer's face on food." Joining a CSA is one way to know where your food comes from and support small-scale farming in your community. A CSA farmer sets a price for a "share" of the farm's seasonal harvest. The CSA members pay for a share in advance of the growing season in order to allow the farmer to purchase all needed farming supplies and mitigate risk. Prices, amount of produce, packing, and delivery or pickup methods vary, but usually a member receives a box of produce each week during the growing season. Many CSA farms use organic growing methods, but not all, so ask.

Multifarm CSAs are becoming more popular as farmers find it beneficial to spread crop risks over multiple farms, and the result is happier customers. Let's say, as an example, that Ben's Organic Farm had a failed crop of green beans due to an early November freeze, but Julie's Organic Farm, being closer to the coast, stayed two degrees warmer and the green beans survived. The members of their Ben and Julie's multifarm CSA benefitted because they got green beans for their Thanksgiving dinner in their CSA box that week. A small, multifarm CSA may also be a good way to balance out the overabundance of certain crops because there are more clients to absorb the extra.

You may wish to enter community supported agriculture as a producer rather than as a member. If you wish to supply a CSA with even just one crop during the year, get to know the CSA farmer or manager and invite her to your garden. CSA policies regarding methods of growing and pest control vary, but if you are using organic methods, you are a step ahead of the game. One potential problem area may be fertilizers that are organic, but that nevertheless violate the principles of certain groups. Blood meal, for example, is organic and provides

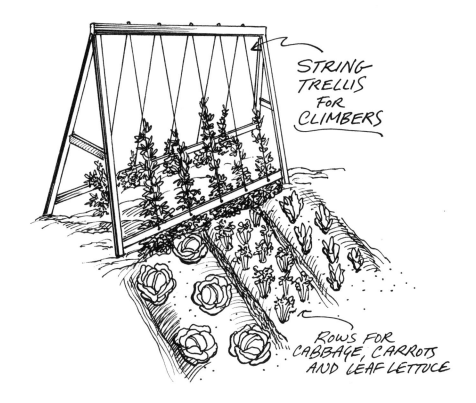

STRING
TRELLIS
FOR
CLIMBERS

ROWS FOR
CABBAGE, CARROTS
AND LEAF LETTUCE

plants with nitrogen and iron. A vegetarian/vegan CSA, however, may have trouble accepting the use of blood meal. Just be honest and open because there is no better certification for a farm or garden than a visit to see how things are really done.

A small piece of land can feed a lot of people. Try starting your own CSA with a small group of friends or family. After you feel confident enough to grow a regular supply of garden produce, try a short-season CSA to start, lasting four to six weeks during the peak of your local season. Find another organic gardener or small farmer who wants to share in the production or provide back up if necessary, and inform your members of the source of everything in their share. Start small, and if you like, invite members to help with gardening and harvesting. It's a low-risk way to find out whether becoming a CSA producer suits your lifestyle.

Farmers Markets

Farmers markets benefit producers, consumers, and the local economy. By shopping at a farmers market, you give your money directly to the farmer or the farmer's representative, and much of that money will stay in the local community. Conversely, in a supermarket, an estimated ninety-one cents of every food dollar goes to middlemen, marketing, distribution, and others in the food chain, while only nine cents goes to the farmer.

Farmers-market sales may provide small- and medium-sized farms with a large portion of their income. So shop at farmers markets, get to know your local producers, and have fun trying new vegetables.

According to statistics from the USDA, farmers markets have shown explosive growth in the last ten years. Restaurants with chefs who support local growers may hold them in their parking lots. Other potential hosts for farmers markets include yoga studios, government buildings, community health centers, parks, food-centered festivals, and even schools. In some areas, the demand is greater than the supply of farmers willing to come to market. You can help fill this vacuum by selling your own beautiful, organically grown produce.

The USDA encourages the managers of farmers markets to accept urban gardeners and other nontraditional growers at their markets: "encouraging urban gardeners to participate in the market creates a tie to the community. Their participation in the market means more awareness of the market among community members; providing opportunities for community residents also generates goodwill for the market." Many markets have special low rates for "card table vendors" who bring their produce to sell. You may find that the market manager has been praying that someone like you would call. Get a group of gardeners together, and take turns at market to make scheduling easier. Remember, fresher produce, not cheaper produce, is the number-one reason people buy at farmers markets. So bring out your best harvest to share and take advantage of the many opportunities for organic gardeners and micro-farmers.

- Before you invest your time and energy in getting ready to sell at a market, speak to the market manager to learn the rules and regulations and to find out if you can sell there.

- Sell only what you, your group, or partner farms produce.
- Tell people how your produce is grown and which organic fertilizers and pest control methods you use. (This is a great opportunity to educate the public about organic methods!)
- Harvest your produce as close to selling time as possible to ensure maximum freshness.
- Make sure your produce, your display, and you are all clean and attractive. Use contrasting colors, interesting crates or baskets, and clean, pretty table covers (or at least a clean table; would you eat off it?).
- Keep your greens moist; mist them regularly.
- Keep produce in the shade; if the market has none, bring a market umbrella or a pop-up tent, if permitted.
- Price it right. Don't undervalue the fruits of your labor! For a regular customer, throw in a free item rather than reduce your price. Even at the end of the market day, keep your prices steady—don't train your customers to wait until the end of the day.
- Sell your own produce to add value. People want to meet the person who grew their food!
- Try to offer uncommon vegetables and products that the other farmers are not offering.

USDA Organic Certification

For most home gardeners, organic certification is not necessary or practical. But for growers somewhere between home gardener and small farmer who plan to sell over $5,000 of produce each year, organic certification is probably worth it. Take, for example, a micro-farmer who has a small three-quarter-acre lot where he plants lettuces for salad mix, edible flowers, and a few varieties of gourmet garden vegetables. He sells directly to a few restaurants and a gourmet shop, and takes his excess produce to a farmers market. (Yes, such gardeners do exist.)

Earning organic certification allows him to sell his gorgeous produce at a premium price—much more than if he used the same organic methods with no certification. He can sell his produce with the

USDA Organic seal. Certification has a reputation for being expensive, but in reality it is not prohibitively so because it adds value to your offerings. At times, there are incentives available like cost-share programs for certification. In Florida, we are fortunate to have Florida Organic Growers (FOG), a nonprofit organization that promotes organic growing in Florida, based in Gainesville. The organization helps growers who wish to become certified organic and manages a separate certifying agency, Quality Certification Services (QCS).

For smaller producers whose gross income from organic sales is $5,000 or less, organic certification is not required, as there is an exemption written into the program regulations. These small growers may tell people that their products are grown using organic methods but may not use the USDA Organic seal. This applies to many who grow edibles for their own use and sell their excess crop at farmers markets. It is important to remember that, by law, even those exempt from organic certification are expected to adhere to the same growing principles as certified organic growers. These non-certified organic growers may sell only directly to consumers, if they wish to use organic claims. Check with FOG/QCS for clarification. The USDA threatens, "A civil penalty of up to $11,000 can be levied on any person who knowingly sells or labels as organic a product that is not produced and handled in accordance with the National Organic Program's regulations."

Foodsheds

Like a watershed, which is the whole area of land where all of the water that is under it or drains off of it drains into a single body of water, a foodshed is the geographical area that supplies food to a single population. For most of us in Florida, our foodshed is actually the entire world. But what if we had to feed ourselves locally? What would our foodshed look like?

For gardening purposes, this book divides Florida into three zones: north, central, and south. Imagine that all of your food came only from the zone where you live. These zones are naturally divided by climate and so lend themselves to natural foodshed divisions. However, north Florida would have at least one east-west dividing line and would probably extend northward over the state line into Georgia as well. And regional foodshed divisions may not always translate into the political divisions on a map since Mother Nature doesn't always color inside the lines.

For our purposes, we can define a foodshed as the area where all of our food *could* be grown, which begs the question: Could we feed ourselves? Estimates suggest that south Florida has a sufficient food supply to feed at any given time its entire population for three days. After that, it gets harder, as we have seen after hurricanes, when stores run out of milk, produce, and other perishables. If we were forced to buy locally, what would our dinners look like? They would certainly look different from season to season. In south Florida, there would be an abundance of familiar vegetables in the winter, and tropical fruits and vegetables in the summer, but there might also be less beef and more seafood.

Envisioning a local foodshed is an interesting exercise for advocates for local food, as well as for those who want to preserve and revive small local farms, those who want to preserve local food culture, and those who simply want to eat fresher food or reduce their carbon footprint. Dr. Mickie Swisher at the University of Florida has talked about the "thirty-mile problem" in which "disadvantaged communities in Florida's urban areas often live only 30–40 miles from areas where fresh produce is grown." When urban areas like these are so close to good food and yet can't get access to it or import much of their food from far away, we know we have a dysfunctional food system.

Food Policy

Imagine a local, state, or federal "Department of Food." It doesn't exist at the time of this writing, but concerned citizens and food-system stakeholders have come together at local and state levels to create food policy councils in Florida and all over the country. Some of these councils are created via government action to act as a sort of citizen advisory council. Others come together as citizen-led, grass-roots efforts that may then be adopted by state or local governments, either officially or extra-officially. Members of food policy councils often include people who are not typically represented in government but are stakeholders in the local food system.

These stakeholders may include people from the restaurant industry, agriculture, nonprofit organizations, health care, schools, passionate gardeners, environmental organizations, and others who want to inform government policy on our food system. For example, a city government may have archaic laws that make it unnecessarily difficult to hold farmers markets within city limits or keep a few backyard hens. A county's policy disallowing agriculture within city limits may date back to a time when "progress" looked like eating a frozen T.V. dinner in front of the Ed Sullivan Show. While our attitudes about knowing where our food is sourced and building sustainable, accessible local food systems have evolved, this evolution has not yet been translated into policy change. Food-policy councils are beginning to address this next step by serving as sources of information for government policymakers when they make decisions affecting food.

In 2011, the Florida Small Farms and Alternative Enterprises Conference, hosted by the University of Florida (UF) and Florida A&M University (FAMU), offered, for the first time, a Food Policy Councils 101 session as part of the conference—proof that this is an idea whose time has come. More than ever, concerned Floridians want to be involved in the decisions that affect what we put into our mouths and into our environment. You can become involved in a food-policy council in your area, or you can start your own.

Beyond Your Garden Gate

Once you learn how to manage a garden using organic methods that consider the health of the surrounding ecosystem, you will have developed a skill worth sharing. There are many opportunities for expanding your operation or helping others learn how to grow their own vegetables organically. So go grow!

Resources

For the Southern SARE (Sustainable Agriculture Research and Education), go to http://www.southernsare.org.

For the Organic Consumers Association, go to http://www.organicconsumers.org.

For information, including a training manual, on farmers markets, see http://nyfarmersmarket.com.

For Florida Organic Growers, go to www.foginfo.org.

For the Farmers Market Coalition, see www.fmc.org.

For the United States Department of Agriculture, go to www.USDA.gov.

For general information and links to local chapters of Slow Food USA, an organization that encourages keeping food traditions alive and raising edibles, see http://www.slowfoodusa.org.

The American Community Garden Association: www.communitygarden.org.

For food-policy councils and more, go to www.foodsecurity.org.

For Small Farms and Alternative Enterprises, go to http://smallfarms.ifas.ufl.edu.

For information on the food-policy council at Drake University go to www.law.drake.edu/academics/agLaw/?pageID=foodPolicyQnA.

For the Urban Oasis Project, go to www.urbanoasisproject.org.

For details on managing school gardens see Arden Bucklin-Sporer and Rachel Pringle, *How to Grow a School Garden: A Complete Guide for Parents and Teachers* (Portland, Ore.: Timber Press, 2010).

Appendix 1

Gardening Calendars for North, Central, and South Florida

These guidelines present to-do lists for gardeners in each of Florida's three regions and provide tasks for two physical locations—in the garden and under shelter. Gardening under shelter includes starting seeds in a garage or in a greenhouse in the winter months. When cold temperatures are not a factor, gardening under shelter could happen at a potting bench, under a shade house, or in another protected area away from the planting areas. Typically, you will start seeds or cuttings under shelter where you can easily monitor them.

Read the seed packages for guidelines on spacing, size, seed depth, and days until harvest on your specific cultivar because different varieties can have very different characteristics. For instance, one variety of basil is ten inches tall, while another one could be three feet tall.

As you plant the seeds, note their location in the garden and the information on their seed packs in your garden log so you will know when to start harvesting and have a ready reference for the leftover seeds that you can use the following season.

The list of seeds, seedlings, and cuttings presented here does not include every crop we cover in this book, but it should provide you with enough suggestions to get started. Your local extension office is a good source of additional information and advice on growing crops in your county and on testing your soil. Find your local office here: http://solutionsforyourlife.ufl.edu/.

These guides start in September, which marks the beginning of Florida's most productive vegetable season. And for many of us, as students and perhaps also as parents or teachers, September also marks a new beginning as we prepare for the new school year.

North Florida Vegetable Gardener's Calendar

SEPTEMBER

In the Garden

Prepare your beds for cool-weather crops:

- Get your soil tested for acidity and for basic nutrient levels. Until you know the results of these tests, you are working blind. Test your beds at least every other year because the soil in intensive vegetable gardens is highly dynamic.
- Rake away leftover mulching material and crop residue, remove summertime solarization plastic from the treated beds, or check the beds where the cover crops were turned under to make sure that they have composted. Next, incorporate compost and composted manures into the soil as necessary for your next crops. For root crops such as beets, parsnips, and carrots, work the soil until there are no lumps, sticks, or stones that could deform your crops.
- Plan out how you will rotate your crops to avoid sowing plants from the same family in the same space as the previous two seasons. Also, be sure to plan for longer shadows as the days begin to grow shorter.
- Arrange a drip irrigation system to support your cool-weather crops.

Some cool-weather seeds can be sown directly in the garden. These include radishes, beets, spinach, chard, carrots, dill, parsley, leafy greens, and cole crops (i.e., cabbage, broccoli, kale, and cauliflower). When you are planting fast-maturing vegetables, such as those you plan to harvest as micro-greens, sow seeds every two or three weeks until March to ensure a continuous harvest. For tender crops like cucumber, zucchini, sugar-snap peas, and beans, plant early in the month and choose fast-maturing varieties; this way, you have a better chance of harvesting them before the first frost in November or December.

Plants to set out in your beds include onion sets or plants, garlic, scallions, and other multiplying onions. You can also plant strawberries from late September through October. Plant your tomato seedlings or cuttings early in the month. Late in the month and through most of the fall is a good time to plant perennial herbs, including rosemary, sage, oregano, chives, and thyme. Plant any cuttings of basil you took earlier in the season for a fall crop.

Harvest summer crops such as sweet potatoes, okra, eggplants, peppers, peanuts, summer peas, and the winter squashes—butternut, pumpkin, or acorn.

Turn late cover crops, summer peas, or peanuts into the soil as a green manure and let them compost for four to six weeks before planting the next crop. Mulch the bare soil to keep the weeds out and the moisture in. Or, if you wish to plant that bed sooner, move spent crops, especially legumes, to the compost pile.

Under Shelter

Start these seeds: leeks, chives, cole crops, and other cool-weather crops that could use a head start. Cole crop seedlings, for instance, could be planted next month in the beds with the newly turned cover crops.

Sharpen your tools and make sure they are in good condition.

OCTOBER

In the Garden

Prepare for your beds for cool-weather crops as they become available:

- Rake away leftover mulching material and crop residue, remove summertime solarization plastic from the treated beds, and where you turned the cover crops under, check to make sure that they have composted. Then, incorporate compost and composted manures into the soil as necessary for your next crops.

- Plan for crop rotation to avoid sowing plants from the same family in the same space as the previous two seasons. Also plan for longer shadows as the days begin to grow shorter.
- Set up a drip irrigation system to support your cool-weather crops.

The seeds to sow directly in the garden include cool-weather, frost-tolerant vegetables such as radishes, beets, spinach, chard, turnips, carrots, dill, parsley, leafy greens, and frost-tolerant cole crops (i.e., cabbage, broccoli, and kale, but not cauliflower). It's too late to plant tender crops like cucumber, zucchini, sugar-snap or English peas, and bush or pole beans.

Thin September's seedlings so that there is adequate room for the remaining seedlings to grow, and fill in sparsely germinated areas with new seeds or seedlings. Irrigate your new seedlings several times a week, but gradually taper off the frequency to encourage the formation of deep roots. Assess the effectiveness of your irrigation by poking your finger in the soil or as you pull up weeds. Ideally, the soil should be moist to a depth of at least two inches.

Plants to set out in your beds include strawberries, onion sets or plants, garlic, scallions, and other multiplying onions. As space becomes available, plant seedlings of the cool-weather crops you started in September. The fall is also a good time to arrange your herb garden; plant perennial herbs such as rosemary, sage, oregano, and thyme.

Harvest your summer crops such as sweet potatoes, okra, eggplants, peppers, peanuts, summer peas, and the winter squashes—butternut, pumpkin, or acorn.

Under Shelter

Start these seeds: leeks early in the month, and chives, cole crops, and other cool-weather crops that could use a head start.

NOVEMBER

In the Garden

Adjust irrigation levels as Florida's seven-month dry season begins. Continue to test how deeply the soil is moistened after irrigation.

The seeds to sow directly in the garden include cool-weather, frost-tolerant vegetables such as radishes, beets, spinach, chard, turnips, carrots, dill, leafy greens, and frost-tolerant cole crops (cabbage, broccoli, and kale, but not cauliflower). This is the last good month to start parsley, which grows as a long-season annual in Florida. Be sure to plant an extra batch for the larvae of the swallowtail butterfly. When you are planting fast-maturing vegetables like radishes, sow seeds every two or three weeks until March to ensure a continuous harvest.

Thin seedlings planted in September and October to the give the remaining seedlings adequate room to grow, and fill in sparsely germinated areas with new seeds or seedlings. Taper off the frequency of irrigation for your seedlings, but water more deeply when you do.

Plants to set out in your beds early in the month include strawberries, onion sets or plants, and garlic. You can still plant scallions and other multiplying onions, but manage your quantities so that you can harvest what you need and still have enough sets to replant. As space becomes available, plant seedlings of the cool-weather crops you started. Early in the month is the last good time to plant perennial herbs like rosemary, sage, oregano, and thyme. If you have an established rosemary bush, clip some branches for dressing your Thanksgiving turkey.

Complete your harvest of the summer crops such as sweet potatoes, okra, eggplants, peppers, peanuts, summer peas, and the winter squashes.

Harvest your warm-weather fall crops, including tomatoes, peas, squash, and cucumbers, before the first frost.

Prepare for frost by harvesting all tender crops such as basil and Malabar spinach. Be ready to move any pineapples or other tender containerized crops under cover—some people move them back and forth to take advantage of warmer days during the winter.

Under Shelter

Start these seeds: cole crops and other cool-weather crops that could use a head start in the garden later in the season.

DECEMBER

In the Garden

As Florida's seven-month dry season continues, adjust your irrigation levels accordingly. Continue to test how deeply the soil is moistened after irrigation.

Seeds to sow directly in the garden include cool-weather, frost-tolerant vegetables such as radishes, beets, spinach, chard, turnips, carrots, leafy greens, and frost-tolerant cole crops (cabbage, broccoli, kale, but not cauliflower).

Thin seedlings planted earlier in the fall, and pull out weeds to give the remaining seedlings adequate room to grow. Fill in sparsely germinated areas with new seeds or seedlings. As your seedlings mature, taper off the frequency of irrigation.

Plants to set out in your beds include scallions and other multiplying onions. As space becomes available, plant the seedlings of the cool-weather crops you started.

Early in the month, before a killing frost, harvest all tender crops. Be ready to move pineapples or other tender containerized crops under cover.

Under Shelter

Start these seeds: cole crops, including cauliflower, and other cool-weather crops that could use a head start.

JANUARY

In the Garden

Perform a mid-season test of your drip-irrigation system for leaks and clogged emitters. It is also the time to perform a thorough test of how deeply the soil throughout your beds is moistened after irrigation.

Do a mid-season renewal of mulch and a thorough weeding for long-term, cool-weather crops.

Start potatoes from mid-month until mid-February. Buy certified seed potatoes from local sources—mail-order companies don't usually ship them early enough.

The seeds to sow directly in the garden include cool-weather, frost-tolerant vegetables such as radishes, beets, spinach, chard, turnips, celery, carrots, leafy greens, and cole crops (cabbage, broccoli, kale, and now cauliflower). When sowing carrot seeds, wait for a warm spell when the soil is likely to remain above 50°F for a few days.

Thin the seedlings you planted earlier in the season, and pull out weeds to give the remaining seedlings adequate room to grow. Fill in sparsely germinated areas with new seeds or seedlings. As your seedlings mature, taper off the frequency of irrigation.

Plants to set out in your beds include scallions and other multiplying onions. As space becomes available, plant the seedlings of the cool-weather crops you started. If your leeks are eight to ten inches tall, plant them in a ten-inch-deep trench.

Under Shelter

Plant your tomato and pepper seeds. You want them to be well on their way by the time you set them in the garden after the last frost.

FEBRUARY

In the Garden

Start potatoes until the middle of the month.

The seeds to sow directly in the garden include cool-weather vegetables such as radishes, beets, spinach, chard, turnips, celery, carrots, leafy greens, English or sugar-snap peas, and cole crops (cabbage, broccoli, kale, and cauliflower). When sowing carrot seeds, wait for a warm spell when the soil is likely to above remain above 50°F for a few days.

Late in the month, plant your beans, squash, and cucumbers.

Thin seedlings as needed, and pull out weeds to give the remaining seedlings adequate room to grow. Fill in sparsely germinated areas with new seeds or seedlings. Taper off the frequency of irrigation for your seedlings.

Plants to set out in your beds include scallions and other multiplying onions. As space becomes available, plant the seedlings of the cool-weather crops you started. If your leeks are eight to ten inches tall, plant them in a ten-inch-deep trench.

Under Shelter

Early in the month plant tomato and pepper seeds, so that they will be six to ten inches tall by the time you set them in the garden after the chance of frost has passed. Start basil and other warm-weather vegetables and herbs.

MARCH

In the Garden

This month, transition your beds from cool-weather crops to mid-season crops like tomatoes that are sensitive to frost and periods of cold but also don't do well in Florida's hot summers. Rearrange your drip irrigation system to accommodate the needs of the next set of crops. Remember that this is still the dry season, so keep up with your crops' needs but ease off on watering crops like carrots as they approach harvest time so that they do not crack. Renew the compost and composted manure in your beds according to the new crops' requirements. This is also a good time to set up some trench composting between your wide rows in order to replenish the nutrients and trace elements—particularly the calcium for your tomatoes.

Plan for less shade from nearby trees and structures as the days grow longer and the sun moves higher in the sky.

As your potatoes sprout, mound up the soil, straw, or compost around each plant or fill in their pre-dug trenches to protect the developing tubers from the sun and to stimulate more vine growth. If you need more plants, you can take cuttings early in their development. Also mound the soil around your leeks, but be careful not to get any soil into the folds of the leaves.

Seeds to sow directly in the garden early in the month include the last of the cool-weather vegetables such as radishes, celery, fennel, carrots, and leafy greens. Leave the sunniest areas of your garden open for the upcoming warm-weather vegetables. Also early in the month, plant your English or sugar-snap peas. Later in the month, plant bush or pole beans, summer and winter squashes, corn, fennel, and other warm-weather crops. Sow some marigold and nasturtium seeds in and around your vegetables.

Set out your tomatoes, peppers, and other tender seedlings, but be sure to have a plan to protect them in the event of a late frost or near-frost. Remember, on the average last day of frost, you still have a 50 percent chance of frost. As space becomes available, plant the last seedlings of cool-weather crops and mid-season crops you started.

As you move through your garden, check the tomatoes for hornworms. Spend some time learning which are the good and bad bugs in the garden. Move the larvae of the black swallowtail butterfly to the parsley or dill you have reserved for the bugs.

Under Shelter

Start basil and other warm-weather vegetables and herbs.

APRIL

In the Garden

Continue to transition your beds from cool-weather crops to mid-season and warm-weather crops. Renew the compost and composted manure in your beds according to the new crops' requirements. This is still a good time to set up some trench composting between your wide rows in order to replenish the nutrients and trace elements.

Plan for less shade from nearby trees and structures as the days grow longer and the sun moves higher in the sky. Provide some artificial shade for plants that are not heat tolerant, or place a trellised crop to the south or west of them.

Continue to mound up the soil around potatoes and leeks.

Seeds to sow directly in the garden include okra, eggplant, bush or pole beans, summer and winter squashes, corn, fennel, Malabar spinach, and other warm-weather crops.

This is the month to stake your tall tomatoes and peppers. Continue to monitor the tomatoes for hornworms and move the larvae of black swallowtail butterfly to the parsley or dill you have reserved for them.

Plan for less shade from nearby trees and structures as the days grow longer and the sun moves higher in the sky. Provide some artificial shade for plants are not heat tolerant, or place them on the north or east side of a trellised crop.

Under Shelter

With the dry season almost over, scrub out your starting pots and flats, dry them thoroughly in the sun, then store them upside down so that they do not collect water.

Spend some time learning to identify the good and bad bugs in your garden.

MAY

In the Garden

Start to transition your beds from mid-season crops to warm-weather crops. Renew the compost and composted manure in your beds according to the new crops' requirements. This is also a good time to set up some trench composting between your wide rows in order to replenish the nutrients and trace elements. Clean up and mulch the meadow garlic beds after the leaves die back; if they have become too crowded, dig out all the bulbs, add some compost, and replant some of them two to three inches apart. Use the leftover bulbs in the kitchen or share them with a neighbor.

Plan for less shade from nearby trees and structures as the days grow longer and the sun moves higher in the sky. Provide some artificial shade for plants that are not heat tolerant, or place them on the north or east side of a trellised crop.

Continue to monitor the tomatoes for hornworms. Be sure to eat some tomatoes right there in the garden, where they taste the best.

Seeds to sow directly in the garden include okra, eggplant, bush or pole beans, summer and winter squashes, corn, fennel, Malabar spinach, and other warm-weather crops.

To attract more pollinators, allow some of your dill, basil, and cole crops to flower. A squash flower, for example, must be visited eight to ten times before pollination takes place.

As the potato vines flower, you may begin to harvest some fingerling potatoes from the side without pulling the whole plant from the garden. Later, when all the leaves have turned yellow, you can start harvesting full-sized tubers to eat right away but leave the remaining crop in the ground for a couple of weeks to allow the skins to toughen up in preparation for longer storage.

Under Shelter

Store some cold drinks for the hot gardeners.

Start seeds for the fall tomato and pepper crop. Unlike tomatoes, many peppers will produce straight through the summer months. Even so, some may have been hit with root-knot nematodes or blight and need to be replaced.

JUNE

In the Garden

This is the beginning of Florida's five-month wet season. Keep track of the rainfall, and adjust your irrigation levels accordingly.

Continue to transition your beds from mid-season crops to warm-weather crops. Renew the compost and composted manure in your beds according to the new crops' requirements. This is also a good time to set up some trench composting between your wide rows in order to replenish the nutrients and trace elements your plants used during the winter.

Monitor the tomatoes for hornworms. However, as nighttime temperatures remain well above 70°F, most tomatoes will stop setting fruit and may also yellow and wilt with summer fungal diseases. Promptly pull out diseased plants, harvesting their green tomatoes to ripen them inside.

Seeds to sow directly in the garden include okra, eggplant, southern beans, lima beans, peanuts, and other warm-weather crops.

To attract more pollinators, allow some of your dill, basil, and parsley crops to flower.

As the leaves of your garlic and bulbing onions start to yellow or fall over, allow these crops to completely dry out. Harvest them when the soil is dry, and do not wash them—just rub the excess soil off of the bulbs.

As you harvest your cool-weather and mid-season crops, prepare some of your beds for solarization, cover crops, or to lie fallow. For the fallow beds, you could remove four to six inches of soil, lay in a three-inch layer of a variety of easily compostable materials, then replace the soil, and top it with a thick layer of easily removable mulch like straw or pine needles and dead leaves for an in-garden composting session. Wait six to eight weeks before replanting.

Under Shelter

Root some cuttings from the best-looking tomato plants in pots filled with new, finished compost. Also, take cuttings of basil and keep them away from the garden for six weeks to avoid fungal diseases.

Continue to store some cold drinks for the hot gardeners.

Hang braids or bunches of onions and garlic in a dry location for at least two weeks.

Early in the month, start seeds for a fall crop of tomatoes and peppers. Unlike tomatoes, many peppers will produce straight through the summer months, but some may be hit with root-knot nematodes and blight. If you end up with a peck of peppers, set up a table at your local farmers market.

JULY

In the Garden

Remove any remaining mulch from around the long-season summer crops and pull out the weeds. Then, lay in some compost and composted manure around each plant or in the center of the mounds for squash and melons to provide some mid-season enrichment. Trim back suckers and diseased plants.

By the time nighttime temperatures remain above 75°F, most of the tomatoes will be finished. When you pull the tomatoes, check for damage from root-knot nematodes. If the roots were attacked, don't use them for compost. Plant a cover crop of marigolds in those beds for the rest of the summer.

As the leaves of your garlic and bulbing onions start to yellow or bend over, allow these crops to dry out completely. Harvest them when the soil is dry, and do not wash them—just rub the excess soil off of the bulbs.

Continue to harvest okra, peppers, squash, beans, and other fruit on a regular basis so that your plants will continue to produce. Harvest summer herbs like oregano, rosemary, lemongrass, and ginger as needed.

When your basil crop begins to show signs of summer stress such as leaf yellowing or leaf edge dieback, pull it out and use for pesto.

Continue to prepare some of your beds for solarization or cover crops, or to lie fallow. For the fallow beds, you could remove four to six inches of soil, lay in a wide variety of other compostable materials, then replace the soil and top it with a thick layer of easily removable mulch like straw or pine needles and dead leaves for an in-garden composting session. Wait six to eight weeks before planting anything in these beds.

Under Shelter

Start some of the more heat-tolerant cole crops including kale, broccoli, and cauliflower.

Continue to store some cold drinks for the hot gardeners.

Monitor your cuttings of basil and tomatoes.

Hang braids or bunches of onions and garlic in a dry location for at least two to three weeks before storing them in a cool, dry place.

Read gardening books, and stay of out of the hot sun! Go to the Small Farms and Alternative Enterprises Conference. Peruse seed catalogs. Eat salads with leaves of Malabar spinach mixed in. Grill Asian eggplants.

AUGUST

In the Garden

Continue to harvest okra, peppers, winter squash, beans, and other fruit on a regular basis so that your plants will continue to produce.

Begin to transition your beds to cool-weather crops. The solarized, cover-cropped, or fallow beds should be ready by the end of the month. Turn your cover crops into the soil and mulch heavily to moderate soil temperatures, keep out the weeds, and reduce regrowth of the cover crop. Wait at least four to six weeks before replanting this bed.

Seeds to plant directly in the garden include summer and winter squash (including pumpkins if you want to have some for Halloween and Thanksgiving), cucumber, corn, onion, and turnips. Select fast-growing varieties of the tender crops so that you can harvest them before the first frost.

Plant your tomato seedlings or cuttings for a fall crop. Set out your basil cuttings in a different bed from your first crop or plant them in large containers—three or four cuttings per pot.

Set out seedlings of your cole crops late in the month.

Get your soil tested for acidity and for basic nutrient levels. Until you know the results of these tests, you are working blind. Ask your extension office for the soil sample boxes, fill them with a mixture of your soils, and send them off. Test every other year or more often because the soil in intensive vegetable gardens is highly dynamic.

Under Shelter

Start some of the cool-weather cole crops including kale, broccoli, and cauliflower.

Break out the cold drinks for the hot gardeners. Whew!!

Central Florida Vegetable Gardener's Calendar

SEPTEMBER

In the Garden

Prepare your beds for cool-weather crops:

- Get your soil tested for acidity and for basic nutrient levels. Until you know the results of these tests, you are working blind. Ask your extension office for the soil sample boxes, fill them with a mixture of soil from your various vegetable beds, and send them off. Test every other year or, ideally, more often because the soil in intensive vegetable gardens is highly dynamic.
- Rake away leftover mulching material and crop residue, remove summertime solarization plastic from the treated beds, and check those beds where the cover crops were turned under to see if they have composted. Next, incorporate compost and composted manures into the soil as necessary for your next crops. For root crops such as beets or carrots, work the soil until there are no lumps, sticks, or stones that could deform your crops.
- Plan for crop rotation to avoid sowing plants from the same family in the same space as the previous two seasons. Also plan for longer shadows as the days begin to grow shorter.

- Arrange your drip irrigation system to support your cool-weather crops.

Starting at the end of the month, sow cool-weather, frost-tolerant vegetable seeds such as radish, dill, parsley, leafy greens, and cole crops (cabbage, broccoli, kale, and cauliflower) directly in the garden. When you are planting fast-maturing vegetables, such as radishes and microgreens, sow seeds every two or three weeks until March to ensure a continuous harvest. For tender crops like corn, cucumber, zucchini, sugar-snap peas, and beans, plant early in the month and choose fast-maturing varieties; this way, you can be sure to harvest them before the frost arrives in December or January.

Plants to set out in your beds include onion sets or plants, garlic, scallions, and other multiplying onions. You can also plant strawberries from late this month through October. Plant your tomato seedlings or cuttings early in the month. Plant perennial herbs including rosemary, sage, oregano, chives, and thyme. These herbs can be planted throughout most of the fall. Plant the cuttings of basil you took earlier in the season for a good fall crop.

Harvest summer crops such as sweet potatoes, okra, eggplants, peppers, peanuts, summer peas, and the winter squashes—butternut, pumpkin, or acorn.

Turn late cover crops, summer peas, or peanuts into the soil as a green manure and let them compost for four to six weeks before planting the next crop. Mulch the bare soil to keep the weeds out and the moisture in. Or, if wish to plant that bed sooner, add spent crops, especially legumes, to the compost pile.

Under Shelter

Start these seeds: leeks, chives, cole crops, and other cool-weather crops that could use a head start. Cole crop seedlings, for instance, could be planted next month in the beds with the newly turned cover crops.

Sharpen your tools and make sure they are in good condition.

OCTOBER

In the Garden

Continue to prepare your beds for cool-weather crops as they become available:

- Rake away leftover mulching material and crop residue, remove summertime solarization plastic from the treated beds, or where you turned the cover crops under check to see if they have composted. Then, incorporate compost and composted manures into the soil as necessary for your next crops. For root crops such as beets, turnips and carrots work the soil until there are no lumps, sticks, or stones.
- Plan for crop rotation to avoid sowing plants from the same family in the same space as the previous two seasons. Also plan for longer shadows as the days begin to grow shorter.
- Set up a drip irrigation system to support your cool-weather crops.

The seeds to sow directly in the garden include cool-weather, frost-tolerant vegetables such as radishes, beets, spinach, chard, turnips, carrots, dill, parsley, leafy greens, and frost-tolerant cole crops (cabbage, broccoli, kale, and cauliflower). When planting fast-maturing vegetables like radishes, sow seeds every two or three weeks until March to ensure a continuous harvest. It's too late to plant tender crops like cucumber, zucchini, English peas, and bush or pole beans, but you could still plant sugar-snap peas early in the month.

Thin seedlings planted in September so that there is adequate room for the remaining seedlings to grow and fill in sparsely germinated areas with new seeds or seedlings. Irrigate new seedlings several times a week but gradually taper off the frequency and water more deeply when you do to encourage the formation of deep roots. Assess your level of irrigation by poking your finger in the soil or as you pull up weeds. Ideally, the soil should be moist to a depth of at least two inches.

Plants to set out in your beds include strawberries, onion sets or plants, garlic, scallions, and other multiplying onions. As space becomes available, plant the seedlings of the cool-weather crops you started. Fall is a good time to arrange your herb garden; plant perennial herbs such as rosemary, sage, oregano, and thyme.

Harvest your summer crops such as sweet potatoes, okra, eggplants, peppers, peanuts, summer peas, and the winter squashes—butternut, pumpkin, or acorn.

Under Shelter

Start these seeds: leeks early in the month, and chives, cole crops, and other cool weather crops that could use a head start.

NOVEMBER

In the Garden

Florida's seven-month dry season begins this month, so adjust irrigation levels accordingly. Continue to test how deeply the soil is moistened after irrigation. The soil should be moist to a depth of at least two inches.

Seeds to sow directly in the garden include cool-weather, frost-tolerant vegetables such as radishes, beets, spinach, chard, turnips, carrots, dill, parsley, leafy greens, and frost-tolerant cole crops (cabbage, broccoli, and kale, but not cauliflower). When you are planting fast-maturing vegetables like radishes, sow seeds every two or three weeks until March to ensure a continuous harvest.

Thin seedlings planted in September and October to the give the remaining seedlings adequate room to grow, and fill in sparsely germinated areas with new seeds or seedlings. Taper off the frequency of irrigation of your seedlings.

Plants to set out in your beds early in the month include strawberries, onion sets or plants, and garlic. You can still plant scallions and other multiplying onions, but manage your quantities so you can harvest what you need and still have enough sets to replant. As space becomes available, plant the seedlings of the cool-weather crops you started. Early in the month finish planting perennial herbs such as rosemary, sage, oregano, and thyme. If you have an established rosemary bush, clip some branches for dressing your Thanksgiving turkey.

Finish up the summer harvest of sweet potatoes, okra, eggplants, peppers, peanuts, summer peas, and the winter squashes.

Harvest your early fall crops, including tomatoes, peas, squash, and cucumbers, before the first frost.

Late in the month, prepare for frost by harvesting all tender crops such as basil and Malabar spinach. Be ready to move any pineapples or other tender containerized crops under cover—some people move them back and forth to take advantage of warmer days during the winter.

Under Shelter

Start these seeds: cole crops and other cool-weather crops that could use a head start.

DECEMBER

In the Garden

As Florida's seven-month dry season continues, adjust your irrigation levels accordingly. Continue to test how deeply the soil is moistened after irrigation.

Seeds to sow directly in the garden include cool-weather, frost-tolerant vegetables such as radishes, beets, spinach, chard, turnips, carrots, leafy greens, and frost-tolerant cole crops (cabbage, broccoli, kale, and cauliflower). This is your last good month to start parsley, which grows as a long-season annual in Florida. Be sure to plant an extra batch for the larvae of the swallowtail butterfly.

Thin seedlings planted earlier in the fall and pull out weeds to give the remaining seedlings adequate room to grow. Fill in sparsely germinated areas with new seeds or seedlings. As your seedlings mature, taper off the frequency of irrigation.

Plants to set out in your beds include scallions and other multiplying onions. As space becomes available, plant the seedlings of the cool-weather crops you started.

Early in the month, before a killing frost, harvest all tender crops. Be ready to move pineapples or other tender containerized crops under cover.

Under Shelter

Start these seeds: cole crops, including cauliflower, and other cool-weather crops that could use a head start. Later in the month, start your tomato and pepper seeds.

JANUARY

In the Garden

Perform a mid-season test of your drip-irrigation system for leaks and clogged emitters. It is also time to thoroughly test of how deeply the soil throughout your beds is moistened after irrigation.

Do a mid-season renewal of your mulch and thorough weeding of your long-term cool-weather crops.

Start potatoes from mid-month until mid-February. Buy certified seed potatoes from local sources—mail-order companies don't usually ship them early enough for Florida.

Seeds to sow directly in the garden include cool-weather, frost-tolerant vegetables such as radishes, beets, spinach, chard, turnips, celery, carrots, leafy greens, and cole crops (cabbage, broccoli, kale, and cauliflower). When sowing carrot seeds, wait for a warm spell when the soil is likely to remain above 50°F for a few days.

Thin seedlings planted earlier in the season and pull out weeds to give the remaining seedlings adequate room to grow. Fill in sparsely germinated areas with new seeds or seedlings. As your seedlings mature, taper off the frequency of irrigation.

Plants to set out in your beds include scallions and other multiplying onions. As space becomes available, plant the seedlings of the cool-weather crops you started. If your leeks are eight to ten inches tall, plant them in a ten-inch deep trench.

Under Shelter

Early in the month plant tomato and pepper seeds. You want them to be well on their way by the time you set them in the garden after the last chance of frost.

FEBRUARY

In the Garden

Start potatoes until mid-month. Buy from local sources—mail order companies don't usually ship them early enough for Florida.

Seeds to sow directly in the garden include cool-weather vegetables such as radish, beet, spinach, chard, turnips, celery, carrot, leafy greens, English or sugar-snap peas, cole crops (cabbage, broccoli, kale, cauliflower, but not Brussels sprouts). Late in the month plant some beans, squash, and cucumbers.

Thin seedlings planted earlier in the season and pull out weeds so there is adequate room for growth. Fill in sparsely germinated areas with new seeds or seedlings. Taper off the frequency of irrigation for your seedlings as they mature, but water more deeply.

Plants to set out in your beds include scallions and other multiplying onions. As space becomes available, plant the seedlings of the cool-weather crops you started. Early in the month, plant your leeks in a ten-inch deep trench. As space becomes available, plant the last seedlings of the cool-weather crops and mid-season crops you started.

Under Shelter

It is now too late to plant tomato seeds. They need to be six to ten inches tall by the time you set them in the garden after the last frost. Start basil and other warm-weather vegetables and herbs.

MARCH

In the Garden

This month, transition your beds from cool-weather crops to mid-season crops like tomatoes that are sensitive to frost and periods of cold but also don't do well in Florida's hot summers. Rearrange your drip irrigation system to accommodate the needs of the next set of crops. Remember that this is still the dry season so keep up with your crops' needs, but ease off on watering crops like carrots as they approach harvest time so that they do not crack. Renew the compost and composted manure in your beds according to the new crops' requirements. This is also a good time to set up some trench composting between your wide rows in order to replenish the nutrients and trace elements—particularly the calcium for your tomatoes—that your garden used during the winter.

Plan for less shade from nearby trees and structures as the days grow longer and the sun moves higher in the sky. Provide some artificial shade for plants are not heat tolerant, or place them on the north or east side of a trellised crop.

As your potatoes sprout, mound up the soil or compost around each plant or fill in their pre-dug trenches or containers to protect the developing tubers from the sun and to stimulate more vine growth. If you need more plants, you can take cuttings early in their development. Also mound the soil around your leeks but be careful not to get any soil into the folds of the leaves.

Seeds to sow directly in the garden early in the month include the last of the cool-weather vegetables such as radishes, celery, fennel, carrots, and leafy greens. Leave the sunniest areas of your garden open for the upcoming warm-weather vegetables. Also early in the month, plant your English or sugar-snap peas. Plant bush or pole beans, summer and winter squashes, corn, fennel, and other warm-weather crops. Sow some marigold and nasturtium seeds in and around your vegetables.

Set out your tomatoes, peppers, and other tender seedlings, but be sure to have a plan to protect them in the event of a late frost or near-frost. Remember that on the average last day of frost, you still have a 50-percent chance of frost; after that, the chances taper quickly.

Under Shelter

Start basil and other warm-weather vegetables and herbs that transplant well.

APRIL

In the Garden

Begin to transition your beds to warm-weather crops. Renew the compost and composted manure in your beds according to the new crops' requirements. This is still a good time to set up some trench composting between your wide rows in order to replenish the nutrients and trace elements.

Plan for less shade from nearby trees and structures as the days grow longer and the sun moves higher in the sky. Provide some artificial shade for plants that are not heat tolerant, or place them on the north or east side of a trellised crop.

Continue to mound up the soil around potato vines and leeks.

Monitor tomatoes for hornworms. Spend some time learning to tell the good from the bad bugs in the garden. Move the larvae of the black swallowtail butterfly to the parsley or dill you have reserved for them.

Seeds to sow directly in the garden include okra, eggplant, bush or pole beans, summer and winter squashes, corn, fennel, Malabar spinach, and other warm-weather crops.

Stake your tall tomatoes and peppers.

Under Shelter

Scrub out your starting pots and flats, dry them thoroughly in the sun, and store them upside down so that they do not collect water.

MAY

In the Garden

Continue to transition your beds to warm-weather crops. Renew your beds with compost and composted manure according to the new crops' requirements. This is also a good time to set up some trench composting between your wide rows in order to replenish the nutrients and trace elements.

Plan for less shade from nearby trees and structures as the days grow longer and the sun moves higher in the sky. Provide some artificial shade for plants that are not heat tolerant, or place them on the north or east side of a trellised crop.

Continue to monitor the tomatoes for hornworms, and learn to tell the good from the bad bugs in the garden. Move the larvae of the black swallowtail butterfly to the parsley or dill you have reserved for them. Be sure to eat some tomatoes right there in the garden, where they taste the best.

The seeds to sow directly in the garden include okra, eggplant, bush or pole beans, summer and winter squashes, corn, fennel, Malabar spinach, and other warm-weather crops.

To attract more pollinators, allow some of your dill, basil, and cole crops to flower. A squash flower, for example, must be visited eight to ten times before pollination takes place.

As the potato vines flower, you may start to harvest some fingerling potatoes from the side without pulling the whole plant from the garden. Later, when all the leaves have turned yellow, you can start harvesting full-sized tubers to eat right away, but leave the remaining crop in the ground for a couple of weeks to allow the skins to toughen up in preparation for longer storage.

Under Shelter

Store some cold drinks for the hot gardeners.

Root some cuttings from the best-looking tomato plants in pots filled with new, finished compost. Also, root cuttings of your basil and keep it away from the garden for six weeks to avoid fungal diseases.

Late in the month, start tomato and pepper seeds for your fall crop. Unlike tomatoes, most peppers will produce straight through the summer months, but some may be hit with root-knot nematodes and blight, so replacements might be necessary. If you end up with a peck of peppers, set up a table at your local farmers market.

JUNE

In the Garden

This is the beginning of Florida's five-month wet season. Keep track of the rainfall and adjust your irrigation levels accordingly.

Early in the month, finish transitioning your beds from mid-season crops to warm-weather crops. Renew your beds with compost and composted manure according to the new crops' requirements. This is also a good time to set up some trench composting between your wide rows in order to replenish the nutrients and trace elements.

Seeds to sow directly in the garden include okra, eggplant, southern beans, lima beans, peanuts, and other warm-weather crops.

Allow some of your dill, basil, and parsley crops to flower to attract more pollinators.

As the leaves of your garlic and bulbing onions start to yellow or fall over, allow these crops to completely dry out, and harvest them when soil is dry. Do not wash them—just rub the excess soil and outer skin from the bulbs.

As you harvest your cool-weather and mid-season crops, prepare some of your beds for solarization, cover crops, or to lie fallow. For the fallow beds, you could remove four to six inches of soil, lay in a three-inch layer of a variety of easily compostable materials, then replace the soil and top it with a thick layer of easily removable mulch like straw or pine needles and dead leaves for an in-garden composting session. Wait six to eight weeks before replanting.

When your basil crop begins to show signs of summer stress such as leaf yellowing or leaf edge dieback, pull most of it out and use the leaves and soft stems for pesto.

Under Shelter

Continue to store some cold drinks for the hot gardeners.

Hang braids or bunches of onions and garlic in a dry location for at least two weeks.

Early in the month, start tomato and pepper seeds for your fall crop.

JULY

In the Garden

Remove any remaining mulch from around the long-season summer crops and pull out the weeds. Then, lay in some compost and composted manure around each plant or in the center of the mounds for squash and melons to provide some mid-season enrichment. Trim back suckers and remove diseased plants.

By the time nighttime temperatures remain above 75°F, most of the tomatoes will be finished. When you pull the tomatoes, check for damage from root-knot nematodes. If the roots were attacked, don't use them for compost. Plant a cover crop of marigolds in those beds for the rest of the summer.

Continue to harvest okra, peppers, squash, beans, and other fruit on a regular basis so that your plants will continue to produce.

Plant some sweet potatoes for a Thanksgiving harvest.

Continue to prepare some of your beds for solarization, cover crops, or to lie fallow. For the fallow beds, you could remove four to six inches of soil, lay in a wide variety of other compostable materials, then replace the soil and top it with a thick layer of easily removable mulch like straw or pine needles and dead leaves for an in-garden composting session. Wait six to eight weeks before planting anything in these beds.

Under Shelter

Start some of the more heat-tolerant cole crops, including kale, broccoli, and cauliflower.

Continue to store some cold drinks for the hot gardeners.

Read gardening books, enjoy tropical fruits, and stay of out of the hot sun! Go to the Small Farms and Alternative Enterprises Conference. Peruse seed catalogs. Harvest summer herbs like oregano, basil, rosemary, lemongrass, and ginger as needed. Eat salads with leaves of Malabar spinach mixed in. Grill Asian eggplants.

AUGUST

In the Garden

Continue to harvest okra, peppers, winter squash, beans, and other fruit on a regular basis so that your plants will continue to produce.

Begin to transition your beds for fall crops. The solarized, cover-cropped, or fallow beds should be ready by the end of the month. Turn your cover crops into the soil and mulch heavily to moderate soil temperatures, keep out the weeds, and reduce regrowth of the cover crop. Wait at least four to six weeks before replanting this bed. The solarized and fallow beds should be ready for planting right away.

Seeds to plant directly in the garden include summer and winter squash (including pumpkins if you want to have some for Halloween and Thanksgiving), cucumber, corn, onion, and turnips. Select fast-growing varieties of the tender crops so that you can harvest them before the first frost.

Set out your tomato cuttings or seedling for a fall crop. Also plant your basil cuttings in a different bed from your first crop or plant them in large containers—three or four cuttings per pot.

Set out the seedlings of your cole crops late in the month.

Get your soil tested for acidity and for basic nutrient levels. Until you know the results of these tests, you are working blind. Ask your extension office for the soil test boxes, fill them with soil from various parts of your garden, and send them off. Test every other year or more often because the soil in intensive vegetable gardens is highly dynamic.

Under Shelter

Start some of the cool-weather cole crops including kale, broccoli, and cauliflower.

Break out the cold drinks for the hot gardeners. Whew!!

South Florida Vegetable Gardener's Calendar

SEPTEMBER

In the Garden

Begin the transition of your beds from warm-weather to cool-weather crops. The beds you solarized, cover-cropped, or allowed to lie fallow should be ready by the end of the month. Turn your cover crops into the soil and mulch heavily to moderate soil temperatures, keep out the weeds, and reduce regrowth of the cover crop. Wait at least four to six weeks before replanting this bed. The solarized and fallow beds should be ready for planting right away.

Prepare your beds at the beginning of the month, but wait until at least late in the month to set plants or seeds out in the garden. September is the rainiest month in south Florida, and historically has the most hurricanes. The other potential drawback to September planting is that insect and disease pressures are still high from the daily heat and humidity. These pressures will decrease as the month passes into the next. If you have your beds ready in August, and want to try early September planting, have some extra seeds and seedlings ready in the event that a storm or pest ruins some of your newly planted garden. That said, no one can control Mother Nature, so if you don't mind the possibility of having to perform some damage control, why not get the garden started as soon as possible? Farmers are constantly trying to get started earlier or continue later in order to have a crop that few others do. Sometimes it works; sometimes it doesn't. By the end of the month, be prepared to plant a variety of crops from the seeds you started earlier, or to seed directly in the garden.

- Get your soil tested for acidity and for basic nutrient levels, even if you are gardening in raised beds with non-native soil and compost. Until you know the results of these tests, you are working blind. Ask your extension office for the soil sample boxes, fill them with soil from various places in your beds, and send them off. Test every other year or more often because the soil in intensive vegetable gardens is highly dynamic.
- Rake away leftover mulching material and crop residue, remove summertime solarization plastic from the treated beds, and check the beds where the cover crops were turned under to see if they have composted. Next, incorporate compost and composted manures into the soil as necessary for your next crops. For root crops such as beets and carrots, work the soil until there are no lumps, sticks, or stones.
- Plan out how you will rotate your crops to avoid sowing plants from the same family in the same space as the previous two seasons. Also plan for longer shadows as the days begin to grow shorter.
- How will you water your garden? If you are using drip irrigation, set it up this month for those cool-season crops.

Plants to set out in your beds early in the month are tomato seedlings or cuttings. Cantaloupe can also be planted now. Late in the month and through most of the fall is a good time to plant perennial herbs including rosemary, sage, oregano, chives, and thyme. Plant the cuttings of basil you took earlier in the season for a good fall crop.

Harvest any remaining summer crops such as sweet potatoes, okra, eggplants, peppers, summer peas, and the winter squashes—Seminole pumpkin or calabaza.

Turn late cover crops or summer peas into the soil as a green manure and let them compost for four to six weeks before planting the next crop. Mulch the bare soil to keep the weeds out and the moisture in. Or, if you wish to plant that bed sooner, add spent crops, especially legumes, to the compost pile.

Under Shelter

Start these seeds: tomatoes, eggplant, sweet peppers, leeks, chives, cole crops, and other cool-weather crops that could use a head start. Cole crop seedlings, for instance, could be planted next month in the beds with the newly turned cover crops.

Sharpen your tools and make sure they are in good condition.

OCTOBER

In the Garden

As beds become available, prepare them for your cool-weather crops:

- Rake away leftover mulching material and crop residue, remove summertime solarization plastic from the treated beds, and where you turned the cover crops under, check to see if they have composted. Then, incorporate compost and composted manures into the soil as necessary for your next crops. For root crops such as beets, parsnips, and carrots, work the soil until there are no lumps, sticks, or stones.
- Plan for crop rotation to avoid sowing plants from the same family in the same space as the previous two seasons. Also plan for longer shadows as the days begin to grow shorter.
- Set up a drip irrigation system for your cool-weather crops.

The seeds to sow directly in the garden include cool-weather vegetables such as radishes, beets, spinach, chard, turnips, carrots, dill, parsley, leafy greens, and cole crops (cabbage, broccoli, kale, and cauliflower). Plant small amounts of fast-maturing vegetables like radishes every two or three weeks until March to ensure a continuous harvest.

Thin the seedlings you planted in September so that there is adequate room for the remaining seedlings to grow, and fill in sparsely germinated areas with new seeds or seedlings. Irrigate new seedlings several times a week, but gradually taper off the frequency of irrigation and water more deeply when you do to encourage the formation of deep roots. Assess the effectiveness of your irrigation by poking your finger into the soil or as you pull up weeds. The soil should be moist to a depth of at least two inches.

You can plant any cool-season crop directly in the garden—the calendar is wide open. This is the best month for cool-season vegetable planting. If it's one of those years when the summer heat just won't let up or the hurricanes are being named into the last letters of the alphabet, wait until later in the month when the rains have stopped. Sow vegetable seeds such as radish, dill, parsley, carrots, leafy greens in the mustard family, and other cole crops (cabbage, broccoli, kale, and cauliflower). Plant fast-maturing vegetables like radishes, or lettuce, every two or three weeks until March to ensure a continuous harvest. Choose fast-maturing varieties of tender crops like cucumbers, zucchini, sugar-snap peas, and beans, and plant them early in the month so that you can harvest them before the low temperatures return in December and January. Even south Florida gets a freeze every few years. If there is no freeze, you can continue the harvest.

Get your herb garden started, and interplant cutting flowers or salad flowers like nasturtiums and pansies.

Order your strawberry plants in early October or buy them from a local organic grower—University of Florida has developed a handful of varieties for Florida. Irish potatoes do best when planted from October to January. Continue to harvest the last of your summer crops such as sweet potatoes, eggplants, and peppers.

Under Shelter

Start these seeds: leeks, chives, cole crops, and other cool-weather crops that could use a head start.

NOVEMBER

In the Garden

This is the beginning of Florida's seven-month dry season, so you will need to adjust your irrigation levels accordingly. Test how deeply the soil is moistened after irrigation to be sure you are not moistening only the top crust.

Any cool-season crop can be planted in November. The seeds to sow directly in the garden include cool-weather, frost-tolerant vegetables such as radishes, beets, spinach, chard, turnips, carrots, dill, parsley, leafy greens, and frost-tolerant cole crops (cabbage, broccoli, and kale, but not cauliflower). Plant fast-maturing vegetables like radishes every two or three weeks until March to ensure a continuous harvest.

Thin the seedlings you planted in September and October to the give the remaining seedlings adequate room to grow, and fill in sparsely germinated areas with new seeds or seedlings. Taper off the frequency with which you water your seedlings, but water more deeply when you do.

If you missed doing so in October, set out strawberries and onion sets or plants early in the month. You can still plant scallions and other multiplying onions, but manage your quantities so that you can harvest what you need and still have enough sets to replant. As space becomes available, plant the seedlings of the cool-weather crops you started. Early in the month, finish planting your perennial herbs such as rosemary, sage, oregano, and thyme. If you have an established rosemary bush, clip some branches for dressing your Thanksgiving turkey.

Begin harvesting the green beans, radishes, lettuces, and other quick harvests from your September–October plantings.

Under Shelter

Start these seeds: cole crops, and other cool-weather crops that could use a head start. Also start tomato, eggplant, and pepper seeds if you haven't already, to give them a chance before colder weather slows their growth.

DECEMBER

In the Garden

As Florida's seven-month dry season continues, adjust your irrigation levels accordingly. Continue to test how deeply the soil is moistened after irrigation.

December, especially the first half, is still a great month to start most cool-weather seeds directly in the garden. If you were too busy or missed out earlier in the season, don't despair—just plant anything that takes seventy-five days or less to mature, from transplants if possible. Calculate the time until harvest, and keep in mind that as the weather gets warm in mid-March, disease and insects will begin to attack your plants. The seeds to sow directly in the garden in December include cool-weather vegetables such as radishes, beets, spinach, chard, turnips, carrots, leafy greens, and frost-tolerant cole crops (cabbage, broccoli, kale, and cauliflower).

Thin the seedlings you planted earlier in the fall, and pull out weeds to give the remaining seedlings adequate room to grow. Fill in sparsely germinated areas with new seeds or seedlings. As your seedlings mature, taper off the frequency with which you water, but water more deeply when you do.

Plants to set out in your beds include scallions and other multiplying onions. As space becomes available, plant the seedlings of the cool-weather crops you started.

Under Shelter

Continue to start seeds for cool-weather crops. This is the last month to plant potatoes.

JANUARY

In the Garden

Test your drip irrigation system for leaks and clogged emitters. It's also the time to test of how deeply the soil throughout your beds is moistened after irrigation.

It's time for a mid-season renewal of mulch and a thorough weeding around your long-term cool-weather crops.

Start potatoes early this month. Buy certified seed potatoes from local sources—mail-order companies don't usually ship them early enough. Try growing them in a porous bag filled with straw or in a hay bale rather than in the garden. Keep adding straw as the plant grows.

The seeds to sow directly in the garden include cool-weather vegetables such as radishes, beets, spinach, chard, turnips, celery, carrots, leafy greens, English or sugar-snap peas, cole crops (cabbage, broccoli, kale, cauliflower, but not brussels sprouts), beans, squash, and cucumbers.

Thin the seedlings you planted earlier in the season and pull out weeds to give the remaining seedlings adequate room to grow. Fill in sparsely germinated areas with new seeds or seedlings. As your seedlings mature, taper off the frequency with which you water them, but water more deeply when you do. January is your last good month to start parsley, which grows as a long-season annual in Florida. Be sure to plant an extra batch for the larvae of the swallowtail butterfly.

Thin the seedlings you planted earlier in the season and pull out weeds to give the remaining seedlings adequate room to grow. Fill in sparsely germinated areas with new seeds or seedlings. As your seedlings mature, taper off the frequency of with which you water them, but water more deeply when you do.

Plants to set out in your beds include scallions and other multiplying onions. As space becomes available, plant the seedlings of the cool-weather crops you started. If your leeks are eight-to-ten-inches tall, plant them in a ten-inch-deep trench.

Under Shelter

Early in the month, plant tomato, eggplant and pepper seeds. You want them to be well on their way by the time you set them in the garden after the last chance of frost if it is a cold year.

FEBRUARY

In the Garden

Early in the month, transition your beds from cool-weather crops to mid-season crops that, like tomatoes, are sensitive to periods of cold but also don't do well in Florida's hot summers. Rearrange your drip irrigation to accommodate the needs of the next set of crops. Remember that this is still the dry season, so keep up with the irrigation needs of your crops, but ease off on crops like carrots as they approach harvest time so that they don't crack. Renew the compost and composted manure in your beds according to the new crops' requirements. This is also a good time to set up some trench composting between your wide rows in order to replenish the nutrients and trace elements—particularly the calcium for the tomatoes—that your plants used during the winter.

Plants to set out in your beds include scallions and other multiplying onions. As space becomes available, plant the seedlings of the cool-weather and mid-season crops you started. Early in the month, plant your leeks in a ten-inch-deep trench.

Seeds to sow directly in the garden early in the month include the last of the cool-weather vegetables as radishes and celery. Also sow fennel, carrots, and leafy greens, but leave the sunniest areas of your garden for the upcoming warm-weather vegetables. Also plant English or sugar-snap peas early in the month. Plant bush or pole beans, summer and winter squashes, corn, fennel, and other warm-weather crops. Sow some marigold and nasturtium seeds in and around your vegetables.

Stake tall tomato, pepper, and eggplants if you haven't already. Eggplants, especially Asian varieties, will continue to bear fruit throughout the summer. Some peppers and eggplants will not bear well until the warm weather sets in, and can be left in the ground, where they will become woody and bushy, and can continue to bear for another two years if there is no frost.

Under Shelter

It's too late to plant tomato and pepper seeds. They need to be six-to-ten-inches tall by the time you set them in the garden, and tomatoes need to have warm days and cool nights to bear fruit. Start your basil and other warm-weather vegetables and herbs.

MARCH

In the Garden

Plan for less shade from nearby trees and structures as the days grow longer and the sun moves higher in the sky. Provide some artificial shade for plants that are not heat tolerant, or place them on the north or east side of a trellised crop.

As your potatoes sprout, mound up the soil, straw, or compost around each plant or fill in their pre-dug trenches or containers to protect the developing tubers from the sun and to stimulate more vine growth. If you need more plants, you can take cuttings early in their development. Also mound the soil around your leeks, but be careful not to get any soil into the folds of the leaves.

Under Shelter

Start your basil and other warm-weather vegetables and herbs.

APRIL

In the Garden

Continue to transition your beds from cool-weather crops to mid-season and warm-weather crops. Renew your beds with compost and composted manure according to the new crops' requirements. This is still a good time to set up some trench composting between your wide rows to replenish the nutrients and trace elements.

Plan for less shade from nearby trees and structures as the days grow longer and the sun moves higher in the sky. Provide some artificial shade for plants that are not heat tolerant, or place them on the north or east side of a trellised crop.

This is a good time to plant sweet potatoes.

Monitor the tomatoes for hornworms. If you find one with white, parasitic wasp eggs (they resemble grains of rice) laid on its back, move it to a papaya plant and let the wasps continue their life cycle by using the worm as food. This way, there will be more parasitic wasps to feed on more hornworms. Spend some time learning to tell the good from the bad bugs in your garden. Move the larvae of the black swallowtail butterfly to the parsley you have reserved for them.

Seeds to sow directly in the garden include okra, eggplant, bush or pole beans, summer and winter squashes, fennel, Malabar spinach, and other warm-weather crops.

As the potato vines flower, you may start to harvest some fingerling potatoes from the side without pulling the whole plant from the garden. Later, when all the leaves have turned yellow, you can start harvesting full-sized tubers to eat right away, but leave the remaining crop in the ground for a couple of weeks to allow the skins to toughen up in preparation for longer storage.

Under Shelter

With the dry season almost over, scrub out your starting pots and flats, dry them thoroughly in the sun, and store them upside down so that they do not collect water.

MAY

In the Garden

By this time in south Florida, many of your crops will have succumbed to heat or insect pressures. Enjoy what is left of your vegetable garden as far into May as Mother Nature will allow, then compost healthy spent plants or dispose of diseased ones. Many south Florida gardeners allow beds to lay fallow from now through August or September, covered with a mulch layer. You may decide to plant cover crops for part of the summer then solarize the soil from July to September. You may also want to keep going, with plants which can take the hot, humid summer weather. The choice is yours. Renew the compost and composted manure in your beds according to the new crops' requirements. This is also a good time to set up some trench composting between your wide rows in order to replenish the nutrients and trace elements your garden.

Plan for less shade from nearby trees and structures as the days grow longer and the sun moves higher in the sky. Provide some artificial shade for plants that are not heat tolerant, or place them on the north or east side of a trellised crop.

Seeds to sow directly in the garden include only the toughest tropical heat lovers: yard-long bean, hyacinth bean, calabaza squash, Malabar spinach, leaf fennel, and calaloo. You may slip in a quick okra crop, and transplant eggplant starts. Many perennial herbs like oregano, marjoram, sage, and rosemary will thrive now, as will some basil varieties. Plant yuca cuttings now.

To attract more pollinators, allow some of your dill, basil, and cole crops to flower. A squash flower, for example, must be visited eight to ten times before pollination takes place.

Under Shelter

Store some cold drinks for the hot gardeners.

Root cuttings of your basil and it keep away from the garden for six weeks to avoid fungal diseases.

JUNE

In the Garden

This is the beginning of Florida's five-month wet season. Keep track of the local rainfall and adjust your irrigation levels accordingly.

Early in the month, finish transitioning your beds from mid-season crops to warm-weather crops. Renew your beds with compost and composted manure according to the new crops' requirements. This is also a good time to set up some trench composting between your wide rows in order to replenish the nutrients and trace elements your garden used during the winter.

Seeds to sow directly in the garden may include okra, jicama, yard-long bean, and other warm-weather crops, depending on the heat and your microclimate.

Allow some of your dill, basil, and parsley crops to flower to attract more pollinators.

Prepare some of your beds for solarization or cover crops, or to lie fallow. For the fallow beds, you could remove four to six inches of soil, lay in a three-inch layer of a variety of easily compostable materials, then replace the soil and top it with a thick layer of easily removable mulch like straw or pine needles and dead leaves for an in-garden composting session. Wait six to eight weeks before replanting.

Under Shelter

Continue to store some cold drinks for the hot gardeners.

Late in the month, start tomato and pepper seeds for your fall crop. Unlike tomatoes, many of the peppers will produce straight through the summer months, but some may be hit with root-knot nematodes and blight and need to be replaced. If you end up with a peck of peppers, sell them at a local farmers market.

JULY

In the Garden

Remove any remaining mulch from around the long-season summer crops and pull out the weeds. Then, lay in some compost and composted manure around each plant or in the center of the mounds for squash and melons to provide some mid-season enrichment. Trim back suckers and diseased plants.

Continue to harvest okra, peppers, yard-long beans, and other fruit on a regular basis so that your plants will continue to produce.

Continue to prepare some of your beds for solarization, cover crops, or to lie fallow. For the fallow beds, you could remove four to six inches of soil, lay in a wide variety of other compostable materials, then replace the soil and top it with a thick layer of easily removable mulch like straw or wood chips and dead leaves for an in-garden composting session. Wait six to eight weeks before planting anything in these beds.

Under Shelter

Read gardening books, enjoy tropical fruits, and stay out of the hot sun! Go to the Small Farms and Alternative Enterprises Conference. Peruse seed catalogs. Harvest summer herbs like oregano, basil, rosemary, lemongrass, and ginger as needed. Eat salads with leaves of Malabar spinach mixed in. Grill Asian eggplants.

AUGUST

In the Garden

Continue to harvest any remaining okra, peppers, calabaza squash, yard-long beans, and other fruit on a regular basis so that your plants will continue to produce.

Get your soil tested for acidity and for basic nutrient levels. Until you know the results of these tests, you're working blind. Ask your extension office for soil sample boxes, fill them with a mixture of soil from your various vegetable beds, and send them off. Test every other year or more often because the soil in intensive vegetable gardens is highly dynamic.

Get your garden beds ready for fall planting.

Under Shelter

Order seeds early in the month for the upcoming cool-weather growing season, and start some of the more heat-tolerant cool-weather cole crops including kale, broccoli, and cauliflower. You can also start tomatoes, eggplant,
and peppers in this hot month, as they can take the heat and are months away from producing a crop.

Break out some cold drinks for the hot gardeners. Whew!!

Appendix 2

Chickens and Rabbits and Worms! Oh My!

Chickens, rabbits, and worms are the three most popular animal companions for the garden. The manure of all three is great for your plants.

Chickens

Keeping chickens in the backyard is more popular than ever, and many Florida cities have changed their codes to allow chickens (hens only) to live in residential neighborhoods. Chickens don't need roosters to produce eggs. Chickens are entertaining to watch and can be very friendly, especially when raised from chicks. A few chickens can contribute so much: they can help you to control insects and weeds and to fertilize and aerate the soil. They provide you with manure and mulches. They can also help you to dispose of your waste, by eating your kitchen scraps. Plus, they give you eggs!

There are times, however, when you should keep your chickens out of the garden: (1) when seedlings are small and vulnerable to chicken scratching, and (2) when it's close to harvest time—120 days for crops that touch the soil and 90 days for crops that do not. During this time, no fresh manure should contact your food for safety reasons.

To keep free-ranging chickens out of your garden, install temporary fencing around the perimeter. The alternative is to fence the chickens with a movable, bottomless pen, or "chicken tractor."

The advantage of using a chicken tractor is that the chickens can scratch and fertilize to their hearts' content in one area, and then you can move them to another as needed. If this is not your style, be sure to provide them with a coop. They can free-range during the day, the ideal condition for a chicken, but be safe in a closed, predator-proof coop at night. Cover the floor of the coop with wood shavings or other organic litter. Continue to place fresh litter on top of soiled litter until it is six to eight inches deep, then scoop it out and compost it for a boost of carbon and nitrogen.

Rabbits

Quiet, social, and intelligent, these creatures deserve a better fate than being relegated to a backyard hutch in sweltering heat and freezing cold. Domestic rabbits (*Oryctolagus cuniculus*) are not related to the wild rabbits of North America (*Sylvilagus audubonii*) but rather are descendants of the European hare, a completely different genus of animal, and do not do well if they are kept outside in Florida's heat.

Rabbits have been gaining in popularity as indoor pets since the 1980s. The feces of cats and dogs must be disposed of very carefully, but rabbit manure (dry, nonstinking "bunny balls") is considered one of the best available for vegetable gardens. Rabbits can use a litter box lined with pine pellets or shavings, or recycled newspaper pellets, and topped with a layer of hay. After about a week, the litter box contents can be thrown into the compost pile. What's more, bunny manure does not have an odor. Bunny urine does, but the litter absorbs that. Like any pet, a rabbit is a commitment; with good care, the average rabbit can live for ten years.

Worms

Worms produce two wonderful products—castings (manure) and worm tea. They also "eat your garbage" and allow apartment dwellers to compost indoors. The species most often used for vermiculture is *Eisenia foetida*, also known as the red wiggler, or the manure worm. This species is not native to Florida, so use a secure indoor worm-farm system to be sure that you do not release them into the wild.

A small worm bin kept under the kitchen sink is a good way to start. Worms will eat anywhere from 50 to 100 percent of their body weight in food scraps each day, turning the scraps into what some call "black gold." Their castings can be top-dressed or side-dressed onto garden plants. The famous urban farmer Will Allen, of Growing Power in Milwaukee, starts all of his seeds in equal parts worm castings and coconut coir.

To make worm tea, pour filtered water over the castings (with or without the worms) and collect the tea-colored liquid. Then, dilute and spray it onto your plants to deliver micronutrients. Research funded by the U.S. Department of Agriculture shows that plants fertilized with worm tea have increased growth and yields. According to researchers, "vermicompost maintains high levels of microbial activity, which produces such valuable plant compounds as growth hormones, plant growth regulators, and soluble nutrients." If you don't want to keep worms (though they are fun!), you can purchase worm compost.

Cats

Unlike chickens, rabbits, and worms, cats have no place in an organically managed garden. They deposit their manure in loose soil and bury it, so you won't know where it is. Because they are carnivores, their manure can harbor dangerous pathogens. The other big problem with cats is the harm they do to the ecosystem as subsidized predators. They catch or harass bug-catching predators such as the birds and lizards. So if you are owned by a cat, keep it inside. Ask your neighbors to do the same. Also, do what you can to rid your neighborhood of feral cats.

Resources

For more information on chickens, see www.aphis.usda.gov/animal_health/birdbiosecurity.

For more information on rabbits, see www.rabbit.org.

For more information on worms, see www.growingpower.org; www.fertileearth.org; and www.vermitechnology.com.

Also see Amy Stewart, *The Earth Moved: On the Remarkable Achievements of Earthworms* (Chapel Hill: Algonquin Press, 2004).

For the USDA-funded research on worm products, see www.csrees.usda.gov/newsroom/impact/2009/sbir/08101_earthworm_tea.html.

Glossary

acidity: Measured on the pH (potential of Hydrogen) scale of one to fourteen, with seven being neutral. Substances whose acidity measures below seven are acidic, while those whose acidity measures above seven are alkaline. When you test your soil, the acidity is one of the characteristics that will be measured. Most plants do best in near-neutral soil. However, some thrive in the extremely acidic soils found in bogs, while others have adapted to the extremely alkaline soils such as the limestone substrate found in the Florida Keys. A soil's acidity determines the uptake rates of various nutrients from the soil.

adventitious roots: Roots formed from an area of a plant that is not its primary root. They may, for example, form on a stem that has come into contact with soil or water. True bulbs, like onions and some grasses, have adventitious roots.

aerobic: A condition in which air, especially oxygen, is present. Aerobic conditions in soils or compost piles support worms, microbes, and other creatures that are important to a healthy soil's ecosystem. Soil or compost under aerobic conditions will have a sweet smell or no smell at all. An aerobic organism is one that requires air to survive. See *anaerobic*.

allelopathy: A phenomenon wherein a plant produces chemicals that are toxic to other plants or organisms. Allelopathic plants can inhibit the germination, growth, or reproduction of competing plant species or can be toxic to soil organisms such as nematodes. In the vegetable garden, there are a number of organic products that reduce the germination rates of weed seeds, such as corn gluten. One reason to rotate your crops is to reduce the problems associated with such residues in the soil. Sunflowers are allelopathic to many other plants, so be aware of where you plant them and what you plant around them. Also be aware of allelopathic trees near your vegetable garden. Black walnut, Australian pine, sycamore, eucalyptus, and hackberry all release compounds through their leaves or roots that are poisonous to most other plants.

anaerobic: A condition in which air or oxygen is absent. When soil becomes waterlogged, anaerobic bacteria will take over, causing it to smell sour or like ammonia. Microbes that exist in such conditions are called anaerobes. See *aerobic*.

biodiversity: Refers to the number of living organisms in an ecosystem. Corn growing alone in a field is a monoculture and has low biodiversity, while healthy soil ecosystems have high biodiversity, containing an immense number of organisms—millions in each gram of soil. Organic gardening promotes high biodiversity in the soil, gardens, and surrounding areas.

blanch, blanching: (1) The process of preventing light from reaching a part of a plant, usually by piling soil around the stem or wrapping it in paper. Photosynthesis cannot take place in the covered tissues, giving them a white or lighter green color. (2) The quick dunking of vegetables in boiling water to prepare them for canning or freezing.

bolt: The growth of a tall shoot for supporting the flowers. Leafy crops, such as lettuce, cabbage, parsley, or mustard greens will bolt when the weather gets warmer or when the days get longer. Growers usually want to prevent early bolting, because the leaves often become bitter once flowering begins.

Bt (*Bacillus thuringiensis*): A common, naturally occurring soil bacterium that can kill insects by paralyzing their digestive systems. Various strains of Bt have been developed for controlling specific insects such as leaf-eating caterpillars, black flies, or mosquitoes. At present, Bt is the only "microbial insecticide" in widespread use that organic farmers favor, mainly because it is not a general poison and it degrades quickly.

bug: True bugs are those insects that belong to the order Hemiptera, whose members have sucking mouthparts such as aphids. Informally, however, the term "bug" refers to various members of the arthropod phylum (animals with exoskeletons), including six-legged insects, eight-legged spiders and mites, crustaceans such as sowbugs and pillbugs, and the many-legged centipedes and millipedes. With apologies to the entomologists, the informal terminology is used in this book.

bulb: A plant embryo encased in fleshy, modified leaves that contain reserves of food. A bulb's roots emerge from a basal plate at the bottom, while the embryonic plant and layers of fat leaves emerge from the top. Onions are true bulbs.

calyx (plural: calyces): The outermost parts of a flower, normally made up of sepals.

coconut coir (pronounced "core"): A coconut product named for the layer of the coconut shell from which it is extracted. Sold in compressed bricks, it expands to many times its size when hydrated. It can absorb up to eight times its weight in water and is easy to re-wet. Its acidity is close to neutral, and it serves as a more sustainable alternative to peat moss in your potting soil mix and to add humus in your soil. Coconut coir is also available as pots for your seedlings, mats for lining hanging planters, and as biologs for controlling water flow.

corm: Modified stems that look like bulbs but lack the basal plate or the layers of modified leaves.

cotyledons: The leaves pre-formed inside the seed and the first to emerge (also called seed leaves). If there are two, the plant is a dicot. If there's only one, it's a monocot. Only true flowering plants (angiosperms) have these leaves.

CSA (Community Supported Agriculture): Usually, a small, independent, labor-intensive family farm (or group of small farms) that solicits prepaid subscriptions from the community for shares of the crops over a defined period. Subscribers usually receive a box of produce each week of whatever is ripe. By providing a guaranteed market through prepaid sales, the community helps to finance the farming operations.

curd: A flower head of cauliflower or broccoli in the form of a mass of tightly packed buds before it blooms. Traditionally, cauliflower curds are protected from the sun to keep them white.

dicot or **dicotyledonous:** An angiosperm or flowering plant that has two cotyledon leaves preformed in the seed. When it sprouts, these two seed leaves emerge first. The next leaves (the first true leaves) generally look quite different from the cotyledons.

drip line: A somewhat circular line around a tree or shrub where water drops from the ends of the widest spreading branches would fall. The drip line is often used as a guideline for locating edible gardens—ideally, well outside the drip lines of nearby trees in order to avoid their shade and competition with their roots for nutrients and water.

dry well: A hole in the ground filled with gravel, rocks, and, maybe, perforated pipe. Dry wells are installed to hold water as part of a drainage system. Water directed into a dry well will soak into the ground, quickly if it's in a sandy substrate. Usually dry wells are most needed in areas with heavy, clayey soil.

earthworm: A segmented worm that eats its way through the soil (one third of its body weight each day), creating tunnels and leaving behind its waste, which is euphemistically called castings. Earthworms aerate the soil and break down the humus. They respire through their skin and prefer damp, rich soil; they'll seek out the best areas, under wet leaves or in your compost pile. Worms can even live in water for a few weeks. Earthworms are hermaphrodites, each having both female and male reproductive organs. If you cut an earthworm in half, only the front part will have a chance of living. Earthworms are not native to this country but have become extremely important in farming.

ecology: The study of the relationship between organisms and their environment. Together, the organisms and their environment are known as an ecosystem. (When people say that they are taking an action for the good of the ecology, they are misusing the term.)

ecosystem: The complex interrelationship of organisms (plants, animals, fungi, and bacteria) in the substrate where they live and die.

endosperm: A cache of food, in the form of starch, protein, or oil, stored in seeds to provide the energy for germination until they form true leaves and the seedling can photosynthesize and produce sugars on its own. In corn, the endosperm takes up the majority of the seed volume, with the small embryo located off to the side. In some plants such as beans, the food is stored within the cotyledons or seed leaves, and there is little or no endosperm.

epicotyl: The portion of the plant embryo in the seed that grows upward above the cotyledons or seed leaves. The epicotyl is the shoot that will bear the first true leaves of the seedling.

evapotranspiration rate: A measurement of the combined output of water vapor from both plant transpiration and area-wide evaporation from soil and bodies of water. Knowing the evapotranspiration rate in your area will help you determine how much irrigation you garden will need. Readings are available on the Florida Automated Weather Network (FAWN) at http://fawn.ifas.ufl.edu/.

exoskeleton: A hard outer coating or shell that protects and provides a rigid shape for the soft body parts on the inside. Animals with exoskeletons include insects, snails, and crawdads.

flaccid: Wilted; not turgid.

foodways: The culture of what is eaten, when, how, and what it means, common to an ethnic or regional group. Foodways are closely tied to individual and group ethnic identity.

frass: Excrement and plant parts that appear after a fruit or stem has been attacked by a burrowing larval pest such as a squash stem borer or a fruit-boring pickle worm.

fungi (singular: fungus): Soil fungi derive energy from other organisms. Those organisms could be dead or alive. Fungi are composed of long filaments called hyphae (singular: hyphus). One gram of soil may contain as many as 100,000 fungi whose hyphae, if strung together, would measure sixteen feet in length. A collective network of hyphal cells is called a mycelium. When hyphae from two individuals meet, they can form a fruiting body that produces spores, which might appear on leaves as a black coating.

Fungi were formerly classified as plants but now belong to their own kingdom. Soil fungi do best in a damp environment. Most are saprophytes that feed on dead organic materials, but some are carnivorous and ensnare nematodes or other soil organisms. Some also invade and reside within plants or animals, such as the fungi that cause fusarium wilts, rusts, and molds on our vegetable crops.

Not all fungi that invade plants are bad. Fungi play an important role in composting and will break down dead materials. Mycorrhizae are various specialized fungi that invade plant roots and aid in the transfer of soil nutrients and water into the plant. In some cases the fungal hyphae will extend the roots' absorptive system tenfold or more. In turn, the plant supplies sugars to the fungus. It's a symbiotic relationship.

green manure: The end product of a fast-growing cover crop that is uprooted and turned into the soil, adding nutrients to the garden bed as the plants decompose.

hardening-off: A multistage process for acclimating potted seedlings to the garden space. This practice is normally associated with cool-weather climates, but it's also a good idea in Florida.

horizon: See *soil horizon*.

microclimate: The different growing conditions on your property are a result of the amount of sun in different seasons, drainage conditions, competition with tree roots, proximity to heat-retaining elements such as foundations, large rocks, or paved surfaces, and acidity-altering elements such as alkaline cement or limestone. Assessing the various microclimates helps you determine the best locations for your crops.

micro-greens: Leafy crops eaten at the seedling stage. You may plant crops expressly as micro-greens or harvest them when thinning a crop to promote the best growth.

mycorrhizae: Mycorrhizae are various fungi that enter into a symbiotic association with plant roots. Fungus (myco) and the roots (rhiza). See more at *fungi*.

node: A spot on a stem where leaves or new shoots grow or have grown. The nodes on a bamboo stem are particularly obvious.

pH: See *acidity*.

photosynthesis: A process of combining carbon dioxide (CO_2) and water (H_2O) with energy from sunlight to form sugar ($C_6H_{12}O_6$) and oxygen gas (O_2). Most vascular plants use the water supplied by transpiration and the carbon dioxide that is available from the air for photosynthesis. Respiration is the opposite chemical reaction, and all organisms, even plants, respire.

priming: See *seed priming*.

radicle: The portion of the plant embryo in a seed that will form the root. The radicle is usually the first part to emerge during germination. See *epicotyl*.

rain garden: A garden sited in a swale with plants that can withstand both standing water and drought. Storm water runoff from roofs, driveways, or other hard surfaces is directed into the rain garden swale. The rainwater is absorbed by the plants or it percolates into the soil.

respiration: The chemical reaction in which plants and animals take in oxygen gas (O_2) and break down sugar ($C_6H_{12}O_6$) to get energy for life. The by-products released are water (H_2O) and carbon dioxide (CO_2). Photosynthesis is the opposite chemical reaction.

***Rhizobium* spp.** (plural: *Rhizobia*): A unique group of soil bacteria that live in a symbiotic relationship with roots of the legumes. The legume plant supplies the rhizobia with energy from photosynthesis, and the rhizobia "fix" nitrogen gas from the air in the nodule, converting it into a form that the plant can use. The rhizobia living in the plant's root nodules are called symbionts.

rhizome: Thickened stems, sometimes called rootstocks, that grow horizontally. Ginger produces edible rhizomes.

seed priming: The process whereby seeds are soaked in water to break their dormancy and induce an earlier germination. Seed priming is recommended for seeds such as parsley or onion that take two to three weeks to germinate if planted in soil without seed priming. The seeds should be soaked just long enough to soften—if the root radicle emerges, you've soaked them too long. After you soak the seeds, dry them for easier handling during the sowing process. Seed priming not only shortens the time to germination, but it usually also produces a more uniform germination rate.

sets: Small bulbs used for propagating some members of the onion family. You can purchase sets or grow the plants from seed and then dry them out as soon as the bulbs reach a diameter of one-eighth to one-half of an inch. Using sets gives you a head start in the garden, and you can plant them at just the right distance apart for ideal growth.

soil horizon: The four layers of soil in an undisturbed landscape. The top layer consists of organic litter, such as dead leaves and twigs that serve as Mother Nature's mulch. Topsoil, the next layer, contains a lot of humus (digested organic materials). Under the topsoil, the subsoil contains very little organic material, and beneath that is the bedrock layer. Only the top two layers are filled with many types of soil organisms—insect larvae, nematodes, earthworms, bacteria, and fungi.

stomata (singular: stomate): Openings or pores in leaf surfaces that allow water to escape through transpiration and air to flow into the leaf tissues to supply carbon dioxide for photosynthesis. Most leaves are arranged with their stomata on the bottom surface, away from the direct sun and water. These pores stay open as long as the guard cells, a pair of kidney-shaped cells located on either side of the opening, are turgid and filled with water. When high temperatures or general drought conditions cause water stress, the guard cells become flaccid and the pores close to prevent further water loss.

symbiotic: A mutually beneficial relationship between two separate organisms. For example, legume plants supply rhizobia bacteria with sugar from photosynthesis, and the rhizobia fix atmospheric nitrogen in the root nodule, converting it into a form that the plant can use.

taproot: A swollen storage root—often formed in a biennial plant to store energy for flowering during the second year. Taproot vegetables include radishes, carrots, turnips, and beets. The taproot is harvested whole.

tilth: A characteristic of a soil's structure. A handful of soil with good tilth will have many differently sized, but mostly rounded, particles. The particles of soil should withstand gentle pressure but should break apart easily. Such soil is neither too sandy nor too clayey. A soil with good tilth is easily tilled with a plow or with a shovel or fork, and is rich in organic material, with both good porosity and the ability to hold water. Seeds grown in soil with good tilth have a high rate of seedling emergence and deep root penetration.

transpiration: The passive evaporation of water from a vascular plant, mostly through the pores (stomata) on its leaves. Water is absorbed from soil into the roots and is sucked through the vessels by the evaporation of water from the leaves. The rate of transpiration is determined by the amount of water in the soil, the humidity, the air temperature, and whether the plant's stomata are open or closed. Less than ten percent of the water pumped through the plant is actually absorbed into the plant's tissues or used in photosynthesis. Transpiration cools both the plant's tissues and the surrounding air.

trench composting (composting in place): The process of digging a trench six or more inches below soil level in your garden, usually between wide rows, and spreading a mixture of kitchen waste such as egg shells, vegetable trimmings, leftovers, and other organic material (but not meat or oily foods) in the bottom of the trench and covering it with soil. This should be done as the bed is being prepared for planting, or when seedlings are still small. For more details, see chapter 3.

true leaves: The set of leaves that emerge after the cotyledons or seed leaves and that have the characteristic shape for the plant.

tuber: A modified, underground stem that stores food and that has a knobby or lumpy surface with growth buds, or eyes, from which the shoots of the new plant emerge. Irish potatoes are the best-known example, but Jerusalem artichokes, true yams, and daylilies also produce tubers.

tuberous roots: Swollen roots, not modified stems. They don't have eyes, and rather sprout from one end (called the "crown") and grow in clumps. Sweet potatoes are the best example.

turgid: The state wherein a plant's tissues—leaves and stems—are firm and filled with fluids. It is the opposite of flaccid or wilted.

vascular plants: Those plants that contain an arrangement of cells that form vessels or tubes for carrying water and nutrients.

vermiculite: A substance derived from rocks containing large crystals of the minerals biotite and iron-bearing phlogopite, a form of mica. These rocks are mined and then heated to produce the worm-like strands that are broken into smaller flakes to produce an inorganic moisture-holding medium that is often added to commercial potting mixes.

Index

Ginny Stibolt, a life-long gardener with a master's degree in botany, is the author of *Sustainable Gardening for Florida*. She writes about gardening for Floridata.com, Florida Native Plant Society, Native Plants & Wildlife Gardens, Lawn Reform Coalition, and on her own blog, www.GreenGardeningMatters.com.

Melissa Contreras has gardened in the challenging south Florida climate since 1998 and is a Master Gardener volunteer in Miami-Dade County. Her fascination with relationships among people, land, and food came from her grandmother who grew enough vegetables for her 10 children on less than an urban acre in Middlesboro, Kentucky, and kept a cow, a pig, and chickens. Melissa is creator of Urban Oasis Project, a non-profit organization which educates people about growing and getting local foods. You can keep up with her at urbanoasisproject.org and southfloridaorganicgardening.com.

*   *   *

The University Press of Florida is the scholarly publishing agency for the State University System of Florida, comprising Florida A&M University, Florida Atlantic University, Florida Gulf Coast University, Florida International University, Florida State University, New College of Florida, University of Central Florida, University of Florida, University of North Florida, University of South Florida, and University of West Florida.